Handbook of Competitive Cyc

To my parents,
Simone, and
Angelika

Achim Schmidt

Handbook of Competitive Cycling

Training/Keep Fit/Tactics

Meyer & Meyer Sport

Original title: „Handbuch für Radsport"
© 1994 by Meyer & Meyer Verlag, Aachen
Translation: Tina Scheufele

Die Deutsche Bibliothek – CIP Einheitsaufnahme

Schmidt, Achim:
Handbook of Competitive Cycling / Achim Schmidt. [Transl. by Tina Scheufele].
– Aachen : Meyer und Meyer, 1998
Dt. Ausg. u.d.T.: Schmidt, Achim: Handbuch für Radsport
ISBN 3-89124-509-2

© 1998 by Meyer & Meyer Verlag, Aachen (Germany)
Olten (CH), Wien (A), Oxford (GB), Québec (CDN),
Lansing/Michigan (USA), Findon/Adelaide (AUS),
Auckland (NZ), Sandton/Johannisburg (ZA)
Cover Photo: Bongarts Sportfotografie, Hamburg
Photos: F. Bodenmüller: S. (50), (51), 101, 169
K. Eweleit: S. 104, 172, 216, 224, 226
H. Pfingsten: S. 16, (52), 169, 170, 171, 223
M. Pöhler: S. 90
P. Erkens: S. (49)
POLAR Electro GmbH: S. 63, 65, 102, 103, 147, 213, 231
Sachs: S. 221
Sigma: S. 221
A. Schmidt: 73, 105, 115, 165, 175, 183, 199, 202, 212, 222
Figures: Stefan Bossier: S. 14, 160
René Marks, Köln: S. 38, 40, 118-125
Manuela Haupt/Alberta Siebertz: S. 42, 228, 232, 234, 235, 236, 241, 243
All others by Achim Schmidt
Cover design: Walter Neumann N&N Design-Studio, Aachen
Cover exporsure: frw, Reiner Wahlen, Aachen
Type exposure: Typeline, Dagmar Schmitz, Aachen
Lektorat: Dr. Irmgard Jaeger, Aachen
Satz: Quai
Printing: Burg Verlag & Druck, Gastinger GmbH und Co. KG, Stolberg
ISBN 3-89124-509-2
Printed in Germany

Table of Contents

Foreword

Bicycle racing in the 90's is experiencing a strong tendency towards professionalism that has an impact on and clearly changed amateur cycling as well. Technical improvements in materials and workmanship and, above all, goal-oriented training plans based on scientific principles, have enhanced performances to levels that were unforeseen 15 years ago. The areas of amateur cycling covered in this book (from juniors to seniors to masters), as well as bicycle touring, have also experienced a similar performance explosion. In today's competitive racing environment, where fitness levels among racers may not vary by much, it's especially important to formulate a good training plan and stick to it. This book provides the necessary fundamental knowledge to allow the reader to design his own training plan. In addition, it provides a plethora of useful information and tips for cycling.

One point must however be mentioned in the foreword. The mileage and training programs indicated for each class of riders presented in chapter 3 are fairly general and apply to the average male or female bicycle racer. The training plans are not sufficient for professional cyclists. This book is not designed, therefore, for the few professional cyclists, since they have experienced coaches to help them in this respect, but rather for the normal bicycle racer who, although he takes his sport seriously and invests a lot of time in it, must still subordinate racing to school or work. If you take the time to work through the chapters on training theory, you either will be able to modify the programs provided or design your own individualized training program. The "Handbook of Competitive Cycling" is available in various English speaking countries and cannot therefore do justice to the special features of each country. Therefore no alterations were made to the original German text as far as competitive types of person, range of training and class distinctions are concerned. Also, if, for example in so-called „developing countries" for competitive cycling it proves difficult to achieve the aforesaid frequency of racing, the book nevertheless shows what is required to keep pace with the best in the world. My special thanks go to Tina Scheufele, herself an active racing cyclist and medical student in Texas (U.S.A), who had the insight, together with a lot of specialized knowledge of her subject and linguistic sensitivity to translate the manuscipt into English. The translation captures accurately for the reader those moments and intentions, which the author wishes to convey in the German edition.

Achim Schmidt, Pulheim, May 1998

1 Introduction

1.1 About the Book

This book about road cycling addresses topics that are applicable and of interest to both the recreational and, in particular, the competitive cyclist and presents them in a well-grounded and understandable manner. For the benefit of the text and figures, it was necessary to forego a colorful edition with many pictures.

The organization and structure of each individual chapter, in particular those that deal with the medical and scientific aspects of training, is such that the chapters build on each other. For this reason, the reader without previous knowledge of these topics might have trouble understanding an isolated chapter taken out of context. Therefore, you should take the time to carefully peruse those chapters and sections that provide the theoretical foundation for the sport of cycling, since only through an understanding of these concepts you can gain insight into the proper training methods.

Topics in this book that may seem complex have usually already been highly simplified and condensed. The goal is to provide the reader with enough information and knowledge so that he can be his own coach and can critique the training methods of others; he should combine his own experience with the knowledge that this book provides to develop his own style of training. Naturally, some topics could only be touched upon; the interested reader can get more information through additional sources (see References) listed at the back of this book.

The Secrets?! The reader who opens this book and immediately searches the training programs for the final secrets to achieve top form should be warned that there are no such secrets. Peak performance on the bicycle is determined by the combination of a multitude of individual factors, many of which are covered in this book, but in the end, only many years of intense training can lead to top performances in cycling.

For example, many cyclists believe that there is a certain heart rate zone that will basically guarantee the individual who trains in this zone phenomenal performances. In regard to this mistaken belief, it must be said that only the knowledge of different training zones and their specific ranges and the combination of these zones and training methods in the context of a structured periodization will lead to success. The same applies to "miracle diets", which are just as fictitious, and also to the overrated influence of equipment on performance.

Listen to your body

Despite all the scientific information and theory, you should never ignore your body's signals, which as a rule are the best indicators of performance ability and the most useful determinants in planning your training. In modern times, this sport has come to rely more and more on instruments, the use of which has served to obscure its real meaning: to provide people with a hobby that is both fun and healthy, in short, to improve one's quality of life. Commercialization and an overly technical approach have also contributed to this trend.

It is time to go back to the roots, to view sports as sports; only then can high-performance sports, which are in general headed for a dead end, survive and continue to evolve.

1.2 Cycling for Health and Fitness

Cycling has experienced a "renaissance" over the last 20 years, and especially since the end of the 1980's, that is apparent not only in competitive cycling but also particularly in the area of recreational cycling. Never before have so many people ridden bicycles, whether road, touring, or mountain bike, as an active hobby or as an alternative mode of transportation. Mountain biking has attracted a wide variety of people to cycling and cautious forecasts predict that road cycling will eventually benefit from this increased interest, since more and more athletes will make the transition to the faster road bike. Last but not least, the long-overdue technical improvements over the last few years have contributed to cycling's success.

Recreational cycling has many benefits, all of which lead to improvements in the quality of life. Cycling's benefits of leading to an improvement in health, not only through exercise alone, but also through the different lifestyle of athletes in general, seem especially important in light of the increasing incidence of many life-threatening diseases (arteriosclerosis, obesity, etc.). Thus, this sport generates an awareness of a healthier lifestyle that puts an end to, or at least reduces to an acceptable level, the ravaging of the body through lack of exercise, poor nutrition, nicotine, and alcohol. This healthier lifestyle, in combination with exercising outdoors closer to nature, leads to a clearly noticeable improvement in well-being.

For many recreational cyclists, riding in the countryside is not only an individual sport, but also a group activity that enables them to meet new people through bike tours, clubs, or weight-loss groups.

In the same way, many athletes in today's stressful environment use cycling as a means of spending some time alone, far away from stress and all obligations. Even if it's difficult to be alone at work and at home, it's always possible on the bike. As just indicated, cycling improves not only physical health, but also mental health and often helps one distance oneself from everyday problems.

Bicycle vacations are becoming more and more popular. While viewing the scenery and nature from the car window is little different from watching television and makes you feel like a mere bystander, riding a bicycle makes you part of the experience.

Many more benefits of cycling as a recreational and health-promoting activity could be listed, but anyone who has ever ridden a road bike and caught cycling fever knows his individual reasons for choosing cycling above all other sports.

1.3 Competitive Cycling

Most of the benefits enumerated for recreational cycling also apply to competitive and highly competitive cycling. Whereas for recreational cyclists, performance and racing play only a subordinate role, bike racers elevate these aspects of cycling to a prominent role.

The bike racer must endure maximal suffering and postponement of gratification both during training and in races. With the exception of several extreme endurance sports (ultra-triathlons, 100 km running races, etc.), road cyclists accomplish the highest possible endurance performances over the course of not only one day, but, as in the case of the Tour de France, three strenuous weeks that stress participants almost to their absolute limits. Bicycle racing illustrates the astonishing adaptability of human beings (Chapter 2) to endurance training. The active, experienced competitive athlete who critically analyzes his sport should be able to perform with distinction.

2 Anatomical and Physiological Foundations of Cycling

2.1 Anatomical/Physiological Foundations

Unfortunately far too many cyclists still know too little about the way their bodies work, and even basic facts, such as the process of digestion, are either completely a mystery or only partially understood.

The purpose of this chapter is to explain the design and function of the human body as it relates to cycling. Processes ranging from muscle contraction to digestion are simplified to improve the reader's knowledge of his own body, since only by learning the structures and workings of the body one can develop a true understanding of the training process, enabling one to evaluate the plausibility of different theories on training. Therefore, the following chapters will cover a lot of scientific topics.

The Musculoskeletal System
The journey through the body will start with muscles, bones, and joints: in other words, with the musculoskeletal system, without which movement, not to mention sports, would be impossible. The importance of a smoothly functioning musculoskeletal system becomes apparent whenever movement becomes painful or even impossible due to sprains, bruises, or even cracked or broken bones. Even something as simple as muscle soreness can significantly impair the performance of an athlete.

Musculature
The approximately 430 muscles in the human body normally comprise between 40 and 45% of body weight and use 20% of the body's energy at rest. During maximal work (athletic peak performance), the energy requirement rises to as high as 90%.

Muscles have the ability to convert chemical energy (in the form of foodstuffs) into mechanical energy (tension), similar to a combustion engine. During a movement, one muscle or a group of muscles never works alone, but rather depends on one or more opposing (antagonistic) muscles.

Figure 2.1:
The cyclist's most-used muscle groups:

1. **Quadriceps**   *extending the knee*
2. **Hamstrings**   *flexing the knee*
3. **Gluteus muscles**   *extending the hip joint*
4. **Calf muscles**   *extending the foot*
5. **Shin muscles**   *lifting the foot*
6. **Back muscles**   *stabilizing the spine*
7. **Neck muscles**   *lifting the head*
8. **Shoulder muscles**   *stabilizing the shoulder*
9. **Hip flexors**   *flexing the hip joint*
10. **Stomach muscles**   *bending and turning the torso*
11. **Triceps**   *extending the elbow*
12. **Biceps**   *flexing the elbow*
13. **Wrist flexors**   *flexing the wrist*
14. **Wrist extensors**   *extending the wrist*

For example, in the leg, the extensors (agonists) and flexors (antagonists) oppose each other. Muscle work is classified into two basic types:
a) static work
b) dynamic work.

Static work means without movement; for cycling, these muscles are the ones that maintain posture. Arm, neck, and back musculature hold the upper body and head still during periods of quiet riding in the saddle and, therefore, perform static work. Turning over the pedals, on the other hand, is a dynamic form of muscle work; more precisely stated, it is dynamic-concentric muscle work, which means that the muscle actually shortens under tension (contraction) as it overcomes the load placed on it.

The opposite, the eccentric load (pliant work) occurs, for example, when one lands after jumping off a wall; the legs must give way, and although the muscles work against this, they still get stretched (lengthened). The leg extensors get stretched a lot under the load generated during the eccentric phase of an act such as running, and these muscles are not used to this type of stress. The result is microscopic muscle tears (microtrauma), universally recognized as muscle soreness.

The most important muscle for cycling is the quadriceps, the leg extensor with four separate heads, whose prominence depends more or less on body type. Road riders tend to have slender, wiry legs. Pulling on the pedals activates the flexors. The lower leg muscles support the pedaling motion: while the calf muscles work during the entire pedal revolution (both during flexion and extension), the shin muscles are only used to fix the foot in place while pulling back on the pedals (see chapter 8.2, The Smooth Pedal Stroke).

Bones

The human skeleton's design enables it to be fairly light; a tough, compact outer layer covers the sponge-like material filling the inside. Bones are relatively elastic, even though they seem very stiff and inflexible. Stretching, bending, twisting, and subjection to pressure are all tolerated up to surprisingly high stress values. Cycling is a "bone and joint sparing" sport, since high-stress injuries, such as stress fractures and sprains, as seen in running, rarely occur.

Joints

The bones, with their cartilage-ensheathed ends, form the joints, which determine the body's range of motion. Mostly two, but sometimes even three, bones meet at a joint and are attached to each other by muscles, tendons, ligaments, and capsules. The cartilage-covered ends of bones form the joint surface on the inside of the joint. Cartilage is a very pliable, smooth substance with a lifespan that has not yet been matched by synthetic substances. The joint space (area between the opposing bone ends) is enclosed by a two-layered capsule, whose function is, first, to help support the joint and, second, to produce the so-called "joint lubricant". A very important joint for cyclists is the knee joint, a modified hinge joint. However, the hip joint is also subjected to the constant motion of the thigh bone (femur). In contrast, the ankle's range of motion is fairly small. The rest of the joints in the body are only used when shifting position and when standing up.

The skin on a road cyclist's legs is very thin.

Heart and Circulatory System

The body's ability to perform endurance type work is limited next by the heart and the circulatory system. In endurance sports, such as cycling, this system has demonstrated an astonishing ability to adapt in response to higher demands (see next chapter).

The Heart

Blood from all regions of the body flows from the superior and inferior vena cavae into the right atrium of the heart and then through a valve into the right ventricle. When the heart contracts, the blood is forced out of the right ventricle into the arteries in the lungs, where it gets oxygenated. Veins then carry the oxygen-rich blood from the lungs to the left atrium of the heart. The pathway of blood flow described up to this point is called the "pulmonary (lung) circulation." Blood from the left atrium then flows into the left ventricle, which, upon contraction (heart beat), expels blood into the aorta, the largest artery in the body, so it can flow into the "systemic (body) circulation." The aorta distributes the blood to all organs and structures via numerous smaller branching arteries.

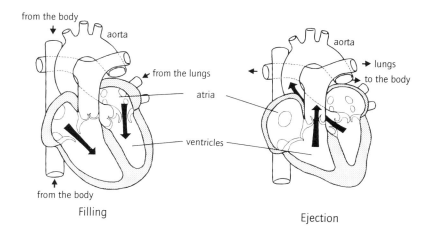

Figure 2.2: Anatomy and work phases of the heart

The heart valves function like trap doors to prevent the backflow of blood, which could be fatal. The heart ejects blood during the contraction phase and fills again with blood during the relaxation phase.

The heart rate is determined by a complicated regulatory and control mechanism: the higher the work load, the higher the heart rate, up to a maximum rate of about 220 minus your age. The excitation of the heart is an automatic pro cess, not under voluntary control; the impulse that causes the heart to beat originates in the sinus node, which lies between the two atria, and spreads rhythmically to the rest of the heart.

An unconditioned heart weighs between 250 and 300 grams, beats about 70 times a minute (about 100,000 times a day), and propels 7,000-8,000 liters of blood through the body every day.

The Vascular System

The blood vessels, especially the arterioles (small arteries) are responsible for distributing the oxygen-rich blood throughout the body. Muscle arterioles and capillaries are actively constricted when the body is at rest to prevent unnecessary blood flow through the musculature, since, at rest, blood is needed principally for other organs (stomach, intestines, kidneys, liver). As soon as a person begins to move, the blood vessels in the working muscles dilate, and more blood, and consequently more oxygen and nutrients, can flow to the muscle fibers. The blood flow to the digestive system is proportionately reduced. The higher demand for blood during muscular movement is met by the greater pumping ability of the heart. From the capillaries, the smallest blood vessels and also the

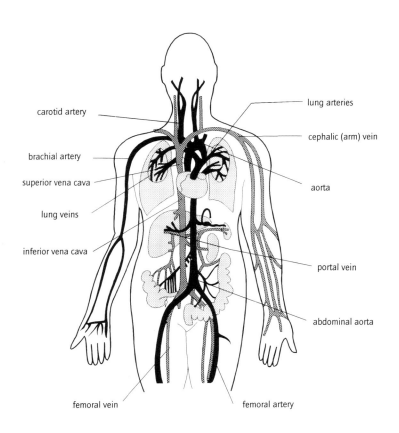

Figure 2.3: Circulatory system

exchange-site of materials (oxygen< $\rightleftharpoons$ >carbon dioxide, nutrients< $\rightleftharpoons$ >waste products), blood flows into venules and finally into veins, which merge to form either the superior or the inferior vena cava. The vena cavae then transport the blood back to the heart.

In contrast to arteries, veins cannot actively constrict to limit blood flow; however, they possess valves that enable the transport of blood back to the heart even against the force of gravity.

Breathing

The lung, which is composed of two lobes, is the organ of external breathing. Oxygen-poor, carbon dioxide-rich blood flows around the lung's air sacks (alveoli) in extremely thin-walled capillaries that enable the exchange of carbon dioxide from the blood for oxygen from the lungs. This process, called gas exchange, takes only about 0.3 seconds. With the help of the breathing muscles, primarily the diaphragm at rest, the lungs expand during inhalation, and air flows through the windpipe and bronchia into the air sacks, in which gas exchange occurs; carbon dioxide is expelled out of the lungs during exhalation. The lungs are very elastic and the work they do during breathing can be compared to blowing up a balloon; active inflation occurs during inhalation and passive emptying during exhalation. Only when under stress, as during rapid breathing (cycling), do accessory muscles in the chest help the diaphragm. A group of accessory breathing muscles strengthens the force of both inhalation and exhalation and raises the energy requirements of the breathing muscles to as high as 10% of the body's total energy requirements. At rest, each breath results in only about 0.5 liters of air being breathed in and out at a rate of 15 times a minute (about 7.5 liters/minute); during intense exercise, a trained cyclist can inhale and exhale over 190 liters of air every minute.

The vital capacity (the volume of air expelled after a maximal inhalation) depends highly on age, sex, and body size. The vital capacity usually ranges between three and seven liters, but predicts only minimally the absolute endurance performance capacity of a cyclist. For example, top runners from Africa have small lungs compared to those of Europeans and yet still usually run faster. As already mentioned, the gas exchange occurring at the lungs is called external breathing, and the use of gases at the cellular level for the burning foodstuffs to provide energy is termed internal breathing.

Organ Systems

This section briefly outlines the structure and function of the nervous system, digestive system, kidneys, and blood.

The Nervous System

Many bodily processes and our reflex responses are controlled by the nervous system, whether we are aware of it or not. The nervous system senses, processes, and responds to stimuli with the help of sense and target organs, which are responsible for interacting with the environment. The nervous system is composed of billions of cells that have lost their ability to divide. The two anatomic divisions of the nervous system are the central nervous system (CNS: brain and spinal cord) and the peripheral nervous system (PNS), whose nerves form the connection to the sensory and target organs. Functionally, the nervous system is divided into voluntary (somatic) and involuntary (autonomic) nervous systems.

The *somatic nervous system* guides all voluntary movement commands to the appropriate target organs, usually muscles. The cerebral cortex is divided into motor (movement) and sensory (feeling) areas. The cerebellum is responsible for balance and coordination of movement (for example, balancing while riding a bicycle). While the brain represents the central switchboard of the nervous system, the spinal cord is the cable that conveys and receives information to and from nerves, while running in the protective vertebral canal, formed by the vertebral bodies; it also performs a function similar to that of the brain, by serving as a switchboard for more basic functions, such as reflexes.

The *autonomic nervous system*, which controls all unconscious activities in the body, is composed of two separate systems that are responsible for two completely different functions. The parasympathetic nervous system, responsible for all resting bodily functions (digestion, repair and regeneration), is localized in the terminal ganglia (nerve structure) near target organs. The sympathetic nervous system, on the other hand, takes over during exercise and improves the performance ability of those organ systems necessary for motion.

Digestion

The process of digestion, from food intake to waste excretion, will now be described, following the path of an energy bar through the digestive system. The times given are meant to provide an overview and differ significantly depending on the situation and concomitant circumstances.

3:30 PM: A cyclist starts a three to four hour training ride. The last meal was over three hours ago and was not very filling.

5:00 PM: The cyclist eats an energy bar. The teeth mechanically break down the food, and saliva mixes with it to form a slippery mush. ❶ The salivary enzymes start breaking down complex carbohydrates in the mouth.

5:01 PM: The "mush" slides down the oesophagus into the stomach. The transport down the approximately 30 cm-long oesophagus is hastened by waves of contraction. ❷

5:02 PM: After reaching the stomach, the "energy bar" stimulates the production of acid and enzymes, stomach fluids that chemically break down the food. ❸ About 1.5 to 2 liters of stomach fluids are produced every day. The stomach enzymes are only able to break down fats and proteins; carbohydrates are not further digested here. The acid increases the rate of food breakdown by converting the enzymes into active forms.

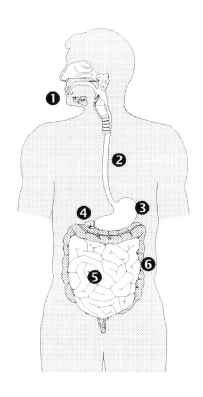

Figure 2.4: The digestive system

5:03 PM: The secretion of water into the stomach dilutes the food "mush", and stomach contractions mix it thoroughly like in a concrete mixer. During strenuous cycling, the body spares no energy for digestive processes, and digestion is postponed until the pace gets slower.

5:09 PM: The stomach still operates like a concrete mixer, but gradually fats rise to the top of the mush, while carbohydrates settle to the bottom.

5:25 PM: The mush becomes even more liquid, but still needs several minutes until it is ready to leave the stomach. Carbohydrate drinks would already be in the small intestine.

5:40 PM: Finally, shortly before the bonk sets in, the stomach opens its muscular pyloric valve, allowing the mush to pass into the duodenum bit by bit. ❹ The pancreas empties enzymes into the duodenum to digest carbohydrates, proteins, and fats; at the same time, the gall bladder secretes bile, which aids in fat digestion.

5:43 PM: Rhythmic (peristaltic) contractions propel the "energy bar" further into the small intestine. ❺ The complex carbohydrates that have now been broken down to glucose get absorbed into the bloodstream by the villus that project into the small intestine and pass through the portal system to the liver. Part of the ingested fat is already in the broken-down form of fatty acids and glycerol, and proteins are mostly present as individual amino acids. The uptake (absorption) of these nutrients begins now.

5:46 PM: The food mush passes further through the small intestine, whose first third is primarily concerned with the absorption of glucose. Glucose travels via the portal system to the liver, where it is used to manufacture glycogen. The liver stores part of the glycogen (100-130 grams) itself, while the rest travels to the muscles to either be stored there or used immediately. Amino acids, fatty acids, vitamins A, B, C, E, and K, and minerals are absorbed into the bloodstream from the small intestine.

6:30 PM: The remnants of the energy bar are still present in the small intestine.

7:00 PM: End of the training ride. Almost all of the glucose has been absorbed, and even the proteins have been partially taken up. Naturally, fat digestion and absorption takes even longer.

7:30 PM: The process begins again when dinner is eaten. The amino acids from the energy bar now reach the liver, where they combine again to form proteins, so called plasma proteins, and enter the bloodstream. Excess protein (as seen during too high a caloric intake or during periods of starvation) is metabolized for energy or converted and stored as fat (see chapter 5).

10:30 PM: The remains of the energy bar leave the small intestine and enter the large intestine. **❻** Up to this point, the food mush has been stripped of about 80-90% of its nutrients. The function of the large intestine is to reclaim the water used to facilitate digestion. The first section of the large intestine is still capable of absorbing some nutrients and minerals. The energy bar finally leaves the body the next morning as stool. A fat-rich meal would require approximately 10 more hours for complete digestion.

The Kidneys

The kidneys, which filter blood to get rid of waste products, are extremely important organs. The kidneys of cyclists, in particular, must work harder to match the doubled caloric intake that is necessary to support athletic performance. The kidneys rid the blood, and hence the body, of excess salt and water, protein waste products, and foreign substances. Of the 1,500 liters of blood that flow through the kidney every day, about 150 liters become the filtrate (the precursor to urine) that eventually gets concentrated and expelled as approximately 1.5 liters of urine.

The Blood

Blood is the body's life fluid. The 5-6 liters of blood contain 55% blood plasma (liquid) and 45% blood cells. Endurance training leads to a blood volume increase of about 15%. The following are the principal functions of blood:

- transport (oxygen, carbon dioxide, nutrients, waste products, hormones)
- transport and distribution of body heat
- blood clotting
- immune defense

Here are a few interesting facts about blood: 1 mm^3 of blood, a vanishingly small amount, contains an incredible 4.5-5 million red blood cells, and about 5,000 - 8,000 white blood cells, the cells of the immune system. In 100 ml of blood, there are 7 grams of protein. The red blood cells (erythrocytes) are responsible for the blood's transport of oxygen and carbon dioxide.

2.2 Performance Physiology

The Effects of Training on the Heart, Circulatory System, and Musculature

This next section discusses the changes that occur during endurance conditioning (cycling) in the heart and circulatory system, as well as in the musculature. It will explain concepts such as athlete's heart, resting pulse, and maximum oxygen uptake.

The body's adaptation process will be divided into two phases: the first phase occurs at low training distances and intensities, as experienced by recreational cyclists, and leads to a *"functional"* adaptation that is characterized by an improvement in muscle metabolism, consequently leading to a more efficient heart/ circulatory system. This improvement in efficiency occurs through a slight reduction in heart rate; i.e. the resting heart rate is slightly decreased and lower heart rates are reached during exercise. The second phase of adaptation is *"dimensional"* adaptation, during which the size of certain organ systems increases.

Many years of regular endurance training leads to an adaptation of the heart called "athlete's heart".
Athlete's heart is characterized by an increase in size and a consequent reduction in heart rate. This adaptation process is a result of an increased metabolism, particularly in the muscles, whose higher oxygen and nutrient requirements can only be met by increased blood circulation, necessitating a more efficient heart.

While the heart of an unconditioned person weighs about 300 grams, the heart of an endurance athlete can weigh up to 500 grams. The increased heart mass reflects a higher heart volume. With training, heart volumes can reach values of 900-1,200 ml, sometimes even more than 1,500 ml, whereas non-athletes have values of 800 ml and 500 ml for men and women, respectively. Some of the biggest athlete's hearts were discovered among road cyclists, as a consequence of extreme endurance conditioning. A larger heart volume results in a greater beat volume. The beat volume is the amount of blood that the heart expels into the aorta with each beat (80 ml for non-athletes; up to 150 ml for athletes). Since the body doesn't require any more blood for the same performance, the heart rate will be lower in a trained than in an untrained athlete performing the same amount of work. The maximum possible heart minute-volume, defined as the amount of blood expelled by the left side of the heart in one minute (heart rate X beat volume; for example, 70 X 80 ml = 5.6 L/min at rest), rises in comparison to that of non-athletes, so that more blood per minute is available to the muscles. The maximum heart rate decreases only slightly through many years of endurance training, so that the larger maximum beat volume results in a much larger maximum heart minute-volume. Non-athletes that are maximally stressed reach heart minute-volumes of about 20 liters, while endurance trained athletes can reach values of over 30 liters.

The reduction of the heart rate (from 60-70 beats per minute (bpm) in non-athletes to 40-50 bpm in competitive athletes) is a clear sign for the development of athlete's heart. Professionals and top amateurs often have heart rates under 40 bpm, and rarely may even have values below 30 bpm. The reduction in the resting heart rate of recreational cyclists to 50-60 bpm is usually not due to an increase in heart size, but rather, as already mentioned, can be attributed to a less excitable autonomic nervous system. After completing an active cycling "career," one cannot stop training altogether, since a life-threatening condition can develop if an enlarged heart's strength is not maintained.

The Advantages of Athlete's Heart

- higher performance ability
- ability to do the same amount of work at a lower heart rate
- lower resting and working heart rate, which protects the heart (comparable to lower rpm's in an automobile)
- more efficient circulatory system
- concurrent with the process of forming athlete's heart, positive adaptations also occur elsewhere in the body

Maximum Oxygen Uptake

The maximum oxygen uptake (**VO$_2$ max**) is a very interesting physiological parameter for cycling, since it is believed to be the factor that most influences endurance. Maximum oxygen uptake is defined as the greatest amount of oxygen – not air – that a cyclist can absorb through his lungs into the bloodstream during maximal exertion. A bicycle ergometer used during a performance test measures precisely the maximum oxygen uptake (see chapter 4). Normal values for non-athletes are around 3 liters of oxygen per minute; this value can increase with appropriate training to 5-6 liters/min.

The VO_2 **max** depends on the conditioning, age, sex, and weight of the athlete. For example, a larger athlete requires more oxygen than a smaller athlete for the same amount of external work, since he has to move more mass. Therefore, values for VO_2 **max** are reported with respect to body weight to allow for more accurate predictions of performance and to facilitate the comparison of different athletes. The weight-based or relative VO_2 **max** indicates the oxygen uptake per minute and kilogram of body weight; professionals reach values between 80 and 90 ml of oxygen per minute and kg body weight, compared to the 40 to 45 ml of oxygen per minute and kg body weight of non-athletic 20-30 year-olds. The maximum oxygen uptake in a non-athletic man decreases by 1% every year; women only lose 0.8% a year. What most non-athletes don't know is that this process can be stopped, or even reversed, through cycling. Thus, an endurance trained 70 year old could still reach the same values as a non-athletic 30 year old. In addition to age, weight, and sex, VO_2 **max** is also influenced by:

- transportation capacity of the circulatory system
- oxygen-carrying capacity of the blood
- breathing and gas exchange in the lungs
- muscle blood supply (vascularization)
- muscle metabolism (enzyme concentration)

The Musculature

The muscles of humans are composed of slow- and fast-twitch muscle fibres, as well as of an intermediate type that is not of much interest in this context. The slow, so-called red, muscle fibres are endurance fibers; they are the predominant muscle type (comprising 70-90%) found in cyclists' legs, with the exception of track sprinters. The fast-twitch, or white, muscle fibres are thicker, tire more easily, and are present mostly in sprinters and weight-lifters.

Non-athletes demonstrate a genetically variable fibre-type distribution, which can be shifted to a certain degree by training. The process whereby white fibres change into red fibres or vice versa is not yet completely understood; for certain, though, is that the type of exercise (endurance or strength) somehow triggers a change. The shifting of muscle types is more easily accomplished in the direction of slow-twitch than fast-twitch fibres. Therefore, training to improve endurance is significantly easier than to develop a good sprint. Only a handful of professional road cyclists possess the combination of both a high level of endurance and a great sprinting ability.

Since the red, capillary-rich, thinner muscle fibres are advantageous for endurance metabolism, the goal of road cyclists should not be to build up muscle mass (for example, through strength training), which would only have to be supplied with oxygen as well.

Improved vascularization (an increase in the number of capillaries per muscle fibre) of muscles is a result of endurance conditioning; as a consequence, the nutrient and gas exchange surface between muscle fibres and the bloodstream enlarges so that the muscle metabolism can speed up and become more efficient.

Metabolism

Muscles have three sources of available energy, which are discussed separately in the following sections for explanatory purposes, but are in reality inseparable and intermixed. The transitions from one type to another are smooth. The two major forms of energy production are **aerobic** and **anaerobic**, which is further subdivided into the categories of *anaerobic metabolism without lactic acid production* and *anaerobic metabolism with lactic acid production*.

Aerobic Metabolism

Aerobic means that energy is liberated with the help of oxygen. This is the most important form of energy for cycling, since it can provide energy for long periods of time, liberates relatively high amounts of energy, and replenishes the two anaerobic metabolic pathways after they have depleted their energy stores. Aerobic metabolism combusts, or oxidizes, fats and carbohydrates.

The most important fuel is glucose, a simple carbohydrate with the chemical formula $C_6H_{12}O_6$. Glucose is the product of carbohydrate digestion (see chapter 5, Nutrition). In a highly simplified explanation of the process, glucose combines with oxygen and gets cleaved to carbon dioxide (which is expelled from the lungs) and water. This reaction liberates a relatively large amount of energy in the form of ATP (adenosine triphosphate, a very energy-rich molecule). ATP is the direct energy storage form of cells and is also used as the "muscle fuel" that powers muscle contraction. The individual reaction steps from glucose to ATP are far too complex to describe in detail here. The body's process of energy liberation can be compared to that of a steam engine:

The combustion materials (fats and glucose) are represented by the water; the fire, sometimes small, sometimes large, symbolizes the metabolic rate. The steam that is formed from the water symbolizes ATP. In order to move or power something forward, the cell uses ATP and the steam engine, steam. Just like the storage of ATP in the body, so, too, is the storage of steam in the engine (tank)

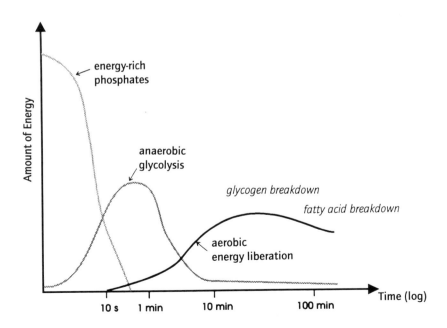

Figure 2.5: The energy forms in relation to exercise duration

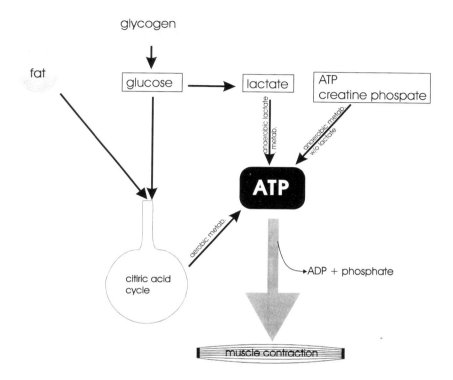

Figure 2.6: Simplified metabolic scheme

limited and constantly has to be replenished. The site of aerobic energy metabolism is the mitochondrion, the so-called powerhouse, of the muscle fibre. The glucose is either removed from the bloodstream or originates from the glycogen stores of the cell (glycogen is the storage form of glucose), from which it is transported into the mitochondria.

In addition to carbohydrates, fats are also combusted aerobically. Fats are made from fatty acids that enter the carbohydrate metabolic cycle at a specific site and are burned together with the carbohydrates. Therefore, the energy from fats can only be used when carbohydrates are oxidized simultaneously. The disadvantage of fats is that they can be used for energy only during low intensity exercise, since their metabolism requires a lot of oxygen. Fats, however, store twice as much energy as carbohydrates, namely 9.3 kcal, compared to 4.1 kcal per gram.

Cyclists must condition their bodies to burn fat to conserve the glycogen stores that are needed for high-intensity efforts and become vastly depleted after about two hours of strenuous exercise. While the unconditioned athlete can use fat to provide about 40% of his energy during exercise, an endurance trained cyclist can generate 60% or more of his energy requirements from fat. With increased endurance training, an athlete can condition his body to use a higher percentage of fat while exercising at the same intensity. This increased fat utilization spares valuable glycogen stores, conserving them for the intense efforts that may decide the outcome of the race. The muscle cells of an endurance trained cyclist can store two to three times more energy-liberating fat than can those of an untrained athlete.

If a good endurance base has not been established, muscle cells will begin to use glycogen stores at relatively low levels of exercise. The combined glycogen stores present in muscle and liver is between 400 and 500 g, most of which is stored in the muscle cells. Cycling performance depends heavily on the amount of muscle glycogen. Muscle glycogen that is depleted after a race must be replenished, a process that takes between 24 and 48 hours with the proper nutrition (see chapter 5, Nutrition). Endurance training improves metabolism in the muscle fibre itself: the enzyme concentrations in the mitochondria rise and the substrates (glucose, fatty acids) are also present in higher concentrations that are more readily metabolized for energy than in an unconditioned individual.

The number of mitochondria per muscle fibre of increases as well and improved vascularization (the number of capillaries per muscle fibre) allows oxygen, necessary for energy liberation, to enter the muscle cell more easily and in larger amounts. Because of these physiologic changes, aerobic metabolism occurs more rapidly and economically.

Anaerobic Metabolism
Anaerobic Metabolism with Lactic Acid Production
Energy production in the absence of oxygen is classified as anaerobic metabolism. This type of metabolism produces lactic acid, the acid of milk sugar. Lactic acid decreases the pH of muscle and leads to muscle pain and eventual cessation of high-intensity exertion. Muscles use the lactic acid-producing metabolic pathways whenever aerobic metabolism is insufficient to produce the amount of energy

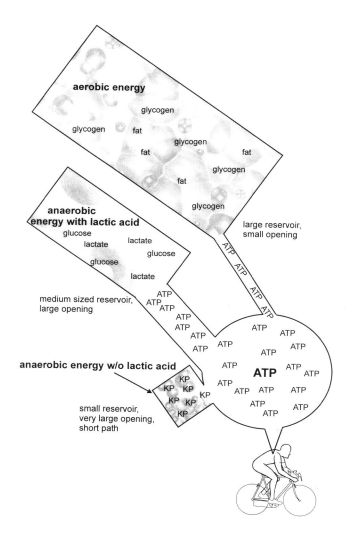

Figure 2.7: The energy reserves of a human (simplified). Energy-liberating systems are interlocked: the large supply of aerobic energy can only be liberated slowly; for larger energy demands, the body must resort to the anaerobic lactic acid-generating pathway, whose energy supply is limited. For brief (lasting several seconds) high energy-requiring movements, the body can use creatine phosphate stores. All three pathways generate ATP, wich is cleaved to ADP to provide energy for muscles contraction. The ATP pool is constantly replenished by these metabolic pathways.

required to meet performance demands. In the absence of oxygen, the cells convert glucose to lactic acid, a process that continues until the "glycolytic enzymes" (responsible for the reaction) become inhibited by the lactic acid and cease to function. The conversion of glucose to lactic acid liberates energy in the form of ATP. It is surprising that although the anaerobic pathway produces only about 5% of the energy generated via aerobic metabolism and does not liberate the energy present in the lactic acid molecule, this pathway still yields a larger quantity of energy per unit of time. This paradox occurs since, theoretically, many glucose molecules can be metabolized at once and their energy used for relatively brief high-intensity bouts of exercise, lasting between 40 and 60 seconds.

At the beginning of a period of exercise, especially at the start of a race and if the cyclist has not warmed-up properly, the aerobic pathway is not functioning efficiently. Under penalty of creating an oxygen debt, the anaerobic lactic acid-producing pathway is activated to prevent an energy deficit. The lactic acid that is then produced, the initial lactic acid, is metabolized when the aerobic pathway starts functioning at a higher rate. Intermediate sprints or attacks are similar situations that generate greater concentrations of lactic acid. If the lactic acid concentration rises above a certain threshold, performance suffers; at this point, the concentration is so great that it blocks muscle metabolism and prevents the aerobic pathway from getting rid of lactic acid. The muscles become acidotic, and the rider is forced to drastically reduce the intensity of his efforts.

Two cycling disciplines are good examples of the production of energy through the anaerobic lactic acid pathway: the kilometer time trial and the track sprint. In road cycling, short time trials up to 1.5 km also completely exhaust energy stores, while generating lactic acid. These forms of cycling require a very brief period of maximum performance, for which aerobic metabolism is too slow and couldn't provide sufficient energy.

Anaerobic Metabolism without Lactic Acid Production

For the sake of completeness, the pathway of anaerobic metabolism without lactic acid production is mentioned, although this pathway plays a subordinate role in cycling. Its importance is seen in strength sports, such as weight-lifting and shot-put, and in sports requiring jumping. As implied in the name, this pathway does not produce lactic acid like the previously discussed anaerobic lactic-acid pathway. ATP and creatine phosphate stores (energy-rich phosphate bonds) provide energy for at most 5 to 8 seconds, during which a few maximal muscle contractions can take place. Every muscle contraction absolutely requires ATP; without ATP, the muscle cannot generate tension. For this reason, cells must constantly regenerate their ATP stores, a process that is primarily accomplished through aerobic metabolism. ATP is also used for other energy-requiring processes in the cell. ATP liberates its stored energy when a phosphate is cleaved off of the molecule. The resulting ADP (adenosine diphosphate) later gets "recycled" to ATP again.

Manifestations of Bodily Adaptations Resulting from Regular Cycling Training (Endurance Training)

    Musculature
↑   higher performance capacity
↑   improved vascularization
↑   larger glycogen stores
↑   more mitochondria

    Heart
↑   enlarged volume
↑   increased mass
↑   larger maximum output
↓   lowered resting heart rate
↓   lowered heart rate at a fixed intensity

    Blood
↑   increased volume
↑   improved flow properties
↑   enlarged oxygen transport capacity

    Lungs
↑   enlarged volume
↑   enlarged maximum oxygen absorption
↓   decreased breathing rate

    Body
↑   more efficient metabolism
↑   strengthened immune system
↑   improved performance capacity
↓   decreased fatiguability
↓   reduced body weight

2.3 The Demands of the Individual Disciplines of Road Cycling

The next section briefly explores the characteristic and distinct physiological demands of different types of racing. The different endurance disciplines are explained in chapter 3.1.

1. Bicycle Touring

The bicycle tour places extremely variable demands on the athlete; the intensity spectrum ranges from a race-paced time trial to an easy training ride at endurance pace, and the distances vary from 40 to 200 km, depending on the fitness and goals of the athlete. Because of this immense variability, it is impossible to provide precise descriptions of the demands of a typical tour; instead, the curious reader should estimate what type of race described below most approximates his tour and read about that type of riding.

2. Road Races of 60 to 120 km

Only the shortest amateur races are less than 120 km long. Races for juniors and women, however, fall almost exclusively in this category. Because of the huge time span covered by the Long-distance Endurance Zone III (90 min-6 hr) (see chapter 3), these races, as well as most amateur circuit races, fall into the category of Long-distance Endurance Type III. As in all bicycle races, the cyclist has the opportunity to draft, whereby he must expend less energy. The proportion of anaerobic energy use can increase with decreasing race duration, up to about 10% for this type of race. The depletion of the VO_2max reaches 95% during short races. The heart rate is between 150 and 195 beats per minute, but this value tends to be higher for juniors, who have higher maximum heart rates.

3. Road Races of 120 to 200 km

Road races covering this distance take 3 to 6 hours, and therefore fall into the Long-distance Endurance Type III category (see chapter 3.1). This race distance requires careful allotment of energy stores, which should be saved for race-determining situations (attacks, hills, and sprints). The aerobic pathway covers 95% or more of the energy requirements through the oxidation of fats and carbohydrates; anaerobic metabolism provides 5%, at most. The heart rate varies between 140 and 180 beats, but may briefly reach higher values (up to 195). The value of the maximum oxygen uptake (VO_2max) decisively determines performance capacity. About 60-90% of the VO_2max is depleted during the race. Eating and drinking are absolutely necessary due to the heavy use of glycogen stores (about 80% get used) and progressive dehydration (loss of body water).

4. Circuit Races and Criteriums of 40 to 60 km

This race distance is especially prevalent in women's and junior's races. High exercise intensities of 80-95% of VO_2max are reached. The heart rate varies from 170 to 195; again, this value is somewhat higher for younger athletes. Aerobic metabolism covers about 90% of the energy requirements, and the anaerobic pathway covers the remaining 10%. Because of the constantly changing race status and the frequent prime sprints, circuit racing requires a riding style that is very dynamic and adaptable to rapid changes in pace. Intermediate sprints and numerous attacks at any point during the race require speed and strength, combined with a well-developed anaerobic capacity. While food intake, assuming adequate pre-race fueling, is relatively unimportant, fluid intake even during short races is critical to preserve performance capacity (see chapter 5).

5. Circuit Races and Criteriums of 60 to 100 km

Circuit races of more than 60 km and less than 100 km are classified into Long-distance Endurance Type III races, and are usually only found in amateur racing. As mentioned above, abrupt changes in the race status are characteristic of this type of race. The demands on the rider change markedly depending on his aggressiveness. Thus, it is possible to race a noticeably less intense race by sitting in the pack than by riding at the front and in breakaways. Frequent surges (up to 320 times in an 80 km race) after coming out of turns heavily tax the muscles, necessitating anaerobic energy production.

6. Stage Racing

Cycling stage races represent the single most exhausting form of sports competition, with the exception of the recently popular extreme endurance sports, such as the triple ultra-triathlon. The riding demands are most often like those of Long-distance Endurance Type III riding. The achievement of such performances over the course of days, or sometimes even weeks (Tour de France: 3 weeks), is an excellent example of human beings' extreme endurance conditioning capacity. With a daily energy expenditure that often exceeds that which the rider can take in through food, metabolism is driven to its limits. It is not uncommon for body fat and even muscle protein to be broken down during a stage race.

7. Time Trialing

The time trial has few tactical considerations, since only true fitness determines success or failure. Time trial distances vary so much that it is not easy to give physiological characteristics that apply to all. Short time trials of under ten minutes

require near maximum functioning of the heart and circulatory system. Heart rates are in the sub-maximal to maximal zones: 190 to 210 beats per minute. Oxygen uptake is near maximum and anaerobic metabolism can occasionally provide over 20% of the energy. Therefore, short time trials result in high muscle acidosis (high lactic acid concentration). The greater the distance, the more the effort approaches that of Long-distance Endurance Type II riding. As a rule, time trialing is typically performed at a steady pace, as shown by a constant heart rate.

3 Training

3.1 Training Fundamentals

The science of coaching, which occupies its own influential branch of sport science, is concerned with providing training programs to athletes to optimize their training. **Training** is, or at least should be, a structured process; "should be" illustrates that this is unfortunately often not the case in cycling or in other sports. Even with the stronger tendency in recent years toward structured training programs, many cyclists still train randomly and aimlessly, although they could have achieved significantly better results in the same amount of time if their training had been more structured.

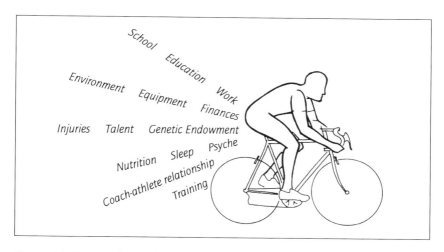

Figure 3.1: Factors that influence cycling performance: training is an important factor in athletic performance.

Proper training and understanding of training programs requires a knowledge of the basic theories behind coaching, enabling the practical application of this knowledge to everyday training. Even top riders who don't have to design their own training programs could benefit from a basic grasp of training fundamentals which would enable them to better understand their training schedule and modify it if necessary. In the same way, recreational riders can use such information to guide their development in a certain direction and improve their fitness. The following section gives simplified coaching advice pertinent to cycling as an endurance sport.

As already mentioned, training is a planned process whose goal it is to improve or maintain a certain level of fitness through appropriate workouts. Athletic fit-ness does not refer solely to physical (conditioned) fitness, but also encompasses and seeks to improve the tactical, technical, and psychological aspects of the sport.

From a biological standpoint, training is the body's response to stress. In response to demands placed on it, the human body develops its physical capabilities; however, physical adaptations waste away again as soon as the body is no longer stressed. Training is most effective when periods of stress and rest are logically alternated. Stress disrupts the body's biological balance; once the body recovers (regenerates itself), this results in adaptation and a higher level of fitness than before.

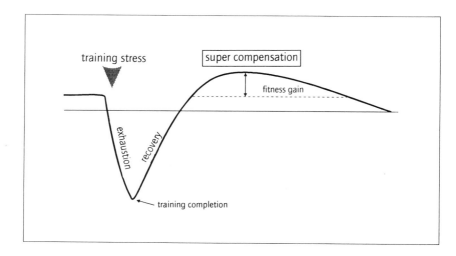

Figure 3.2: The principle of super-compensation

The diagram explains the principle of super-compensation, one of the most important principles of coaching; training stress, exhaustion, recovery, and super-compensation must follow each other in the proper time intervals.

Recovery is the process that compensates for the exhaustion phase and lasts until the previous level of fitness has been reached.

Super-compensation is the improvement in fitness that occurs after recovery: in effect, it is an "over-recovery". This higher fitness level is achieved by extending the recovery phase until a level of fitness is reached that would now easily accommodate the stress that caused the compensation to occur in the first place. This process is termed adaptation.

This concept appears very simple in theory and as illustrated in the diagram, yet in reality it is much more complex: extending the idea of super-compensation, it appears as if an "endless" improvement in fitness should be possible. In reality, though, super-compensation is especially noticeable in beginners and at the beginning of a period of training. Every workout results in improved fitness. However, after the fitness reaches a certain level, further improvements are less and less noticeable until performance finally plateaus. This phenomenon is the reason that highly conditioned cyclists must ride many miles and follow clever training programs to preserve, and possibly raise slightly, their level of fitness; simply increasing the intensity of workouts alone cannot help one attain peak fitness. Chapter 2.2 explains more about the physiological processes of adaptation. An explanation of training terminology follows.

Description of Training

Training intensity is the amount of stress a workout places on the body. The simplest way to measure the training intensity is by using the heart rate (high intensity = high heart rate). Training intensities below a certain percentile of maximum are not useful for improving any of the five conditioned abilities: *strength, endurance, speed, flexibility*, and *coordination*. High intensity workouts condition primarily strength and speed, whereas low intensity workouts improve endurance.

Training scope is the sum of all loads or training stresses within one workout or within a specified training period (a week or a preparation period). In cycling, the

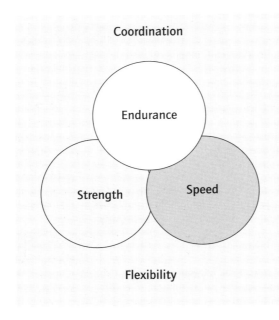

Coordination

Endurance

Strength   Speed

Flexibility

Figure 3.3:
Fitness is the combination of five abilities.

training scope is equivalent to the mileage (i.e. 100 km a day or 400 km a week), or, better yet, to the time spent training; any additionalworkouts off the bike (indoor training, gymnastics, running, etc.) are also added to the training scope.

Workout density is the relationship of periods of stress to periods of rest and, therefore, the duration that separates the individual training stresses; rest breaks are classified as complete and incomplete. Training with complete rest breaks entails waiting for complete recovery, as determined by heart rate or body feeling, before starting the next workload. The incomplete, or short, rest break lasts until the heart rate drops to 120-130 beats per minute, at which point one begins the next stress period (i.e., 1 km intervals).

Effort duration is the duration of a workload, such as an interval (3 minutes) or a sprint series (6 times for 20 seconds).

Training frequency indicates how many times a week one trains. For cycling, the number of workouts per week should not be less than four and can, if time restraints necessitate training two times a day (i.e. before and after work or an appointment), increase to over ten. Good amateurs usually have a training frequency of six or seven workouts per week (including races).

These five principles of athletic training enable a precise description of the training process; make sure you understand them, since they will come up again and again in this chapter on training.

As already elucidated, training is an interchange of stress and recovery; this presents the problem of determining the optimum amount of stress and recovery. The recovery phase is viewed as the most important phase, since improvement in fitness takes place during this period of time; the stress phase serves solely to trigger the recovery phase and the subsequent super-compensation. The main reason that many cyclists fail to achieve results appropriate to the amount of time spent training, is that they train too strenuously and ignore the recovery phase. If you continue to break down your body through strenuous training and never allow it time to recover, you may "ride yourself into the ground", which means that fitness actually declines, despite intense training. However, setting the appropriate workload allows the performance to improve up to an *individually-determined performance level*, which requires a few years of training for an endurance sport such as cycling. It is impossible to reach peak performance within a year, especially without a background in endurance sports. Beginning cyclists often have difficulty understanding this concept, and this frequently leads to frustration.

Figure 3.4 diagrams one more time what was just explained: the top figure shows the consequence of too brief of a recovery interval: when a new stress is applied during the recovery phase, it prevents an improvement in fitness and causes a decline instead.

The consequence of too little stress is fitness stagnation; the next workload is applied only after the super-compensation phase is over, and training begins anew from the same level at which the previous workout started. This type of training results in very little, if any, improvement in fitness. As figure 3.4 shows, the next stress must be applied in the middle (peak) of the super-compensation phase in order to maximize fitness improvement. In order to raise fitness level, the recovery phase must be appropriate not only between workouts, but also between training and competition; the next chapter will explain more on this subject. Training at too low of an intensity does not trigger an adaptation phase – training at too high of an intensity can eventually lead to overtraining; only the

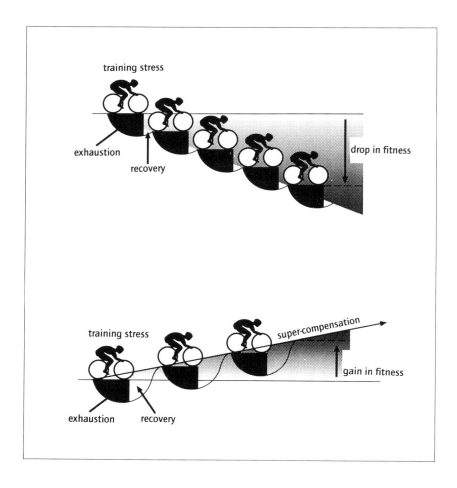

Figure 3.4:
Above: Workouts spaced too closely together lead to a regression of fitness.
Below: The appropriate amount of stress during the super-compensation phase leads to a desirable gain in fitness.

right amount of stress will lead to the desired adaptation and super-compensation. The "right" stress is the proper coordination of workout intensity and amount with periods of rest.

Body feeling plays a big role in the choice of rest periods and the design of a training plan. Training program suggestions, as made in this book, must be modified for different individuals. You should never feel obligated to follow a training program precisely.

Recovery

What influences the duration of the recovery phase? A simple ground rule for recovery is that the more intense or exhausting the training or the race, the longer the required rest period, since the body needs longer to fix the damage done to the tissues to restore balance. Disease states, such as infection or inflammation, negatively influence recovery. Daily stresses may then become intolerable, and the recovery phase may take much longer. After a bad cold, recovery throughout the body can be disrupted for two to three weeks, significantly impacting performance. Even stress and other psychological factors can negatively alter the body's ability to recover. The recovery duration varies quite a bit between individuals: some can perform at their peak the day after a hard race, while others won't recover completely for three days or even a week. This variability explains why some cyclists can perform well in one-day races, but can't compete effectively in stage races, which demand short recovery times.

What influences recovery? Meeting certain criteria after training and competition may improve recovery time; however, there is no "wonder drug" whose consumption enables lightening-fast recovery. What criteria should you watch?

Factors that improve recovery:

- sufficient rest (sleep)
- athletic diet (appropriate for nutrition needs)
- stretching
- massage
- warm baths
- recovery training

These factors are all included in the term "athletic lifestyle". *Sufficient rest* means that unnecessary stress is not placed on the body after a workout; however, it also includes getting enough bed rest. The *proper nutrition* is a diet rich in carbohydrates, vitamins, and minerals (see chapter 5, Nutrition), which allow the body to replenish the depleted energy reserves. *Stretching* loosens up sore muscles, preserves flexibility, and, when combined with *massage*, a *warm bath*, and, above all, *recovery training*, greatly increases the speed with which waste products are transported out of muscles.

Endurance training greatly improves recovery ability: conditioned cyclists are usually fairly well-recovered only a few minutes after crossing the finish line at the conclusion of a difficult race; beginning cyclists, on the other hand, may hardly be able to recover after a mountainous ascent and may even be forced to quit their race or training ride.

Adaptation, the body's adjustment, is divided into metabolic adaptation (the oxidation of foodstuffs) and morphological adaptation (physical changes, for example in muscle and heart). An endurance sport such as cycling leads to significant metabolic and morphological adaptations, discussed more in detail in the section on Performance Physiology.

Fundamentals of Endurance Theory

Endurance is the general improved capacity of an organism to resist exhaustion and recover after exertion. The ability to resist exhaustion has physical, as well as psychological, components. Endurance is, as already seen, one of the indices of fitness, but it is not the only important attribute for cycling, since strength and speed are absolutely necessary for good race results. The quality of strength has been neglected in the past, and only recently has scientific training emphasized the importance that strength has in all sports (see 3.8).

Endurance is divided into many types, not all of which are relevant to cycling; for completeness, though, all of them will be discussed. For example, the opposite of *generalized endurance* is *localized endurance*, which is endurance work that is confined to less than 1/6 of the total musculature. Cycling uses large muscle groups (in the legs), and is therefore classified as a generalized endurance sport. Metabolism is classified into *aerobic* (sufficient oxygen available) and *anaerobic* (too little oxygen present) endurance; cycling requires both aerobic and anaerobic endurance. Yet another classification is that of *static* (work without movement) and *dynamic* (resulting in motion) endurance. The most important distinction in cycling, however, is the exercise duration, which lasts from 35 seconds to over 6 hours.

The Individual Endurance Types:

1. Short-distance Endurance (35 sec to 2 min)

The short-distance endurance (SDE) is characterized by a high rate of energy production; cycling has only a few disciplines that fall into this category: the kilometer time trial on the track and extremely short prologue time trials, as found in amateur stage races, fit into this classification. On the other hand, a match sprint on the track may be long enough to be classified here as well if the sprint was initiated early enough. Lactic acid concentrations up to 20 mmol/litres blood, for example, are reached in the kilometer time trial; these are values that would drastically impair a road cyclist. About 60% of the energy is generated anaerobically.

The following criteria are critical for Short-distance Endurance:

- excellent speed and strength

- high aerobic performance

- coordination

- high lactic acid tolerance (tolerance of muscle acidosis)

2. Intermediate-distance Endurance (2 to 10 min)

Intermediate-distance endurance is necessary for individual and team pursuit on the track for all categories (2,000-5,000 meters) and short road time trials (individual or team). Energy production is still very high, but it is less than that generated in short-distance endurance work. All oxygen requirements of the body cannot be met, necessitating that part of the energy be supplied anaerobically. The shorter the exercise duration, the higher is the proportion of anaerobic energy use (around 20%). The process of training for intermediate- and short-distance endurance is significantly more complex and different from that of long-distance endurance, since high demands are placed on both aerobic and anaerobic systems. As is the case for short-distance endurance riding, strength and speed are also important requirements for this type of riding.

3. Long-distance Endurance

Because of different distinguishing characteristics, there are four separate types:

Long-distance Endurance Type I (10 to 35 min): Long-distance endurance type I riding places maximum demands on the heart/circulatory system and breathing, so that a good aerobic capacity (measured by a high VO_2 max) is the key determinant for success. Heart rate and breathing are almost in their maximum zones. Time trialing, short junior races, and many races on the track (the points race of several categories, missing out races, etc.) fall into this classification. Since aerobic metabolism covers about 85% of the energy requirements, glycogen stores (muscle glycogen) is a limiting factor. Moderate concentrations of lactic acid have to be tolerated for relatively long (up to 35 min) periods. The oxidation of fatty acids does not play an important roll.

Long-distance Endurance Type II (35 to 90 min): Events lasting between 35 minutes and an hour and a half are quite common in cycling, and include all races up to about 60 km; almost all juniors' races (except the longer road races of older junior riders that may be up to 120 km) and individual time trials are of this type. Muscle and liver glycogen, but also fat, supply energy, resulting in an increase the proportion of aerobic to anaerobic metabolism to 9:1. However, tactical moves, such as prime sprints, attacks, and the final kilometers and finishing sprint of a race, all require a good anaerobic capacity.

Long-distance Endurance Type III (90 min to 6 hrs): The long-distance endurance Type III zone encompasses almost all amateur road cycling and recreational touring, as well as road races in other categories that are over 60 km long and amateur classics such as the german classic "Around Cologne" (200 km). Even most professional races don't exceed the 6 hour limit. The flow of energy is low in comparison to the other types and allows the body to burn a higher percentage of fat.

The period of time from 90 to 120 minutes does not show the same characteristics of the LDE III; it is a transition zone between LDE II and LDE III. In general, the transitions from one type of endurance category to the next are smooth.

The anaerobic threshold for well-conditioned cyclists is over 90% of the VO_2 max, enabling them to continue riding at a fast pace even with 3 mmol of lactic acid per litre of blood. Muscle and liver glycogen stores are limiting factors of performance, thus necessitating the intake of food (carbohydrates). To avoid compromising performance, one must also replace water and electrolytes that are lost through heavy perspiration.

Long-distance Endurance Type IV (over 6 hrs): Riding times of over six hours occur in professional racing and extreme bicycle touring, where distances of 250 km may be commonplace; there are even races, such as "Paris-Bordeaux", that cover distances of over 500 km. After muscle and liver glycogen stores are exhausted, the body resorts to high levels of fat metabolism (80%), supplemented by gluconeogenesis (the formation of glucose from lactic acid, protein, and fat). The intake of large amounts of food (carbohydrates) and water is absolutely necessary for such an extreme endurance feat.

The existence of triple ultra-triathlons and the "Race Across America", should necessitate the creation of the category long-distance endurance type V.

Fundamentals of Strength Theory

This section briefly explains the different types of strength. In addition to many minor types, sports science distinguishes among three main types of strength: a) maximum strength, b) speed strength, c) endurance strength.

Maximum strength is the strength an athlete can generate with a maximum muscle contraction.

Speed strength is the ability of the athlete to overcome high resistance with great muscle contraction speed; this type of strength depends heavily on the *maximum strength*. New research has shown that the maximum strength is even more important than previously thought as a foundation for the other types of strength – even for road cycling. *Speed strength* is especially valuable in road cycling, in particular during sprints and attacks.

Endurance strength is the athlete's ability to resist exhaustion after repeated strength-taxing activities. For mountainous ascents and breakaway attempts, which may require pushing gears of 53 x 13 or larger, *endurance strength* is critically important. A simple comparison of strength and pedal cadence is possible: at a certain speed, a higher pedal cadence requires less muscle strength; a lower pedal cadence necessitates a greater use of muscle strength. Strength training on and off the bike is explained in detail in chapter 3.8.

Fundamentals of Speed Theory

Speed is divided into two main types: the speed of a single movement (movement speed) and the propulsive speed of an athlete. Depending on the type of motion, speed is classified into *rotational* and *linear*. Cycling is a repetitive circular, or *rotational* motion, for which *rotational speed* is of primary importance. The *rotational speed* (movement speed) depends on the gear size: when pushing a large gear (i.e. 52 x 12), the pedal cadence and, therefore, also the movement speed is low; however, the propulsive speed can be very high. If a high pedal cadence can be sustained for a longer period of time in combination with great strength (large gear, endurance strength) the propulsive speed will be high. This statement illustrates how much speed depends on strength; without the appropriate amount of strength, high speeds are not attainable. Training should emphasize both strength training as well as speed training.

Speed is limited through:

- muscle strength
- reflex speed
- general aerobic dynamic endurance
- coordination
- muscle contraction speed
- muscle elasticity

Fundamentals of Flexibility Theory

Flexibility is the capacity of a person to carry out a movement with a large possible range of motion. Although flexibility is obviously more important for sports such as gymnastics than for cycling, flexibility's importance for high levels of performance on the bicycle should not be underestimated. General flexibility should be conditioned through special exercises and should be better than that of non-athletes.

Warming up on the rollers before the individual time trial

Flexibility is an absolute requirement for high-quality movement. The main consequence of inadequate flexibility is a higher risk of injury. If the joints and ligaments have no movement latitude during a crash, injuries such as sprained or even torn ligaments or tendons and also broken bones occur more frequently. Insufficient flexibility hinders an athlete's development of conditioning and coordination.

Flexibility increases the efficiency of movement and stimulates repair mechanisms. It depends to a large degree on the elasticity of muscles; therefore, this book devotes a whole chapter to stretching and gymnastics.

In a comparison of two "equally strong" athletes, the one who can't completely utilize his conditioned abilities (endurance, strength, speed) due to his limited flexibility, will always come up short. The conditioned abilities influence one another: too much strength training decreases both flexibility and endurance, and it is hypothesized that too much stretching negatively influences speed. As always in athletic training, an individual must find his own balance.

Foundations of Coordination Theory

Coordination is the athlete's ability to achieve a maximum effect (result) with a minimum of planned muscle involvement.

There are two types: *intermuscular* and *intramuscular coordination*. Intermuscular coordination is the interplay of muscles, both agonist and antagonist (flexors and extensors); intramuscular coordination is the collaboration of the central nervous system with a muscle unit (motor unit). The goal of intramuscular training is to involve as many muscle units as possible, so that the cyclist can reach maximum speed in a sprint (see chapter 3.8, Strength Training).

Cycling demands a high level of cycling-specific coordination, although the general coordination of a cyclist is usually poorly conditioned. In the past, coordination and flexibility training was often completely ignored at the beginning of a cycling career and was, consequently, never learned. Even so, the cycling specific coordination is often excellent; for example, the smooth pedal stoke and the jump, as well as attacking, cornering, and track-standing all illustrate that coordination is highly developed. To prevent a loss of general coordination that can result from focusing too much on cycling-specific training, a winter indoor training program should be begun when athletes are young.

3.2 Training Methods

Endurance Training Methods

Endurance training is divided into four training methods, which can be further partitioned into sub-methods:

1) The duration training method serves, above all, to improve basic endurance, and is divided into 1. the continuous method, 2. the alternating method, and 3. the random method. The duration training method is cycling's main training method, especially during the pre-season preparation period, since training at the appropriate intensity will improve aerobic capacity and repair mechanisms. The training time should be over an hour and can reach up to 5-8 hours. The training intensity can be steady or can vary within a certain range.

a) *The continuous method:* steady intensity; the use of a heart rate monitor to guide the level of intensity is most accurate.

b) *The alternating method:* On previously determined ride sections, the tempo is increased into the anaerobic zone.

c) *The random method:* the tempo is adjusted according to the terrain and the wind.

2) Interval methods consist of the planned alternation of periods of stress with periods of rest; the rest interval, however, is not carried out to complete recovery, but instead is cut short by the initiation of another stress interval once the heart rate drops to around 130 bpm. The interval method is used, for example, in sprint training (i.e.: 8 x 7 sec or 6 x 30 sec). If the workout calls for multiple sets of intervals, a training method used less frequently in cycling, longer rest breaks are necessary between sets. Since the 1980's, interval training (in particular, with long intervals) has lost importance, since its effectiveness was called into question.

3) The repetition method is characterized by complete recovery (heart rate under 100) between periods of stress that simulate or exceed race-pace. In road cycling, this method is less frequently used; in track cycling, on the other hand, it is more frequently employed (i.e. 3 x 1000 m).

4) The race simulation and control method involves a one-time stress that should be equal to the intensity and duration of the race. The physiological training stress is very similar to the race stress; when the training distance is longer than the race, the pace is less intense, and when the distance is shorter, the pace is harder. The race simulation method requires a high level of motivation in order to duplicate the difficulty of a race. Training races are especially useful, since they simulate not only the physical demands of racing, but also the technical, tactical, and psychological aspects. The race simulation method should only be used at the end of the preparation period and may not be employed until the beginning of the competition period. Time trials (over- and under-distance) are used to control (control method) and diagnose fitness (see also chapter 4.3).

Strength Training Methods

In strength training, stress is measured in repetitions and sets; a set can be composed of up to 20 repetitions, carried out one after the other without rest breaks. There are rest breaks between sets.

Speed Training Methods

For speed training advice, see the section on "Speed training" in chapter 3.3.

Flexibility Training Methods

A high level of performance demands good flexibility. The goal is to develop a high level of cycling-specific and an adequate amount of general flexibility. Even after the desired amount of flexibility has been reached, stretching exercises cannot be discontinued, since flexibility will then quickly return to the previous level. One should choose exercises that are appropriate to the type of stress experienced during competition or training. These exercises should be done while either warming-up or cooling down. More about improving flexibility in chapter 3.9, Stretching.

Coordination Training Methods

Coordination and riding technique are closely related; therefore, many tips on coordination training are also included in the technique sections. Coordination training without the bicycle takes place in the winter in the gym, but should be continued during the competition period as well. Coordination training should, as a rule, be done when the body is well-rested, and, therefore, not after a hard workout, since this could in some circumstances worsen coordination.

A workout designed to create a smooth pedal stroke, for example, is best combined with a recovery workout. Also, riding technique exercises, such as avoiding obstacles, tapping the back wheel of the rider in front of you with your front wheel, or cornering, can easily be incorporated into a rest day (training break). While working on cycling-specific coordination, you should not neglect general coordination, since it is beneficial for learning new skills on the bike.

3.3 Training Zones

For better structured workouts, training is divided into training zones, which are classified mainly by the intensity and the type of stress they create. This section introduces the different zones, while sections 3.5 and 3.6 explain how to combine and distribute the training zones and give examples of training programs for each main category of riders. Thoroughly reading chapters 2, 3.1, and 3.2 should vastly improve your understanding of the following sections.

Compensatory Training CO	
Description	regenerative training to restore performance capacity after a strenuous workout or competition; for warming-up before workouts
Heart Rate	80 - 120 beats/min
Metabolism	aerobic lactic acid concentration below 2.0 mmol/L
Distance/Profile	15 - 50 km, flat
Duration	0.5 - 2 hrs
Pedal Cadence	70 - 100 rev/min
Gear Ratio	4.60 - 6.00 meters 42 x 20 - 16
Training Method	endurance
Periodization	applicable the whole year round; less important during the preparation periods (PP) I and II; more important in the competition period (CP) as a component of the micro cycle
Workout Cycle	especially after a strenuous competition or workout; as a rule on Mondays and the day before a race
Ride Organization	individual and group training
Tips	apply as little pressure to the pedals as possible; dress warmly; incorporate technique training into CO-training; this is a very important component of the training camp

HR
120
80
Time

Compensatory Training CO (Knock out)

Compensation means balance; compensatory training, therefore, is used to balance fitness or to regenerate the body after a hard workout. The goal is active, sport-specific recovery. Compensatory training should follow when the body is exhausted, or "knocked out". The CO -zone is the lowest training intensity zone.

Basic Endurance Training BE

Basic endurance training is the most important type of training for all endurance sports, and especially for cycling, since it provides the critical performance base, namely a high aerobic capacity, without which a high level of fitness is not possible in cycling. Depending on age, training level, and cycling discipline, cyclists put in 70-90% of all their training miles in the basic endurance zone. Also, a large portion of winter training off the bicycle falls into this zone. BE -workouts are characterized by easy gears with low intensity. The basic endurance category itself is divided into two intensity levels: basic endurance 1 and basic endurance 2.

Basic Endurance I BE I

Description	most important training zone for cyclists; creates a high aerobic capacity to serve as a base for high-level performance; used for warming-up before workouts	
Heart Rate	115 - 145 beats/min	
Metabolism	aerobic lactic acid 0 - 3.0 mmol/L	
Distance/Profile	50 - 250 km, flat to hilly	HR 145 115 Time
Duration	2 - 8 hrs	
Pedal Cadence	80 - 110 rev/min, preferably 100 rev/min	
Gear Ratio	4.70 - 6.40 meters i. e. 42 x 19 - 14	
Training Method	endurance	
Periodization	applicable the whole year round; especially important in the PP's; for cross-training during the PP; main component of the spring training camp	
Workout Cycle	if possible, train in blocks: 3:1, 4:1, or 5:1, i.e. 1. 90 km, 2. 120 km, 3. 150 km 4. 40 km CO; during the CP this training ist best done Tues. through Thrus. or on free weekends, and in the PP from Fri. to Sun.	
Ride Organization	Training alone is best; use heart rate to guide intensity; group training: take short pulls (1 - 2 min) to keep intensity constant	
Tips	Determine individual heart rate range, depending on fitness level; if possible, don't train over 150 beats/min; a range of 20 beats is desirable	

Basic Endurance 2   BE 2 (Strength)

Description	medium-intensity training zone for developing competition-specific endurance, improving lactic acid metabolism, and optimizing the aerobic-anaerobic transition zone; strength- and motor-conditioning
Heart Rate	about 145 - 180 beats/minute
Metabolism	aerobic-anaerobic transition lactic acid 3.0 - 6.0 mmol/L
Distance/Profile	50 - 70 km, hilly to mountainous
Duration	0.15 - 2.00 hrs
Pedal Cadence	70 - 95 rev/min
Gear Ratio	6.20 - 8.60 meters i. e. 52 x 18 - 52 x 13
Training Method	repetition
Periodization	in PP II and III and in the CP, especially while preparing for a race; the longer the races, the less the BE 2 training
Workout Cycle	during the CP, advisable Wed. or even Thurs.
Ride Organization	solo training: self-motivation not easy; control intensity using heart rate and cadence group training: frequent change of leaders (1-2 min) to keep the intensity constant
Tips	important to determine individual heart rate zones using fitness diagnosis; a range of 10-15 beats is best; speed should not be used to guide intensity; flat land inhabitants: headwind training; distance is total of all BE 2 training

HR 175 145 Time

For example, 3 x 8 km BE 2 with 15 minute-long CO training in between (HR about 100); important: entering and leaving this zone

Basic Endurance 2   BE 2 (Pedal Cadence)

Description	medium-intensity training zone for developing competition-specific endurance, improving lactic acid metabolism, and optimizing the aerobic-anaerobic transition zone; motor-conditioning
Heart Rate	about 145 - 185 beats/minute
Metabolism	aerobic-anaerobic transition lactic acid 3.0 - 6.0 mmol/L
Distance/Profile	5 - 70 km, flat to hilly
Duration	0.15 - 2.00 hrs
Pedal Cadence	100 - 120 rev/min
Gear Ratio	5.60 - 7.60 meters i. e. 42 x 16 - 52 x 15
Training Method	repetition
Periodization	in PP III and in the CP, especially while preparing for a race; the longer the races, the less the BE 2 training
Workout Cycle	during the CP, advisable Wed. or even Thurs., as well as a short BE 2 ride the day before a race
Ride Organization	solo training: self-motivation not easy; control intensity using heart rate and cadence group training: frequent change of leaders (1-2 min) to keep the intensity constant
Tips	important to determine individual heart rate zones using fitness diagnosis; a range of 10-15 beats is best; speed should not be used to guide intensity; use as a warm-up before short races (criteriums or time trials); distance is total of all BE 2 training

HR 175 145 Time

For example, 3 x 8 km BE 2 with 15 minute-long CO training in between (HR about 100); important: entering and leaving this zone

Basic Endurance 1 BE 1
For distances from 70 to over 200 km, the body uses almost exclusively aerobic metabolic pathways and burns a high percentage of fat. This training zone is excellent for conditioning the body to burn fat and is, therefore, also the most useful zone to improve health (i.e., through weight loss).

Basic Endurance 2 BE 2
The BE 2 zone trains the aerobic-anaerobic threshold. One distinguishes between strength- and pedal cadence-oriented zones.

The individual heart rates of each training zone are given in the tables. The mixing in of BE 2 intervals into a BE 1 workout is wise. A long training ride exclusively in zone BE 2 is very tiring and depletes glycogen stores, as is desirable for carbohydrate loading (see chapter 5 Nutrition).

Competition-specific Endurance CSE
Training in the CSE zone – as implied by the name – is at race pace and race intensity. Distances are ridden at race intensity or, depending on fitness, above race intensity. Training in the competition-specific zone can be carried out with very high cadences and little use of strength, with race-appropriate cadences and

Competition-specific Endurances CSE	
Description	high-intensity training zone for improving stamina and lactic acid metabolism and tolerance, and getting used to riding fast; even races can be used for training
Heart Rate	over anaerobic threshols > 175 beats/min (160 - 185 bpm)
Metabolism	aerobic lactic acid over 5.0 mmol/L
Distance/Profile	10 - 80 km, flat to hilly
Duration	0.20 - 2.30 hrs
Pedal Cadence	80 - 120 rev/min, ideally 100 rev/min
Gear Ratio	6.20 - 9.20 meters i. e. 52 x 18 - 52 x 12
Training Method	repetition, competition
Periodization	in PP III and in the CP, especially important for time trial preparation
Workout Cycle	during the CP, advisable Wed. or Thurs (use sparingly, since it is very strenuous)
Ride Organization	solo training: as time trial training, use heart rate to guide intensity group training: as team time trial practice
Tips	important to determine individual heart rate zones using fitness diagnosis; a range of about 20 beats is best; speed should not be used to guide intensity; training races

(chart: HR, 185, 160, Time)

Speed Training   ST

Description	high-intensity training zone above anaerobic threshols for improving speed and speed endurance, as well as stamina and lactic acid tolerance
Heart Rate	over anaerobic threshold > 175 beats/min
Metabolism	anaerobic lactic acid over 6.0 mmol/L
Distance/Profile	0,5 - 5 km, flat
Duration	40 sec - 8 min
Pedal Cadence	120 - max rev/min
Gear Ratio	5.20 - 7.50 meters i. e. 42 x 17 - 52 x 15
Training Method	interval
Periodization	at the end of PP II and III and in the CP; especially important preparation for track and criterium racing
Workout Cycle	during the CP, advisable Tues. or Wed. (use sparingly, since it is very strenuous)
Ride Organization	solo training: use heart rate and cadence to guide intensity group training: motivation is easier; it's easier to maintain high cadences
Tips	important to determine individual heart rate zones using fitness diagnosis; speed should not be used to guide intensity; train in this zone regularly; a measure of progress; maximum cadence test

For example, 3 x 1000 m ST with CO/BE 1 rest breaks in between, gear ratio 42 x 16; or 3 x 1 min. important: entering and leaving this zone

gears, or with large gears and the resulting lower cadences and greater use of strength. When training as a group, individuals should not ride in front longer than 60 seconds, so that each cyclist can ride at a fairly constant intensity. Motor-pacing, training at high speed by drafting off of a motorcycle or car, is another form of **CSE** training.

Specialized Training Zones

The specialized training zones occupy only a few percent of the total amount of training.

Speed Training **ST**

Speed training belongs in the category of specialized training zones and is different from speed-strength training. Speed training does not refer to riding speed, but rather to movement speed, which in cycling is equivalent to the pedal cadence. This type of training conditions both speed and speed endurance.

Wind sprints, or "ins and outs", are a form of speed training; in this workout, the cyclist rides in an easy gear (see table) and then "jumps" 6-12 times for 20 to 30 meters, with about 50 meters of easy pedaling between each effort.

Speed-strength Training SS

Description	specialized high-intensity training zone for improving speed, maximum strength, and anaerobic metabolism without lactic acid production
Heart Rate	not relevant
Metabolism	anaerobic without lactic acid production
Distance/Profile	incorporate into 60 km BE 1 ride
Duration	6 - 12 x 6 sec. , 1 - 3 sets
Pedal Cadence	maximum, out of the saddle
Gear Ratio	6.20 - 7.20 meters i. e. 52 x 18 - 52 x 15
Training Method	interval, rest breaks of 3 - 5 min
Periodization	in PP II and III and in the CP, especially important preparation for track and criterium racing
Workout Cycle	during the CP, advisable Tues. or Wed.
Ride Organization	solo training: time (6 sec) guides intensity group training: motivation is easier, it's easier to do lots of repeats
Tips	jump with maximum (100%) effort for 6-8 sec; start with easy gears; speed does not reflect intensity; do this workout regularly

For example, 8 x 6 sec. SS with CO/BE 1 rest breaks; gear ratio 52 x 15; rest duration 3 - 5 min; important: entering and leaving this zone

Speed-strength or Sprint Training SS

Speed-strength training serves primarily to improve sprinting and jumping abilities. The training types will be discussed in more detail in section 3.8, Strength Training.

A workout of this type requires sprinting all-out for 6 to 8 seconds in a moderate gear from a slow rolling start or a stand-still, then riding easy, and repeating the drill after 2 to 3 minutes.

SS training is especially important for criterium and track racers.

Strength-endurance Training SE

The goal of strength-endurance training is to improve the resistance to exhaustion in the face of repeated assaults on strength. Training with increased resistance can be accomplished by riding up a mountain or mountain pass with a low-grade incline. Using a large gear (big cog), climb the relatively small incline in the saddle with a pedal cadence between 40 and 60 rev/min. This exercise is excellent for

Strength-endurance Training   SE

Description	specialized high-intensity training zone for improving strength endurance; hills are climbed in the saddle at low cadences	
Heart Rate	about 145 - 175 beats/min	
Metabolism	aerobic-anaerobic lactic acid 3 - 5 mmol/L	
Distance/Profile	3 - 30 km, hilly	
Duration	20 min - 1.5 hrs	
Pedal Cadence	40 - 60 rev/min	
Gear Ratio	5.20 - 8.00 meters i. e. 52 x 21 - 52 x 14	For example, 1 x 20 km SE with gear ratio 52 x 15; important: entering and leaving this zone; if no long hill available, use several short hills or a long stretch (30 km) into a strong headwind
Training Method	repetition; as a rule, not more than 3 repeats	
Periodization	In (PP I, II) and III and in the CP, especially important preparation for hilly road races, time trials, and circuit races; during PP I - if at all - only train in flat SE	
Workout cycle	during the PP, Wed. or Thurs. or during a race	
Ride Organization	solo training group training: motivation is easier; problem: don't race each other up the hill	
Tips	ride up the hill sitting quietly in the saddle, pay attention to pedal stroke (pulling); start with easy gears, speed does not reflect intensity; perform regularly; stop if joint pain occurs, but build up slowly if no problems (slowly increase the load)	

working on a smooth pedal stroke, in particular, the pulling back phase. If the heart rate is in the highest zone, the load is too small and the pedal cadence is too high; you should choose a larger gear.

To work on competition-specific endurance, climb a hill at least 4 km long using race-appropriate gearing and simulating 3-5 high gear attacks of over 300 meters each. The last 500 meters should be a finishing sprint. This final method of training should be only occasionally employed, since it is very strenuous.

If there are no mountains available for SE -training, you can also use a flat stretch with a constant, strong headwind, but this method is less effective.

Strength training has gained importance in recent years, since using larger gears results in attaining even higher speeds. Due to the high load and low cadence, the intensity remains in the sub-maximal zone.

The high load causes a large elevation in blood pressure; therefore, people cycling for the benefit of their health should not do this type of training. Sections 3.5 and 3.6 explain more about the use of the individual training zones.

3.4 The Use of Heart Rate Monitors

This chapter explains the benefits and use of heart rate monitors, or pulse watches. In addition, it gives helpful advice on determining your individual training zones. Finally, it addresses the most frequent training mistakes.

How does a heart rate monitor work? As recently as 20 years ago, the control of training through the determination of heart rate was a "game of luck", since heart rate could only be estimated by taking the pulse at certain locations (wrist, neck); constant monitoring of the heart rate was, therefore, impossible. In the succeeding years, the first pulse watches were worn only by top athletes, whose great success was attributed to this training device. The unbelievable success of the East German cyclists was due, among other things, to the development and implementation of heart rate-guided training. In the mid 70's, the East Germans experimented with the first wireless heart rate monitors. In the mid 80's, the first, fully functional pulse watches made by POLAR appeared in stores, and today they have become an affordable training instrument for everyone (around $100). The range of pulse watch users spans from the top amateur or professional to the recreational rider.

The transmitter in the chest strap registers the heart rate and sends radio waves (wireless) to the watch (receiver). The recording of the heart beat through chest electrodes in the strap uses EKG technology and surpasses all other methods as the most precise form of measurement. Higher-end models allow training intensity zone programming and emit an audible

The POLAR INTERFACE makes a data transferences into child's play and represents the best technology for heart rate-oriented cycling.

signal when the heart rate is either higher or lower than the set zone. The top models made by POLAR allow heart rate data to be stored during the workout or race. At home, the data can then be transferred through an interface to a PC, which can graphically represent and evaluate the information. These values provide important information for effectively guiding your training.

The watch is attached to the handlebars while riding, so that the heart rate can constantly be controlled. When using a pulse watch, pay attention to the correct, not too tight fit of the strap; your breathing should in no way be obstructed. The electrodes can only sense the heart beat when they are moist. Either wet the electrodes with a little water before the ride or wait until natural perspiration moistens the contacts after a few minutes of riding. In the immediate vicinity of strong sources of electricity (power lines, rail road lines), the heart rate monitor may temporarily show a very high number, which is unrelated to the actual heart rate.

Sometimes during two-abreast or group training, the individual senders and receivers may overlap or disturb each other.

How does the heart rate vary during cycling? The heart rate of a cyclist – regardless of the road profile, the weather, and the road surface – is already subject to relatively large variations on flat stretches. Normally, cyclists use speed as a gauge for level of intensity; due to the above-mentioned factors, this is problematic, especially when you consider how much the intensity increases into a headwind and how much it decreases in the succeeding tailwind section. Therefore, training intensity must be measured by a value other than speed.

In modern, scientific-oriented training, the intensity is only judged by the heart rate, not by the speed. By shifting gears and adjusting the pedal cadence, you can reach the desired intensity zone.

A consequence of heart rate-oriented training is that you may have to ride slower, for example when riding into a headwind or up a hill, so that you do not exceed the desired intensity range (i.e. **BE 1**). Of course, the heart rate zones should not be viewed as strict boundaries that cannot be violated under any circumstances. Periodic deviation is permissible as demanded by the situation, as long as the bulk of training still takes place as planned in the desired zone (usually **BE 1**).

The Resting Pulse

As already mentioned in chapter 2.2, the pulse changes as a consequence of the training process. In particular, the lowering of the resting pulse is viewed as a sign of improved endurance fitness. You can measure your resting pulse to familiarize yourself with the use of a heart rate monitor. The resting pulse is not only an indicator of endurance fitness, but also of imminent illness, infection, and overtraining. Only by taking a resting pulse every morning before getting up, can you detect changes. If the resting pulse is usually between 45 and 48, and one morning, it is 55, this finding could signal approaching illness, even when symptoms are not yet present. On the other hand, if the resting pulse gradually rises throughout the course of the day, the diagnosis would be overtraining; in any case, recovery is affected. After hard races or during stage

The POLAR INTERFACE transfers the heart rates stored in the POLAR VANTAGE NV to a PC, which evaluates and graphically represents training using appropriate software.

races, the resting pulse is often slightly elevated due to the very high stress and short rest periods. In general, you should check for the above-mentioned factors whenever your resting pulse is elevated by 6 to 8 beats per minute; especially when your exercising pulse is elevated as well, you should proceed carefully or even interrupt your training or racing, since an endurance ride while the body is fighting infection can damage the heart or other organs.

Take Your Pulse Every Morning

Taking a resting pulse every morning is part of a cyclist's daily training program; the value is recorded in the training diary (chapter 3.10), so that cyclists, beginners in particular, can follow resting pulse changes over the course of months and years. In high performance-level sports, the resting pulse can be related to and graphically compared with other parameters, such as racing results. Those who don't wish to put on their heart rate monitors in the morning

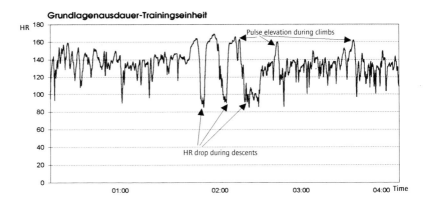

Figure 3.5: Basic Endurance: although the training intensity was intended to be BE 1 (2) the HR varies strongly, depending on the course profile and wind.

can take their pulses manually, on the carotid artery at the neck, at the wrist, or directly over the heart for 15 seconds; multiply this value by 4. Placing pen and paper next to the bed is a good way to remember to measure the resting pulse. The approximate normal values are given in chapter 2.2. Juniors and children have resting pulses that are, on average, 10 beats higher than those of adults. Rarely, very successful cyclists who have been training for many years may have consistently high resting pulse values of up to 80 beats per minute. This phenomenon is not worrisome, as there are always physiological exceptions to the rule, but nevertheless should be looked at by a doctor.

Determining the Training Zones

The training zones mentioned in the previous chapter serve largely as a guide for the heart rate. The given values are applicable to 18 to 35 year-old conditioned cyclists with a maximum heart rate of 200. Younger and older cyclists, but also athletes with lower maximum heart rates cannot use the given values, as they would constantly be training in the wrong zones. Therefore, you must determine your training zones individually through fitness testing or by knowing your maximum heart rate. The following sections explain how these zones can be derived from the maximum heart rate and the resting pulse.

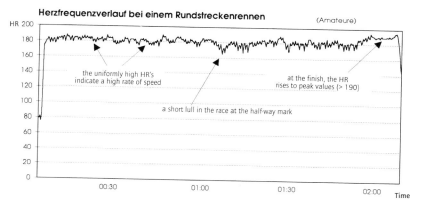

Figure 3.6: Heart rate behaviour during a circuit race (amateurs). The rider with a MHR of about 200 rides almost for the entire duration of the race at the limits of his endurance performance capabilities.

Determining the Maximum Heart Rate (MHR)

The most accurate and safe method is determining the MHR during a stress test supervised by a physician. Because of the inherent risks, older (40+) and beginning cyclists, in particular, should not undertake the max test alone, but should rather seek a doctor's supervision. For persons cycling for health and rehabilitation reasons, determining the maximum heart rate is impractical and would pose an unnecessary health risk. For this group of cyclists, the MHR is calculated by the formula **220 – age = MHR**. This formula, however, is only a very rough approximation (+/−10) and is totally useless for the serious athlete.

Performing the Test

After a 30-minute warm-up period, you can begin the test to determine your maximum heart rate. Although the test is usually performed on the bike in the summer, it can be performed as a running test in the winter. To reach the MHR, you must increase the load over the course of many minutes (about 4-5 min) and then exercise at maximum intensity for the last minute.

A three to four kilometer long gradual incline is ideal; ride at least at race pace and use race-appropriate gearing. The last 600 meters are a sprint to the finish in which 100% effort is required to reach the maximum heart rate. A high cadence is crucial for reaching the MHR. As a rule, the heart rate is highest as soon as this test is stopped or shortly thereafter. This test should be done on different days to minimize the influence of variable factors. In most cases, the MHR is around the zone of 220 – age; exceptions are common, though, since conditioned cyclists age 35 or even older often still have maximum heart rates of around 200.

The running test is ideally performed on a one to two kilometer long flat or slightly uphill course. Similar to the cycling test, the last 400 meters are run at maximum intensity and the MHR is measured at the end of the test. The measurement is only accurate enough and useful for further calculations when made with a pulse watch. The extreme exhaustion at the end of the test makes manual measurement hardly feasible.

Calculating the Intensity Zones

The formulas used in calculating the intensity zones are based on lengthy comprehensive studies of endurance athletes, and therefore represent a fairly high degree of accuracy. Determining the training zones through this simple method is an alternative to the expensive and complex fitness test, which, nevertheless, is more exact and is used especially for top athletes. However, even very.good amateurs can use the method presented here without any reservations.

The resting pulse and the maximum heart rate are used to calculate a cyclist's individual heart rate zones. Do the following:

- 1. subtract the **resting pulse rate** from the **MHR**
- 2. multiply this number by the **training-intensity factor**
- 3. add the **resting pulse number** to the result
- **Example:**   **1.** 200 – 45 = 155
                           2. 155 x 0.52 = 80.6
                           3. 80.6 + 45 = 125.6

The calculated value is the upper heart rate limit of this person's compensatory zone (recovery training). These are the factors for each intensity zone:

These factors can be used to calculate the lower and upper limits of each zone. The compensatory zone and, above all, the basic endurance zone are especially important for the proper control of training intensity.

Gears, cadence, and time and distance are more important than heart rate when training in the last three specialized high-intensity training zones (SE, ST, SS) , since

Training Zone		Factor
• Compensatory Zone	CO	up to max. CO 0.52
• Basic Endurance 1	BE 1	0.52 to 0.65
• Basic Endurance 2	BE 2	0.65 to 0.77
• Competition-specific Endurance	CSE	0.75 to 0.95
• Strength-endurance	SE	0.75 to 0.90
• Speed Training	ST	0.85 to 1.00
• Speed-strength training	SS	0.85 to 0.95

Table 3.1: Intensity factors

a heart of 180, for example, can be achieved through many different training methods and loads. Even so, the heart rate still will indicate the appropriate intensity level.

The Worst Training Mistakes

The following enumerates different training mistakes.

- Too strenuous training, mainly in BE 2 and competition-specific zones. The emphasis should be on developing a high aerobic capacity through BE 1 training. Too strenuous training during the week results in less than peak performance on the weekend. This state of overtraining is characterized by poor recovery (constant exhaustion) and empty glycogen stores.
- Training at too low an intensity in BE 1.
- Not using periodization; athletes have approximately the same fitness throughout the whole year.
- Ignoring the rules for proper recovery.
- Increasing intensity too rapidly early in the year leads to fitness stagnation.
- Not reducing training during sickness (infection) often leads to a collapse in fitness.
- Ignoring strength and strength-endurance training.
- Training monotony often impedes training.
- Partial ignorance of new scientific training knowledge.

This list could be continued; however, the reader will soon discover these and other mistakes himself by carefully reading this book.

3.5 Training Periodization

What Is Meant by Periodization?

Periodization is the division of the training year into periods, or phases, with different goals, to achieve good form for certain races or one main race. Training achieves structure through periodization. A constant, enduring top level of fitness is unfortunately not feasible, since the body needs rest and recovery periods. The training intensity, especially the milage, should gradually be increased over a span of years to develop a peak level of personal fitness. This time factor explains why beginning cyclists, despite riding many kilometers, have very little, if any, success in their first year.

For the recreational or hobby cyclist these training guidelines are flexible, since he will schedule his training around his free time and vary it depending on his cycling enthusiasm; however, he should still adhere to a simplified periodization. The classical three-step periodization is as follows:

1. **Preparation Period (PP)**

2. **Competition Period (CP)**

3. **Transition Period (TP)**

The *preparation period* is characterized by basic training of all conditioned zones, but especially endurance, which provides a foundation for the competition period.

In the *competition period*, training is geared towards racing, and is, therefore, appropriately more specialized and intense. Normally, the goal is a season peak (for example, national championships), although this is difficult in cycling due to the large number of important races. Top athletes, for example Olympic candidates or World Championship participants, focus their preparation on reaching a peak, which is usually only sustainable for a few weeks or even days, for a single race.

Such a periodization, with only one peak, is called a one-peak periodization; there are also two-peak and multi-peak (many) periodizations. The problem with multi-peak periodization is that none of the peaks can reach the absolute highest performance level, since fitness must be maintained over too long of a time period. Even so, the multi-peak periodization is ideal for road cycling, especially for circuit racers, for whom this provides a new opportunity of placing well every weekend. A good example of two-peak periodization is the elite athlete, who must already be in top shape in May for a qualification race and must prove himself again in the summer at national and international championships. A two-peak periodization with two competition periods – one on the road in the summer and the other on the track or in cyclo-cross in the winter – is seldom achievable in top fitness, since this feat requires two separate preparation periods, which overlap with the previous competition period.

The fading competition period is closely followed by the *transition period*, whose purpose is active recovery and also psychological distancing from cycling.

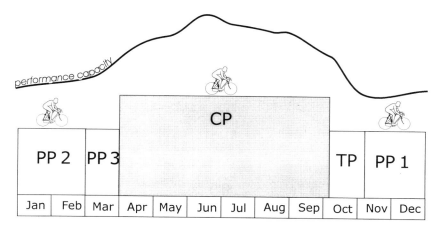

Figure 3.7: Periodization scheme for road cycling

Before the training programs for each individual category are presented, the different periods should be examined closer, since the fundamental principles are the same for all categories. This analysis is carried out using a periodization with only one competition period as an example.

Seasonal Division

Training over the course of a whole year is the first priority of a training program, since continued performance enhancement can only be achieved through regular training; a winter off-season from October to March is out of the question even for recreational athletes.

Preparation Period

This period begins around the middle of November and lasts until the beginning of the season at the middle to end of March – a period of about five months. As already mentioned, this period lays the foundation for the recreational or competition period. The biggest problems during the entire preparation period in the fall and winter are the short days and the bad weather. Many athletes are, therefore, only able to train on the bike on the weekends and are forced to exercise indoors. Running or jogging is an indoor alternative, although the first running workouts are especially hard for cyclists (muscle soreness). Running is still very feasible at dusk and in the rain, and one can stay fit with 30 to 60 minute runs during the week. The preparation period is divided again into several parts – so called macrocycles – with different goals.

The **first macrocycle** (1st preparation period) from the beginning/middle of November to the end of December is the time to be involved in many sports. Exercise should include not only cycling but, more importantly, other forms of exercise, in particular endurance sports, to create a welcome diversion for the bicycle training that has become boring by the end of the season. Other sports such as running, swimming, mountain biking, skiing (rollerskiing), and ice skating (rollerblading) can be pursued. A well-structured indoor training program with a knowledgeable coach can improve coordination, strength, speed, flexibility, and even endurance. A sensible training program can prevent or correct the posture damage that may ensue after a long riding season by toning the muscles that support the skeleton. A few more comments about novel endurance sports such as rollerskiing or rollerblading:

Rollerskiing represents an excellent endurance and complete body workout for the cyclist during the winter, since, unlike cross-country skiing, it can be regularly done in areas that do not get much snow in the winter. It is significantly more pleasant than cycling in very cold weather (due to the slower speeds). The relatively high cost of a pair of rollerskis is worthwhile, and the technique can be mastered after just a few workouts.

A welcome diversion during winter training (preperation period): cyclo-cross and mountain bike training

Rollerblading, on "in-line skating" that has recently become very affordable, is oriented more toward training cycling-specific muscle groups. Not without reason, do Dutch cyclists train on ice skating rinks in the winter and ice skaters train on the bicycle in the summer. The multiple-time Olympic speed skating champion, Eric Heiden, competed in the Tour de France, and women's cycling also has many examples of medal-winners on the bike as well as on skates. Because of the lack of ice skating rinks in Germany, athletes must train on in-line skates, which are a perfect simulation of ice skating. Distances of 10 to 40 km in the basic endurance zone can be covered on sparsely-traveled streets and bicycle paths.

In the first preparation period, the focus should be on having fun with other sports. The intensity is almost exclusively in the **BE 1** and **BE 2** zones, with a clear preponderance of **BE 1** training. Naturally, higher intensities also occur, for example in mountain biking and indoor training, that trigger certain adaptation processes. During the winter, the mountain bike can be used on the road on cold days. The greater rolling resistance allows you to reach the same intensity at lower speeds, which has the benefit in extremely cold weather of cooling off your body less. **Mountain biking** off-road visibly improves bicycle handling and riding technique. In spite of all this other training, you should train on the road bike at least once a week, probably best on the weekend. Training regularity is also important in this phase of the training year; periods of several days or even weeks without training should be avoided if possible (exception: illness). The duration of the workouts is significantly less than during summer training and is between one and three, with a maximum of four, hours. Near the end of the first macrocycle, the training scope increases markedly.

The **second macrocycle** (2nd preparation period) lasts from the beginning of January until the end of February. It begins with a recovery week, during which relatively little training takes place. Without at first reducing the other general training methods, the second macrocycle increases the amount of specialized bicycle training in the **BE 1** zone. Not until February, does bicycle training gradually replace the other sports, one or even two of which should occasionally be used for cross-training during the racing season.

A macrocycle is divided into multiple microcycles that represent weekly training plans. The scope and intensity of individual micro- and macrocycles must not remain constant, a requirement that gives special meaning to the structuring of these workouts. Stress and rest distributions of 2:1, 3:1, 4:1, or even 5:1 have proven effective. The first number is the number of weeks of increasing stress and the second number is the subsequent recovery week of lower intensity. The same scheme is also carried over for individual daily workouts (microcycle), in which stress is increased over the course of 2-5 days, followed by a day of compensation. Specialized training (**SE** , **ST** , **SS**) is often carried out during the preparation period, as well as during the season, in blocks of 2 to 4 days with increasing stress (i.e.: 1st day: 3 km **SE** ; 2nd day: 8 km **SE** ; 3rd day: 2 x 8 km **SE**). During the course of the second macrocycle, the training scope and frequency increases, while the intensity remains for the time being in the basic endurance zone. The end of the cycle is followed by a week or several days of reduced training to stimulate regeneration.

The **third macrocycle** (3rd preparation period) starts in early March and lasts until just before the races begin or may even include the first preparation races. Depending on his objectives, the cyclist must either already be in race shape after this cycle or can build-up his fitness during the initial weeks of racing. A top amateur (in Germany: Bundesligafahrer) must already be fit around the end of March or beginning of April for the first Classics, while a rider in a less competitive category with less pressure to succeed can take longer. This generalization applies in particular to the recreational cyclist. A top cyclist must ride more and increase the intensity of his training earlier. The cycle described here is the normal, classical periodization that is determined by the racing season. It is debatable whether such a long season is wise, since it is also conceivable to postpone the periodization so that the race phase does not start until May or June; such a late start would enable the rider to carry his season through until the end without problems. The benefits hereof are obvious: first, the period of high milage is postponed to a warmer time of the year, and, second, top fitness is achieved when many others are already resigning with sunken heads. Through this method, good results can still be obtained, especially into September and the beginning of October. This periodization is ideal for young cyclists and beginners. However, this example should only be thought-provoking for the numerous variations possible.

Back to the classical model: if possible, a two-week training camp should be scheduled for the beginning of March (see chapter 3.7, The Training Camp), although this is also possible at a later date. The training of specific abilities such as strength, speed, and competition-specific endurance are the focus of the two to three weeks before and at the beginning of the season. In preparation, the training intensity is increased and varied in a goal-oriented manner during the third macrocycle.

Competition Period

The racing season lasts from the middle of March to the middle of October, a long time to master without performance collapse. The division of the competition period depends on the goals of the rider. An individual training program can be designed once you have chosen a time frame to achieve peak fitness. For example, if the peak should occur at the beginning of June, direct preparation already begins in April. There are two phases, each three to four weeks long, in which the stress load is increased for the first two or three weeks and then is drastically reduced for a few days at the end of the period, especially right before a race. The second phase begins at a stress level equivalent to the middle stress level of the first phase and increases the stress far above the highest level of the first phase. The last week before the race consists mainly of recovery training and may include carbohydrate loading (see chapter 5.3). The choice of races or tours should also progress from easy to hard (longer, hillier) to help create the peak. Fitness can usually be maintained for one or two weeks after the peak at the beginning of June. Thereafter, fitness declines slightly as less stress is applied. Beginning again in July, the whole process can be repeated, so that top fitness can again be reached in September and October.

The shaping of the **microcycle** is critically important during the competition period:

Monday

Monday is generally devoted to recovery; compensatory training is appropriate. Many bicycle racers take Mondays completely off or use it to cross-train.

Tuesday

Tuesday workouts should be sprints or strength training in combination with a short to medium-length **BE 1** workout.

Wednesday

Wednesdays are, in general, higher milage days than Tuesdays. The intensity is in the **BE 1** and **BE 2** zones. Intervals in the **CSE** zone can be incorporated (i.e. 3 x 5 km with 52 x 15, complete recovery).

Thursday

Thursday training should be a long **BE 1** ride, significantly longer than the race distance (over distance). Young juniors (16 and under) can ride distances up to 120 km, older juniors up to 180 km, and amateurs up to and over 220 km. The distances given represent upper limits and should not be regularly undertaken by riders under 19, since weekly training rides of 180 km would be too much for the average junior. However, during vacations, when the riders have enough time, workouts of this length should be incorporated into a several-week training program.

Friday

Training on the Friday before a Saturday race should consist of a relatively short **CO** zone ride. A few sprints or tempo intervals can indicate your fitness level and prepare your body for the next day's competition stress. If the race is not until Sunday, do a **BE 1** zone ride on Friday with several sub-maximal tempo intervals.

Weekend

On Saturday, then, the **CO** training should be carried out, and on Sunday is the race. A race-free weekend should be used for one or two long endurance rides, which are often not possible during the week due to time restrictions.

At the beginning of the racing season in April and May, many amateurs and professionals attach additional **BE** training onto their races; for example, they may ride their bicycle home or just ride around for one or two more hours **(BE 1)**.

This training method is also useful in other phases of the competition period for performance enhancement. Caution should be exercised, however, in over-trained states and after an extremely stressful race, since additional training may then provoke the opposite response.

Transition Period

In October, the competition period fades into the transition period. The training that was already reduced during the last weeks of the competition period is reduced even further during the transition period and specialized (bike) training ceases almost entirely. The athlete must consciously stay away from cycling during this period, lasting from October to the middle of November, or even longer, and engage in other sports that he enjoys.

If a cyclo-cross or winter track season is planned, then the transition period is significantly shorter or even non-existent. A wise plan would be to end the road season early, in August or September, take a few rest days, and then start with an abbreviated specialized preparation period. After the transition period, the pleasure of riding a racing bike is renewed, and the new season's preparation period can start with much enthusiasm. A break from the bike is especially important for young juniors, since it allows them to pursue other interests and hobbies. Variety is most important here and should not, under any circumstances, be sacrificed for hard-headed performance ambition.

Be Your Own Coach

The phrase "be your own coach" represents the typical American endurance athlete's viewpoint. You know your body best, you feel its exhaustion and its strength, and you can therefore decide better than any coach what is best for you. Being an effective coach for yourself, however, requires knowledge, which this book seeks to convey. A sensible, self-constructed training program based on a few important training guidelines guarantees good performance. You have to find your own balance of casual and serious training in order to achieve good results while still having fun. This goal cannot be accomplished through a strict training plan with completely inflexible rules. You must listen to your body and decide what is and what is not good for you; if you do not feel like training or racing, skip a day. The following section also offers the coaches, guardians, and parents of young cyclists tips and ideas, as well as constructive criticism, that should help them design a sensible training program.

Overview of Yearly Plan

Training Zones	BE 1 (BE 2)	BE 1 BE 2 (CSE) SE ST	CO BE 1 BE 2 CSE SE ST SS	CO BE 1 BE 2 CSE SE ST SS	CO BE 1
Training Types	• road bike • MTB • jogging • swimming • indoor trainining • health club • weight room • rollerskiing • in-line skating • water jogging stretching cross-training	• road bike • MTB • jogging • swimming • indoor training • health club • weight room • cross-country skiing • in-line skating stretching cross-training	• road bike • (MTB) • (jogging) • swimming • (indoor trainining) • health club • in-line skating stretching cross-training	• road bike • weigth room • swimming • (in-line skating) • as well as cross-training stretching cross-training	• anything fun • MTB • jogging • swimming • athletic games stretching cross-training
Methods	endurance methods	endurance methods interval methods repetition method (competition method)	endurance methods interval methods repetition method competition method	endurance methods interval methods repetition method competition method	endurance methods
Goals	↑ general performance base	↑ general performance base ↑ specialized performance base	↑ general performance base ↑ specialized performance base	↑ general performance base ↑ specialized performance base ↑ developing competition form	Regeneration psychological distancing
Mistakes	• too much training • too high intensity • monotonous training	• too high intensity • too short recovery periosd • lack of strength training • monotonous training	• lack of strength training • too short recovery periods • no periodiszation • monotonous training	• too less training • too short recovery periods • poorly chosen race • monotonous training	• complete break from training • continuing to bicycle • too high intensity
	PP I	PP II	PP III	CP	TP

3.6 Category-specific Training

This chapter goes into more detail than the previous one about training for the recreational and hobby cyclist, as well as for the different racing categories. A section is also devoted to the health-conscious athlete who has chosen cycling as his sport. For each group, training advice is given in the form of two sample training weeks, one during the preparation period and the other during the racing season, as well as a year-long plan. However, one problem must be pointed out: the training plans given are relatively general and are not appropriate for everyone; rather, they should serve as broad guidelines for when and how much to train. Some cyclists have more time and desire to ride, others have less; some need to train more, others less, and the goals of different individuals vary as well. This list of factors that influence training programs could be continued further and shows the difficulty, or impossibility, of creating a generally applicable training plan, even for just one class of riders. Individuality is the key. This book would have to contain 500 pages and a confusing number of different programs, if it were to cover all possibilities. Rather than providing "the" training plan, this book provides a good starting point and the knowledge to create a personal training plan. Again, training principles are important for helping you construct your own plans.

Training for the Bicycle Tour Rider and the Recreational Cyclist

Bicycle tour riders (BTR) and recreational riders are concerned mainly with the health benefits and fun of cycling as a form of exercise. Therefore, thoughts about performance and competition luckily move into the background. Touring rides can be an ideal family sport, since both women and men, as well as children, often participate. The training is influenced by the goals of the recreational cyclists, who can be divided into different groups: 1. occasional cyclist, 2. tour rider (regularly), 3. BTR cyclist, whose hobby is very important to him and who seeks high performance at this level. The BTR is similar to the racer in that he is usually on the road every weekend during the season to participate in a tour. His primary concern is being in the company of friends and people who share this interest, as well as the pleasure of the exercise. Unfortunately, the performances of hobby cyclists are often scoffed at by racers.

The **occasional cyclist** does not have a strict training plan, since he rides when he feels like it. The winter break should, however, not be passive, but active

Touring Cyclist			
Yearly kilometers	5,000–10,000	10,000–15,000	15,000–20,000
Number of tours	10–20	20–30	30–50
Max. training distance	< 150 km	< 180 km	< 200 km
Training zones	BE 1, BE 2, CSE	BE 1, BE 2, CSE, (SE)	BE 1, BE 2, CSE, SE
Tips	a lot of technique training; important:: cross-training & gymnastics to work other muscle groups		

Weekly Cycle in PP and CP (10,000 – 15,000 km)		
	PP	CP
Monday	stretching, gymnastics, strength exercises	swimming 500 m or off
Tuesday	30-50 km BE 1 or running (30-60 min)	40-60 km BE 1 2 km SE
Wednesday	stretching, gymnastics, strength exercises, another sport	30-50 km BE 1/2, stretching, strength exercises
Thursday	cross-training or 30 km BE 1	50-80 km BE 1
Friday	swimming 500-1,000 m	30 km CO/BE 1 or cross-training
Saturday	30-60 km BE 1 or MTB	50-150 km tour
Sunday	< 80 km BE 1 or MTB	50-150 km tour

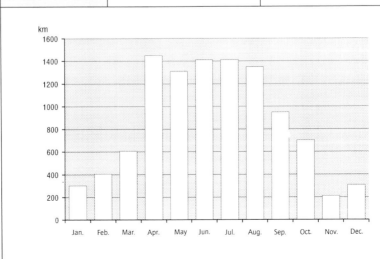

(athletic games, running). Spring training consists mostly of short rides, which can be gradually lengthened over the course of the year. A planned cycling vacation requires more preparation training, since the relaxing rides could otherwise turn into torture. The occasionally cyclist rides almost 100% of his kilometers in the **BE 1** zone to derive the most health benefits out of the sport.

A **tour rider** spends significantly more time in the saddle of his iron horse (2,000-8,000 km) and occasionally participates in a tour. As mentioned above, mileage should be increased gradually over the course of the year, and summer rides can occasionally be at higher intensities.

The **BTR cyclist** rides between 6,000 and 20,000 km a year, whereby he attempts to achieve as high a level of fitness as is possible within the limitations of his training. The conscientiously-training and performance-concerned BTR should model his training more after the program given for Juniors 17-18, except for a reduction in the speed and speed-strength areas. Some tours are very similar to time trials or races. Low training intensities can significantly improve performance capacity of most cyclists.

All three groups have a greater risk than even active bicycle racers of developing back problems, especially with advancing age, from the one-sided, bicycle-centered athletic activity. This risk makes cross-training in one or two other sports important for preventing one-sidedness. Since mostly older athletes develop these problems, they should concentrate on strengthening muscles in the back, arms, and stomach and improving flexibility by callisthenics (stretching) (see chapter 3.9). Such exercises can prevent, or at least reduce, back pain. Regular physicals with stress EKG's and an athletic diet are equally essential for the program of a health-conscious athlete.

The Health-conscious Athlete

The health-conscious athlete pushes performance motivations far into the back-ground. His primary goal is the use of sports for preventative or rehabilitative health care. Exercising outdoors and with friends increases the recuperative effects of the sport. As a health-promoting sport, cycling is superior to running, since it spares the bones and joints and its intensity is easier to control. Higher speeds can be attained and the longer routes can be varied more. The relatively long routes provide much opportunity to enjoy the scenery along the way.

Especially persons suffering from obesity or atherosclerosis can benefit from cycling. Unfortunately, health-conscious cycling is not as much a group sport as, for example athletic games or hiking, since cycling takes place mostly in traffic and a group would be torn apart by the differing fitness levels. Health-conscious athletes must stay in the **BE 1** and **CO** zones, since they often belong to high-risk groups that should not be stressed too much. A rule of thumb for the exercising pulse of these athletes is 180 minus their age, a value that is usually around 130. High strength-taxing exercise (hills), which is accompanied by strong blood pressure elevations, should be avoided. Cross-training should be emphasized. Callisthenics, or other appropriate sports such as volleyball, racquetball, running, and swimming can be incorporated into the exercise program. The health-conscious athlete should be evaluated by a physician before beginning an exercise program.

The Racing Classes
The reader should work through the plans given for all classes, since many fundamental facts and tips are dispersed throughout the sections for the different categories and are not repeated in each section. Female racers are grouped into the male categories, and training-specific differences are pointed out.

Juniors under 11 and under 13
The youngest category in bicycle racing is divided into two categories both for boys and for girls: under 11 and under 13. Racing boys and girls together is not a problem at this age. Often, same-aged girls even have an edge on boys. The pros and cons of bicycle racing for such young children are debatable, but there is clearly no need for 9 year-olds to compete in many races, for which they may end up sacrificing part of their childhood. Often children this young are driven into the sport by ambitious parents and have little personal motivation. Young athletes must be treated with care, since training mistakes and bad experiences can often spoil the sport for these children for the rest of their lives. At the club-level, these children need sympathetic and specially-trained coaches and trainers. The child is in great danger of developing prematurely. Especially for cyclists who started relatively early with the sport, "burn out" is a problem. "Burn out" means that the children get tired of the sport before they reach adulthood, and so miss the most important phase of the sport. Parents should carefully consider whether the risks are worth letting their child participate in races at such an early age.

Juniors under 13				
Age	11 (m)	12 (m)	11 (f)	12 (f)
Yearly kilometers	2,000-3,000	3,000-4,000	2,000-3,000	3,000-4,000
Number of races	5-10	< 15	5-10	< 15
Max. training dist	< 50 km	< 70 km	< 50 km	< 70
Training zones	BE 1, BE 2, (CSE), (ST)	BE 1, BE 2, (CSE), (ST)	BE 1, BE 2, (CSE), (ST)	BE 1, BE 2, (CSE), (ST)
Tips	• many-sided training; a lot of cross-training; a lot of technique training, only few races			

Weekly Cycle in PP and CP (12 years)		
	PP	CP
Monday	other sport or off	other sport or off
Tuesday	indoor training 1 hr	30 km or athletic games technique training
Wednesday	off	other sport
Thursday	indoor training 1-2 hrs	30-50 km BE 1 with playful CSE intervals
Friday	athletic games 1 hr or off	15 km CO/BE 1 or off
Saturday	30 km BE 1 or MTB	30-50 km BE 1 + 2
Sunday	30-45 km BE or MTB	race or 30-60 km BE 1

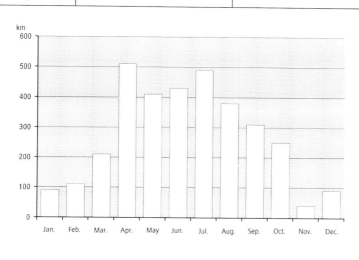

A general cycling program without race participation has no draw-backs, but rather leads to very positive mental and physical developments for the young athlete when the extent of the training and coaching is appropriate. There are large developmental differences in the participants within the classes under 13 years and the juniors 13-14, 15-16, and sometimes even 17-18. Early, late, and normal maturers with up to two-year age differences have to compete against each other, resulting in races whose outcomes are predictable from the start due to the tremendous variations in performance. The biological age is differentiated from the calendar age. The last decades show clearly a tendency for the biological age to precede the calendar age (maturational acceleration).

The training of the classes under 13 years of age is focussed on athletic versatility and must be organized in a child-appropriate manner. Under no circumstances can the training be based on the same principles as for adults, since this would be too hard and monotonous. Aside from bicycle training (about 50%), children are trained in general sports (running, swimming, games) with the help of athletic games. Team sports are most important, since they teach new coordination skills while fostering social behavior. Bicycle traffic safety and technique training must be taught, and wearing hard-shell helmets is mandatory for children as well as for other groups of riders and will eventually become habitual.

Because of childrens rapid growth spurts, you must often check and if necessary, adjust, their saddle height. To protect the growing body from too much stress, there are gear restrictions in some countries for classes of riders under 19 years of age. For the classes under 13 years old, gearing is limited in Germany to 5.66 meters per pedal revolution. Bicycle training should lay the foundation for high performance levels later on and accomplishes this goal primarily through endurance training. Tempo rides and sprints are built into training rides in a playful manner, but specific strength, speed, and interval training is omitted completely. The individual workouts are mostly about 30 km long on a course that can easily be visualized by a child. A fixed route on sparsely-traveled roads is ideal. Cyclists under 13 years of age can ride up to 70 km long stretches at low intensity. Training rides are almost exclusively in the small chain ring. These young cyclist do not start regular road training until March. Until this time, if they have trained on the bike at all, it was only in good weather, and they have focussed mostly on other sports. This next generation of cyclists competes in 5 to a maximum of 15 races. Boys and girls of this age train about equally much.

Juniors 13-14

The 13 and 14 year-old boys and girls race in the Junior 13-14 category. The training programs for girls of this age are similar to those for boys, except that the mileage can be somewhat reduced. Circuit races are mostly 20 km long, and road races can be up to 40 km long. The basic comments in the previous section about the athletic performance of children are, naturally, also applicable to this class of young riders. The Junior 13-14 category is the best time to get introduced to cycling and get a taste of racing.

When cycling is done in moderation at a young age, enough motivation is left over for the later years of performance-oriented training. Therefore, these juniors should compete in no more than 10-20 races per season. Unfortunately, it is not uncommon for there to be 35-40 races per season, but since Junior 13-14 races are relatively rare, children must spend most of their weekends in the car traveling to these often distant races. Ambitious parents must be slowed down. The child's personality development must take precedence over performance enhancement.

Bicycle training for this category of riders takes on a broader scope and should encompass 60-70% of total training. Aside from the unspecific, general winter indoor training, one or two sports should be used for cross-training in the summer, as well as in the winter. It would be desirable for bicycle clubs to offer one workout a week during the racing season to improve general athletic skills in conjunction with team-oriented games. Special emphasis should be placed on developing parts of the body (arms, upper body) that do not get used enough in cycling. Mondays or Wednesdays are ideal for this type of training for Junior 13-14 riders.

The transition period with reduced bicycle and general athletic training can easily be extended for the Junior 13-14 category until the end of November. During the preparation period, these athletes should run and swim quite a bit. No class of riders should have the idea that reduced bicycle training is equivalent to little or no training of any type. Cycling begins again with low intensity and mileage in the middle of February.

The racing season for Junior 13-14 riders must not start until the beginning of April; likewise, the end of the season can also be shortened – to the middle of

Juniors 13-14				
Age	13 (m)	14 (m)	13 (f)	14 (f)
Yearly kilometers	4,000-6,000	5,000-7,000	3,000-5,000	4,000-6,000
Number of races	10-15	< 20	10-15	10-15
Max. training dist	< 100 km	< 120 km	< 80 km	< 100
Training zones	BE 1, BE 2, CSE, ST	BE 1, BE 2, CSE, ST	BE 1, BE 2, CSE, ST	BE 1, BE 2, CSE, ST
Tips	• many-sided training; a lot of cross-training; a lot of technique training			

Weekly Cycle in PP and CP (13-14 years)		
	PP	CP
Monday	other sport or off	other sport or off
Tuesday	20 km BE 1 or indoor training 1 hr	30-40 km with 3-5 sprints technique training
Wednesday	other sport or off	30 km BE 1 or other sport
Thursday	indoor training 1-2 hrs	40-60 km BE 1 with tempo intervalls (BE 2, CSE)
Friday	other sport 1 hr or off	15 km CO/BE 1 or off
Saturday	30-50 km BE 1 or MTB	race or 30-60 km BE 1 + 2
Sunday	30-60 km BE or MTB	race or 30-90 km BE 1

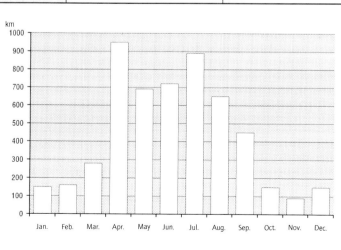

September – to further decrease the stress on these young athletes. This season also precisely avoids the bad weather that occurs in March and April, as well as in fall. During the racing season, these juniors train mostly in the **BE 1** and **BE 2** zones. The **BE 2** zone is more important for juniors up to 15 years old and for beginning cyclists than for any other category of racers. Strength training, as for the younger classes, is forbidden; sprints (i.e.: city-limit sprints) and **CSE** training (i.e.: 3 x 1 km tempo) should, however, be incorporated (in the middle of the week) into the training program. Particularly for beginning cyclists, riding technique training should not be lacking and should be taught in the form of games. The ideal training distance is a 30 to 50 km course on sparsely-traveled well-paved roads. During the preparation period, 20-40 km training rides are sufficient, but in summer, as fitness increases, children can undertake rides or bicycle tours of up to 80 km or even 120 km with longer rest breaks; however, it is crucial that they not struggle to keep up with a faster group of adults, but rather ride at a pace appropriate for their age (but not alone on longer rides). This mismatched-ability training, by the way, represents a big problem, since these young children normally train with older riders (Juniors 15-16 or 17-18, or even amateurs), a practice that not uncommonly results in complete overexertion and often leads to frustration and loss of motivation. Previous beliefs that this would benefit the development of the young athlete have been replaced by the tenet that the most pain does not always bring maximum gain. What was just said is applicable in general to weaker riders who train with significantly stronger cyclists; by doing so, they usually exert themselves too much during training.

Juniors up to 14 years old do not necessarily have to follow a scheduled training plan; rather, they should focus on having fun, while adhering to loose training guidelines, but at the same time not forgetting the crucial points just discussed.

Juniors 15-16

Junior boys 15-16 years old compete in races up to 80 km; races for girls in this category are up to 60 km long. Circuit races for these male juniors are generally 40 km and usually take the form of criteriums.

The transition from the Junior 13-14 category, in which the races are usually still relatively slow, to the Junior 15-16 category, is a significant one. Motivation may be a problem for these new juniors, especially small "late-bloomers", who must compete against riders up to 16 years old, which may represent a four-year biological age difference. Due to the larger permissible gear ratio of 6.99 m, these junior races can reach high speeds, for which the strength to turn over the pedals in large gears becomes increasingly important. Therefore, 15 and 16 year-olds should begin regular specific strength-training both on the bike and in the gym (using their own body weight). The initial goal here is not to improve maximum strength: low weights and many repetitions are employed. From the beginning, correct technique should be given the most attention.

The development of speed is also important at this age: therefore, speed workouts should be done about 1-2 times a week, especially during the racing season. High pedal cadences over 90 rev/min during base mileage training can also improve speed and smooth out the pedal stroke.

The yearly training mileage increases from 4,000-7,000 km for Junior 13-14 riders to about 7,000-9,000 km in the first year and 8,000-10,000 km in the second year of the Junior 15-16 category. Girls in this category ride 6,000-9,000 km a year. The yearly, monthly, and individual workout mileage given here and in the following pages depends strongly on personal goals and time available for this hobby, but nevertheless provides a framework for the type and amount of riding for each class of riders. Elite riders in each category will usually train more, and sometimes significantly more, than the sample training programs. However, their training programs cannot be applied to just anyone, and for most, less training often accomplishes more.

The goal of Junior 15-16 training programs is to build a cycling-specific performance base, characterized by a significantly increased aerobic capacity. In addition, athletic participation should be many-sided, both in the sport of cycling and in other sports used for cross-training. Junior riders in this category should avoid specializing in a single cycling discipline, for example cyclo-cross or the 500 m time trial on the track. Especially for the road cyclist, track riding is a welcome diversion that can improve technical skills. In the winter, the same applies to mountain biking, which can help a rider develop an excellent feel for his bike. Technique training can now concentrate on learning and mastering difficult skills. If not already begun in the Junior 13-14 category, training now becomes heart rate-oriented through the use of a pulse watch. The athletes should be informed (with the help of scientific theory) about the benefits of heart rate-

Juniors 15-16				
Age	15 (m)	16 (m)	15 (f)	16 (f)
Yearly kilometers	7,000-9,000	8,000-10,000	6,000-8,000	7,000-9,000
Number of races	20-30	< 35	15-20	< 25
Max. training dist	< 130 km	< 140 km	< 110 km	< 120
Training zones	BE 1, BE 2, CSE, ST	BE 1, BE 2, CSE, ST, SS, (SE)	BE 1, BE 2, CSE, ST	BE 1, BE 2, CSE, ST, SS, (SE)
Tips	a lot of technique training; cautious SE and strength training starting at 16; get used to higher mileage, important: cross-training			

Weekly Cycle in PP and CP (15-16 years)		
	PP	CP
Monday	other sport or off	other sport or off or 20 km CO
Tuesday	30 km BE 1 or indoor training 1 hr	40-60 km with 5-7 sprints or 2 km SE (52 x 17) technique training
Wednesday	other sport or 30 km BE 1	40-50 km BE 1 and other sport
Thursday	indoor training 1-2 hrs	60-90 km BE 1 with tempo intervalls (BE 2, CSE)
Friday	other sport 1 hr or off	20 km CO/BE 1 or off
Saturday	30-60 km BE 1 or MTB	race or 40-90 km BE 1 + 2
Sunday	30-90 km BE or MTB	race or 40-120 km BE 1

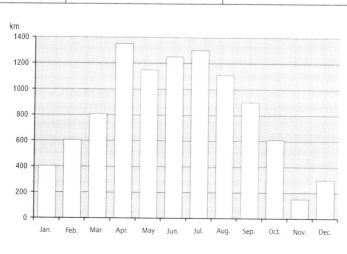

guided training. Junior riders in the 15-16 category train almost throughout the whole winter on the bicycle and ride 80% of their training miles in the BE zone. Strength-endurance training does not begin until April, while speed training has already begun in January. During the season, sprint training (5-7 repeats) **(SS)** is employed. The general athletic training hour with gymnastics and games continues to be important, even in the summertime. During the course of the season which may be shortened a bit in the spring, these riders compete in 20 to 30, with a maximum of 35, races.

Juniors 17-18

The Junior 17-18 category is the beginning of serious cycling. The 17-18 year-old young men and women must train quite a bit to even be able to ride in a race, not to mention being able to place.

There are few sports that require as much training in all age categories as cycling does, a fact that is difficult for beginning cyclists, especially those who have previously participated in team sports, to understand and which often leads to

The junior riders concentrate as they enter the turn.

frustration. Young athletes who don't start cycling until they are in this age category have a hard time adjusting to the high training mileage, especially if they have not previously participated in any endurance or competitive sports. Often, they may go through an entire season without being able to finish a single race. Even so, there are, again and again, very talented riders who are exceptions to this rule. Unfortunately, beginners' races are only very rarely organized to allow these juniors to slowly acclimatize to real racing. There are no separate categories for different levels of junior cyclists under 19 that could make getting started in this sport easier.

In recognition of this special situation, which occurs in almost no other form of sport, coaches, parents, and guardians must be exceptionally sympathetic to prevent these young cyclists from losing motivation; these youngsters must receive a steady stream of encouragement to undertake the high training stresses required.

For those who have raced as young juniors, the phase of training that will lay the foundation for a successful amateur carrier now begins. For this reason, the long-term goals (for amateurs or women) should not be forgotten by coach and rider, since now the tendency may be to train so much and so hard to achieve tangible success that improvement in later years is hardly possible. The long-term improvement of the young male and female athletes must be considered.

Although yearly mileages of 20,000 km are recommended for juniors in their second year in this category, this amount of training is unrealistic for 95% of the athletes, since, on the one hand, they are still in school and have a limited amount of free time and, on the other, they hopefully have other interests besides cycling. Top performances can certainly be reached through yearly mileages of 10,000 to 16,000 km for males and 8,000 to 13,000 km for females. With a well-structured training plan, you can do well while training much less than 14,000 km a year.

After a 6-8 week transition period lasting until the beginning/middle of November, these juniors begin systematic indoor training on the bike and occasionally also in the weight room. In addition, a regular running program lasting until about the end of January should help facilitate training on cold and wet days. Especially during the transition period, before indoor training (which includes a lot of

Juniors 17-18				
Age	17 (m)	18 (m)	17 (f)	18 (f)
Yearly kilometers	10,000-13,000	12,000-16,000	8,000-10,000	10,000-13,000
Number of races	30-40	30-45	20-30	25-35
Max. training dist	< 160 km	< 180 km	< 130 km	< 150
Training zones	BE 1, BE 2, CSE, ST, SS, SE	BE 1, BE 2, CSE, ST, SS, SE	BE 1, BE 2, CSE, ST, SS, SE	BE 1, BE 2, CSE, ST, SS, SE
Tips	SE and strength training important; get used to high mileage; road races and stage races; don't forget cross-training			

Weekly Cycle in PP and CP (17-18 years)		
	PP	CP
Monday	other sport or off	other sport or off or 30 km CO
Tuesday	30 km BE 1, indoor training 1-2 hrs/stenght training 1 hr	50-80 km with 5-8 sprints or 2-4 km SE (52 x 15) technique training
Wednesday	30-60 km BE 1 or 1 hr running	60-90 km BE 1 with 3 x 5 km CSE or training race
Thursday	indoor training 1-2 hrs	80-130 km BE 1 with a few tempo intervalls (BE 2, CSE)
Friday	other sport 1-2 hrs or off	30 km CO/BE 1 or off
Saturday	40-70 km BE 1 or MTB weekend = 2nd BE block	race or 60-150 km BE 1 + 2 race-free: BE block
Sunday	70-120 km BE 1 or MTB weekend = 2nd BE block	race or 80-180 km BE 1 race-free: BE block

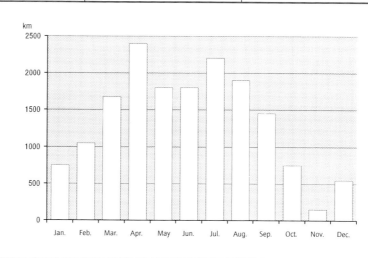

running and jumping) begins, the athletes must get used to running by doing several (< 1 hr) runs through the woods; otherwise the lower extremities, in particular, may sustain injuries and stress-related symptoms. As a rule, running on asphalt should be avoided.

The emphasis of training during the preparation period, with its macrocycles, is the continuous improvement of aerobic capacity through endurance conditioning. Coordination, strength, flexibility, and speed are improved through indoor training and cross-training. The relatively low mileage during the months of December and January in no way means that the athletes are inactive, but rather that they are improving their endurance base through other sports and are riding their bicycles in addition.

A training camp in March or April (Spring break) with very high mileage marks the end of the preparation period. Depending on when the camp is and the amount of training done prior to it, the training camp can also be used to develop competition-specific fitness. In general, this camp represents the only time that most young athletes will have to ride the high mileage that is absolutely necessary for good fitness.

For very successful juniors, a training periodization based on a few important races (regional championships, national championships, and, possibly, world championships) is recommended. The age of 17 or 18 years is appropriate for specializing in a cycling discipline in which one does particularly well or enjoys most. Even so, the rider should not carry this specialization to the extreme, and should also compete in other disciplines. In addition to trying to improve those areas of performance (sprinting, climbing) that are particularly well-developed already, juniors in this category, but younger juniors as well, should also work on their weaknesses. A weak sprinter should do more sprint workouts, whereas a good sprinter but weak climber should try to improve his climbing skills. Starting in the middle of February, athletes begin sprint (SS) and strength-endurance (SE) training. Both training zones should be used at least once a week during a workout. Competition-specific endurance is improved on Wednesdays or Saturdays through short (3 x 3 km) intervals in relatively small gears (52 x 17).

The month of May generally has the highest race density of any month during the competition period; riding in as many long road races as possible is especially important at this time to improve fitness. Even during the competition period, 70-

80% of the training miles are in the endurance zones. Strength, sprint, and speed training, as well as **CSE** training, are built into the weekly schedule. Cyclists should not ignore cross-training, which helps to maintain whole-body fitness, or stretching and strengthening exercises.

Strength training in the weight room is done once a week during the racing season. Riders can compete in 30 to 45 races over the course of a season. Especially at the beginning of the racing season, participating in training races (during the week) is useful. Summer vacation is a good time for riders in all junior categories to add long workouts to their training regimens, undertaking, in effect, a form of base-mileage training camp at home.

The longest basic endurance 1-rides during the preparation period are 120 km for young men and 90 km for young women, while the maximum distances at the end of the PP (training camp) and during the competition period are 180 km for men and 150 km for women. To avoid overtraining during these long rides, pay attention to staying in the low-intensity zone **BE 1**. A general rule of thumb is the longer the training ride, the lower the intensity. The desired training effects are not achieved by riding mammoth distances of 150-180 km at 30 km/hr; an average speed of 25 to 28 km/hr is sufficient. Young athletes must be slowed down, especially on ascents, since their ambition could otherwise cause them to ride themselves into the ground.

Junior 17-18 women ride fewer miles than their male counterparts, and their training during their first year of racing in this category is closer to that of male Junior 15-16 riders.

Amateur C and 1st Year Beginners

The amateur class C is the category with the largest field size, which has increased even further due to the new up-grade restrictions enacted in 1991 in Germany. Those who want to get upgraded to class B, must often compete and be successful against 300 opponents in Germany, a task that requires great fitness, as well as tactical and technical finesse. Austria and Switzerland are similar. Class C is composed of young amateurs who have just recently graduated from the junior category, down-graded class B riders, and amateurs who have been in the C class for years. Additionally, there are cycling newcomers, who understandably have a difficult time, and masters riders ages 41 and up, who occasionally want to compete in the amateur class and sometimes have great success. Providing a training program for such a non-homogenous group would be impossible. Individual goals vary from just wanting to enjoy racing, to earning as many primes as possible while not getting enough points to upgrade, to wanting to up-grade to A-category racing as quickly as possible. You must decide on individual goals and time-restraints to create your own training plan based on the principles outlined for the other racing categories. It is always important to train according to specific training principles and to avoid the most common training mistakes by keeping them ever in mind.

For the former junior-category rider seeking to advance to the A, or at least the B, class, the pattern of long-term training and performance build-up continues. During the first amateur year, the yearly mileage is once again increased to 14,000-18,000 km. This increase is represented mostly by higher mileage during the preparation period. The competition period should include 2-3 stage races if possible. Competition now stands in the foreground of this sport. Up-grading to the B-class is impossible with less mileage, and some athletes, particularly elite riders, who have lofty goals and compete in harder and longer races, have to train more than the amounts indicated. By riding many miles, cyclists try to become good enough to up-grade to the A-class, which is even more competitive than the C-class.

Theoretically, the yearly mileage should increase by 2,000-4,000 km for each of the first four amateur years. However, this quantity of riding is possible only for cyclists who can focus completely on this sport, so that the mileage of most A- or B-class riders plateaus at 20,000 km/year. The amount of time spent training in each of the individual training zones increases proportionately to the mileage increase. Especially the competition portion increases tremendously, but strength-endurance training also increases proportionately more than other types of training. The race density in the C-class rises to 40-60 races every season. For riders with high ambitions, the longer road races are mandatory, and racing in criteriums and circuit races should only be infrequent. Since the outcome of most races is determined by the ascents, climbing ability becomes critical for road racing and stage racing, and young amateurs should focus their training (SE) on this. Reducing body fat and therefore weight improves climbing ability and overall performance. Basic endurance workouts can be over 200 km long.

Don't Train Improperly

A surprising number of riders in the C-class ride over 20,000 km a year and still have not placed once. How is this possible? As the section on training mistakes already pointed out, these riders have either no training plan or a completely wrong yearly training program and often train at too high intensities. Minimal fitness variation over the course of the year, in other words fitness levels that are almost the same in the winter as in the summer, is characteristic for such riders. Performance enhancement is impossible with this constant, overly-intense training. Such riders must radically change their thinking and "renovate" their training. In general, performance can improve markedly with the same mileage incorporated into a well-structured training program. On the other hand, riding significantly less than 20,000 km but beginning a well-structured training plan will result in at least maintaining the same performance as before the training modification.

Riders in all categories and areas of cycling must always have a good basic endurance foundation upon which specific conditioned abilities can be built. If the basic endurance fitness level is too low, competition-specific training often leads to a reduction in fitness. With the proper training, late maturers catch up to, and frequently surpass, the early maturers in the amateur class.

The "normal" C-rider, who wishes to place occasionally, can ride at the front of a race with a yearly training mileage of 12-14,000 km. The training program given for Juniors 17-18 is more than sufficient in most cases for good performances.

If you have failed for years, you should reduce your intensity, periodize your training, and emphasize strength and speed training. The need for a complete change in your tactical thinking or the learning of new tactics is not unusual. Psychological blocks are discussed in detail in chapter 7. A training program cannot be provided due to the variations in individuals' goals.

Amateur A/B, Elite and U 23

The races in the A/B- or elite-classes are 70-200 km long, of which most circuit races are 80-110 km, and road races are 120-180 km long. The longer race distances, especially road races, require more training than for races in the C-class.

Yearly mileages ranging from 15,000 for B-amateurs to 40,000 km for absolute top riders become necessary. An average rider in the A/B-class will do alright by riding 20,000 km, even though some riders can train less and still ride at the front of the field. The biggest problem in the A/B-class is that the near-professional athlete who only rides his bicycle and the athlete who works or attends school have to compete against each other.

Race-mileage increases due to longer and more frequent races. Each season, cyclists compete in 40 to 100 races, a few of which are stage races. The amount of time spent in all training zones increases, with special emphasis on strength-endurance, competition-specific endurance, and, as already mentioned, racing. The larger gears and greater percentage of climbing during races makes strength-endurance very important; consequently, training in this area varies throughout the whole year (less at the beginning of the preparation period, more at the end of the competition period, none during the transition period). Speed-training is less important for road racers. Basic endurance workouts should be over 100 km long and can be as long as 250 km. The principles of periodization discussed earlier apply as well. In the A/B-class, time restrictions confine training almost entirely to the bicycle from the 2nd preparation period through the racing season, forcing general athletic activities, with the exception of strength training (1-2 workouts a week), to fall by the wayside. Even so, you should cross-train during the season to gain psychological and physical distance from cycling. The importance of daily gymnastics for strength and flexibility is often ignored, particularly in the elite ranks.

Specific strength training with weight machines is covered in the section "Strength Training". An athlete can only be as strong as his weakest body part. For example, if the shoulder/arm muscles are poorly trained, hill climbing and sprinting performance will be affected. If stomach and arm muscles are too weak, the body cannot generate the necessary tension for a hard jump or a sprint, and the results remain mediocre. Moreover, well-developed back muscles protect the athlete from stress damage to the spine. However, these statements do not imply that a cyclist should use the weight room to build more muscle mass, which would rob his working muscles of oxygen, but rather that he should tone the muscles that are already present.

The young, second-year amateurs must now concentrate on reaching the A-class, or, if they have already accomplished this in the first year, they should focus on important races. The mileage increases of 10-20% per year are primarily

Amateurs U 23				
Age	19 (m)	20 (m)	21 (m)	22 (m)
Yearly kilometers	16,000-20,000	20,000-24,000	22,000-26,000	24,000-28,000
Number of races	40-60	45-65	50-70	50-70
Max. training dist	< 200 km	< 250 km	< 250 km	< 250
Training zones	BE 1, BE 2, CSE, ST, SS, SE	BE 1, BE 2, CSE, ST, SS, SE	BE 1, BE 2, CSE, ST, SS, SE	BE 1, BE 2, CSE, ST, SS, SE
Tips	SE and strength training important; get used to very high mileage; road races and stage races; don't forget cross-training			

Weekly Cycle in PP and CP (19-22 years)

	PP	CP
Monday	other sport or off	other sport, gymnastics , 30 km CO
Tuesday	60 km BE 1, indoor training 1-2 hrs/stength training 1 hr	70-120 km with 7-12 sprints or 4-15 km SE (53 x 14)
Wednesday	50-80 km BE 1 or 1 hr running or 1-2 hr running/cross-country skiing	80-140 km BE 1 with 3 x 8 km CSE or training race
Thursday	indoor training 2 hrs	120-200 km BE 1 with a few tempo intervalls (BE 2, CSE)
Friday	other sport 1-2 hrs or off	30 km CO/BE 1 or off
Saturday	70-130 km BE 1 or MTB weekend = 2nd BE block	race or 90-180 km BE 1 + 2 race-free: BE block
Sunday	80-160 km BE 1 or MTB weekend = 2nd BE block	race or 90-200 km BE 1 race-free: BE block

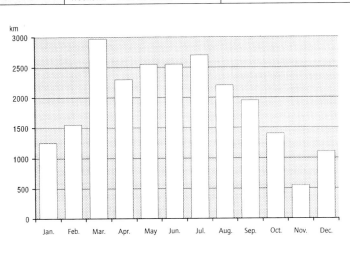

due to the longer races and stage races. At this level of racing, belonging to a club that can send teams to stage races becomes important. The higher the performance level climbs, the more obvious it becomes that a further increase in fitness can only be accomplished through raising the proportion of race mileage, assuming that the rest of the training is conducted properly; this is especially true when the time limit for training has already been reached.

One training method in the amateur class is motor-pacing, which involves drafting behind a motorcycle at high rates of speed (race speed or higher) on sparsely-traveled streets. Although not risk-free, this type of training is well-suited as a race substitute or for learning to ride fast.

Some A/B-riders are circuit-racing specialists, whereas others are road racers. While the first group of riders can get away with low yearly mileage and only compete in road races occasionally to improve their endurance, the riders in the second group only occasionally race in circuit races and criteriums to improve their speed and partake in the rich prime prizes. If possible, road racers should compete in few circuit races and should concentrate completely on long road races and stage races.

Women

Most of what was said for amateur men also applies to women. Due to the smaller field sizes, Germany and Austria don't divide the women into different categories, whereas Switzerland does; this lack of separation leads to significant performance discrepancies within a field of riders. Races are similar in length to those for the Juniors 17-18 category. Cycling rules also permit women to compete in the Juniors 17-18 category, when no women's race is held. Shorter women's races generally lead to a reduced yearly mileage, which has, however, increased in recent years for many elite women riders. The mileage for a first-year women's category rider should be about 14,000 km. Elite women's yearly mileages are around 22,000 to 28,000 km a year.

In the traditionally male sport of cycling, women had to fight hard to gain equality, which even today is absent from certain areas. After many years of debate, it was finally acknowledged that women could perform almost as well as men, particularly in endurance sports (for example, marathons). However, they are comparatively far

Women				
Age	19 (w)	20 (w)	21 (w)	22 (w)
Yearly kilometers	12,000-16,000	14,000-18,000	16,000-20,000	18,000-22,000
Number of races	25-40	30-45	35-50	35-50
Max. training dist	< 160 km	< 180 km	< 200 km	< 200
Training zones	BE 1, BE 2, CSE, ST, SS, SE	BE 1, BE 2, CSE, ST, SS, SE	BE 1, BE 2, CSE, ST, SS, SE	BE 1, BE 2, CSE, ST, SS, SE
Tips	SE and strength training important; get used to very high mileage; road races and stage races; don't forget cross-training			

Weekly Cycle in PP and CP (19-22 years)

	PP	CP
Monday	other sport or off	other sport, gymnastics , 30 km CO
Tuesday	60 km BE 1, indoor training 1-2 hrs/stength training 1 hr	60-100 km with 7-12 sprints or 4-15 km SE (52 x 15) technique training
Wednesday	40-70 km BE 1 or 1-2 hrs running/cross-country skiing	60-100 km BE 1 with 3 x 8 km CSE or training race
Thursday	indoor training 2 hrs	90-180 km BE 1 with a few tempo intervalls (BE 2, CSE)
Friday	other sport 1-2 hrs or off	30 km CO/BE 1 or off
Saturday	70-130 km BE 1 or MTB weekend = 2nd BE block	race or 90-150 km BE 1 + 2 race-free: BE block
Sunday	80-130 km BE 1 or MTB weekend = 2nd BE block	race or 90-180 km BE 1 race-free: BE block

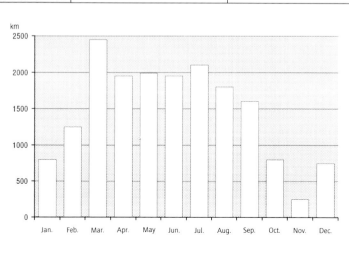

Pedro Delgado with autograph-seekers: handling success is not simple; often the pressure to succeed becomes a burden to the athlete.

Phil Anderson

Pauli Kiuru

Olaf Ludwig

removed from equal performance in cycling, so the future promises a large performance increase. Once performance improves, the race distances at the elite level must then also be increased.

The emphasis here, too, is on basic endurance training, which helps increase aerobic capacity. For a long time, strength and strength-endurance training was, and still is for the most part, neglected in the women's category, which leaves much room for improvement as this performance reservoir is tapped.

Compact women's field

Strength-endurance training occurs with lower gears and somewhat reduced mileage than for amateur men. Female racers must place special emphasis on low body weight. Riders with lean body types are usually clearly at an advantage, since, among other things, they possess a higher relative maximum oxygen uptake capacity.

Masters

The masters class A, 41 and up, and the masters class B, 51 and up, are comprised mostly of former amateur racers, whose desire to race motivates them to still be very involved with their hobby. Cycling newcomers are only rarely found in the masters class. Therefore, in general, these riders are "old hares", who are tactical experts in their field. Often, the extremely short race distances, which rarely exceed 50-60 km, are criticized. Because of the highly similar fitness levels and short distances, these races often end in field sprints. However, longer distances would do more justice to the age of the athletes, since as the distance increases, the intensity drops. Most masters cyclists have ridden so many race and training miles in the course of their cycling carriers that they know exactly what is beneficial and what could be detrimental to them. Even so, and despite old training ideas, the emphasis here should still be on basic endurance training. Cross-training (swimming, ball games) and daily basic gymnastics to protect the older athlete from overuse and misuse injuries are highly important. Specific back exercises can prevent back pain. Due to the very different goals and individual time restraints, a sample training plan is once again not provided for this group.

3.7 The Training Camp

Why Have a Training Camp?

Training camps in the sunny South, but also in the homeland, offer cyclists, most of whom work or go to school, the opportunity to totally immerse themselves in their sport for two or three weeks. The main purpose is a performance enhancement that would only be possible with great difficulty at home, where it is rare to be able to ride as many miles in as short a time span as during a training camp. Most amateur cyclists could hardly imagine not having a training camp in the sunny South at the end of the preparation period. A change of scenery injects new enthusiasm into the relatively boring preparation period training that often takes place in the same home-town surroundings.

Where Should the Training Take Place?

The warm climate of the Mediterranean countries predisposes them to a spring training camp. The daily temperatures at this time of year often reach a pleasant 20'C or more, often allowing cycling in shorts only, while it is still cold at home. For this reason, there is a large congregation of cyclists on Mallorca every spring near the end of February. Bicycle racers as well as hobby cyclists use the mild climate and the sparsely-traveled streets of the island to improve their fitness. However, training camps are also possible in Central Europe in the spring and summer, even though you must be prepared for any kind of weather. Some amateur teams are now conducting training camps in their homelands to use the harsh weather for developing the necessary hardness for the Spring Classics and to save money on the side. Training camps in the homeland are especially recommended for Juniors 15-16. The biggest problem in having a training camp in March in Central Europe is the danger of catching a cold, a risk that can be minimized with proper clothing and vitamin-rich nutrition. After training in the South, riders usually catch a cold during the first week after coming back.

When Is the Best Time for a Training Camp?

As already mentioned, the training camp is usually viewed as the conclusion of the preparation period. Therefore, the best time for racers is between the end of February and the end of March. The best time for students is spring break, although this break usually occurs somewhat later. Hobby cyclists can participate in training camps as early as mid-March. Training camps can even occur in the winter in the form of ski vacations. Elite riders also enter training camps during the season before important season high points, and the altitude training camp is an often-used method of providing the decisive push to their fitness.

Duration of the Training Camp

Two weeks has proven to be the most effective time period; although one-week camps are sufficient for young juniors (13-16), elite athletes may extend their camps to as long as four weeks.

How Should You Train in a Training Camp?

That depends a lot on how much you have already trained at home during the preparation period. During a training camp at the end of February, most of the kilometers will be in the basic endurance zone, while a camp in April or during

Table 3.2: The training camp for amateur riders

	1st Week			2nd Week	
1.	arrival 30-60 km to loosen up		8.	180 km	BE 1
2.	110 km	BE 1	9.	2nd rest day, 50 km	CO
3.	140 km 4 km	BE 1 SE	10.	140 km 15 km SE (i.e. 3 x 5 km)	BE 1
4.	160 km	BE 1	11.	160 km several intervals of	BE 1 + 2 BE 2
5.	1st rest day, 50 km CO		12.	180 km	BE 1
6.	130 km 10 km	BE 1 + 2 SE	13.	220 km	BE 1
7.	150 km	BE 1	14.	return flight if possible, 30-50 km	CO

the season will emphasize special conditioning skills; the purpose of the late camp is to finely tune the existing fitness level with goal-oriented, intense training methods. It would be useless to carry out intense training in February, when a rider may not even have a training base of 2,000 km. The training camp should generally be used to put in lots of mileage, something for which there is rarely time at home. If the mileage base is good, several intense workouts (**SE** , **CSE**, **ST**) can be incorporated into the training regimen. At the appropriate fitness level, participation in local races becomes possible.

Each three- or four-day period of steadily increasing mileage is followed by an easy two hour **CO** ride. Another three- or four-day work cycle with greater mileage follows the first. More details are given in the training plan for the two-week training camp. Strength-endurance training should definitely be included in the training program; the better the fitness, the more strength training can be done (see Table 3.2 for an example).

In addition to cycling, stretching and basic gymnastics should not be short-changed. Exercising before breakfast is a chore for many athletes, and everyone should decide individually if they can benefit from it. Athletic games (table tennis, tennis, volleyball), as long as they are not played too intensely, can provide a welcome diversion for cyclists and a well-balanced free-time program prevents boredom. Cyclists should exercise caution when going swimming, since

Table 3.3: The training camp for Juniors 15-16

Day	Workout
1.	arrival, 70 km **BE 1** , technique training
2.	80 km **BE 1**
3.	100 km **BE 1**
4.	50-70 km **BE 1+2** , techniques and tactics training
5.	100 km **BE 1+2**
6.	110 km **BE 1**
7.	30-50 km , time trial (5 km), departure

susceptible individuals who cool their bodies off too much may catch a cold and miss the rest of the training. If you nevertheless wish to go swimming, this should be postponed until the last few days. Warm, relaxing baths are always acceptable.

During the training camp, but also at home, nutrition is especially important. Feasting orgies at the hotel buffet prevent the desired reduction in percent body fat, and some persons have even gained, instead of lost, weight. The food must not only be nutritious but should also contain plenty of carbohydrates. Getting enough sleep is a basic provision for successful training, since high mileage requires long regeneration times. The following two training programs are for the training of amateurs or Juniors 17-18 in Southern Europe and Juniors 13-14 and 15-16 in Central Europe. Both assume that base mileage training has taken place.

The mileage indicated is based on the assumption that much training has already taken place in the weeks immediately before the training camp. Depending on fitness, category, and weather, cyclists should train between 1,600 and 2,100 km during these two weeks. The long workouts should be strictly **BE 1** zone training, even when mountainous ascents and the finish line tempt riders to go faster. More intense training at such high mileages would stress the riders too much.

Except for during the first cycle, strength-endurance training is done the day after the rest day when the workout distance is relatively short. Other categories should adhere to the same training principles but reduce the given workout lengths proportionately. For organizational reasons, the distances can be divided into two workouts per day; however, the long workout at the end of each block should be ridden as one single workout.

3.8 Strength Training

The importance of strength training for endurance sports in general, and cycling in particular, was discounted for a long time, since only few elite athletes followed a strength training regimen, which was mostly confined to only the winter months. This attitude corresponded to the belief that strength has very little influence on performance in endurance sports. Today, on the other hand, the general opinion is that strength contributes quite a bit to a good endurance performance, providing the ability in cycling to turn over large gears. For this reason, it should not be ignored, since good endurance capacity is of little use without the strength to push a certain gear. During Ergometric testing, cyclists with a high level of strength can clearly maintain a set performance longer than cyclists with poor strength. No consensus has yet been reached in scientific training knowledge about "how to train", although "traditional" methods yield fairly good results. In particular the definitions of the different strength types and their training methods are subject to controversy; some positions espoused by the conventionally accepted literature are directly contradictory. However, the methods and exercises given here correspond essentially to the commonly-taught opinions. Based on new findings, maximum strength is now thought to be far more important for the level of other strength types (speed-strength, strength-endurance, explosive strength, etc.) and also for specific performance abilities than previously assumed.

Train Year-round

Year-round strength training should be promoted not only for elite athletes but also for "normal" racers and hobby cyclists, even when their goals differ: while the elite athlete or bicycle racer seeks mainly to improve his cycling performance, the hobby cyclist uses strength training more for its preventative character and to protect against overuse and misuse injuries. This aspect is, however, not trivial for serious athletes, since specific training of support and posture muscles (torso, shoulders, arms) effectively eliminates back problems.

Functional Improvement of the Musculature

The demand for strength training in cycling, however, does not mean that muscle mass should be increased, but rather that the existing muscles should be toned, whereby body weight should increase very little, if at all. This functional improvement goes along with an increase in maximum strength and is accomplished through an improvement in the coordination within a muscle and between the individual muscles involved in a movement (inter- and intramuscular coordination). Only long-term training with heavy weights will obviously increase cross-sectional area (muscle enlargement), something that road cyclists should avoid in most cases through specific training.

When to Train?

Often the strength potential laboriously built up during the preparation period returns quickly to previous levels through a lack of strength training during the season. Even regular strength training just once a week could maintain the strength level and hereby improve cycling performance. Thus, everything is in favor of riding a few kilometers a week less and devoting this time to strength training instead. An hour, for example on a Wednesday before an easy road ride, completely suffices and strength training can also be done on bad weather days. The strength base is always formed during the preparation period in the weight room or through indoor training. Since strength training is usually highly stressful and incorrect technique can easily result in injuries, you must pay attention to several training rules and learn proper form. Strength training in cycling is divided into strength training in the weight room or in the gym (with weight machines or with body weight) and strength training on the bike, which was already discussed in detail in section 3.3.

Strength training Rules

- A good warm-up must precede strength training, regardless of the type of trai-ning you choose. The higher the stress load, the longer the warm-up should be.

- Strength training follows the same principle of gradual stress-increase as endurance training does; only after a muscular foundation is present, can specialized strength training begin.

- Strength training must be done regularly (1-3 times/week)

- Similar to endurance training, the load must be varied in cycles, since applying the same stress in each workout will not trigger any more adaptation and, therefore, will have no additional training benefit.

- Strength training must be appropriate to the performance ability and, above all, to the age of the athlete; children under 15 years old should only train with their own body weight; avoid over-stressing the body.

- Correctly- and smoothly-executed exercises require a high amount of concentration.

- Breathe quietly during the exercises; no forceful breathing.

- Pay attention to the body's regeneration; for example, don't train when the body is very exhausted from a race or workout; between strength training sets, take rest breaks of 2 to 4 minutes to recover.

The following exercise suggestions for a strength training program do not indicate a fixed number of repetitions and sets due to individual differences among athletes, but rather provide a range from which each individual can choose the most appropriate values. Start out with low weights and gradually increase the weights.

1. In the Weight Room
The following briefly introduces a strength training program that covers the whole training year.

Determine Your Maximum Strength
The stress load is given in percent of maximum strength, which must be determined – after a thorough warm-up – separately on each machine and for each exercise in order to be able to calculate each load's percentage. When doing a maximum strength test, use three or four attempts to approach your maximum load. Note these values and use them to calculate and then record your training program. Repeat this maximum test each month, so that you can adjust the weights to your changing strength levels.

The following muscle groups should be trained:

- **thigh muscles** *(extensors:* various leg presses, knee bends with dumb-bells (not too far); *flexors:* leg curl, squats)

- **lower leg muscles** (calf machine, calf raises with barbell)

- **hip flexors**

- **Gluteal muscles** (see thigh muscles)

- **arm, shoulder, and chest muscles** (biceps curls, bench press, triceps curls, pull-downs, rowing machine, push-ups)

- **back muscles** (back machine without weights, see section "Stretching", push-ups)

- **stomach muscles** (crunches, ab. machines, stomach exercises in section "Stretching", push-ups)

An experienced health-club or weight room strength trainer should explain the exercises named above, and these exercises should be combined with those found in the sections "Stretching" and "In the gym or at home". A strength training workout is composed of a **warm up**, a **main part** (always stretch between exercises), and a **cool down**. The main part concentrates on training one or two muscle groups using many different exercises; back and stomach exercises are interspersed throughout and are part of daily gymnastics anyway.

Preparation Period I (adjustment phase)
In *November*, the muscles are trained with low weights (45-55%), a high number of repeats (15-20), and 2 to 4 sets, to accustom them to the subsequent period of more intense training. During this time period, train two to three times a week in the weight room. A maximum strength test is absolutely necessary after this phase.

Preparation Period II (growth phase)
In *December* and *January*, the muscles are stressed more, at 60-70% of maximum strength. Three to four sets of 8-12 repeats are carried out. When training two times a week, you don't have to fear building too much muscle mass.

Preparation Period III (maximum strength phase)
February and *March* are used to improve maximum strength; for example, training with very high loads (80-100%) and only 1-5 repeats with 4-6 sets stresses the body immensely and leads to an increase in maximum- and speed-strength capacities. This strength training should be done two to three times a week. Test your maximum strength several times during this period and adjust the weights accordingly.

Competition Period (strength maintenance phase)
As already mentioned, the competition phase beginning in *April* seeks to conserve strength capabilities through one or two workouts a week of eight repeats and three sets at 60-70%. During the long competition period, the strength training stress, just like the endurance stress, must be varied by occasionally including a maximal strength workout, reducing training after difficult races, and also by varying the workouts.

Table 3.4: Yearly strength training program for cyclist

	Intensity	Repetitions	Sets	Workouts/week
PP 1	45-55%	15-20	2-4	2-3
PP2	60-70%	8-12	3-4	2-3
PP3	80-100%	1-5	4-6	2-3
CP	60-70%	8	3	1-2

Only 30 to 45 minutes of training time per strength training workout is required to maintain strength, which leads to more effective riding (sprinting, climbing, time trialing) and allows you to push the large gears necessary for a high performance level. Recreational and health-conscious cyclists should limit strength training to low weights and high repetitions (Phase 1, eventually also 2).

2. In the Gym or at Home
Effective strength training can also take place in a gym or even at home – predominantly using your own body weight – and it can even replace weight room training, if done properly and used in combination with strength training on the bike; even better is strength training using a combination of machines and free weights. Two different methods predominate strength training in the gym or at home: dynamic training (resulting in motion) and static strength training (work without movement). It is important to do strength exercises not only for the leg muscles, but also to include arms, stomach, back, and shoulder in the program (for competitive cycling: whole-body training with an emphasis on leg muscles; for recreational cycling: emphasis on back muscles). The following provides an exercise list, divided by body parts, for strength training in the gym.

What Should You Heed?
The number of repetitions and sets are determined by age, fitness, and goals; thus, the hobby cyclist will prefer the lower numbers of repetitions and sets, whereas the conditioned serious athlete will gravitate towards the higher numbers. If you train so hard that your muscles are sore after each workout, the load is too great; sore muscles or extreme exhaustion should be avoided.

Legs
Calf Muscles

Facing a wall, stand on the ball of one foot and repeatedly extend and relax your foot; the other foot can either be held in the air or rested on the heel of the working leg. Keeping the knee of the working leg stiff is important, so that the calf muscles are solely responsible for raising and lowering the body. This exercise is even better if performed on a step or drop-off. Per leg, 15 to 50 repeats in 2 to 4 sets.

This track stand requires Michael Hübner's (front) complete concentration.

Shin Muscles

While sitting on the ground and keeping your heels touching the floor, flex your feet at the ankles to bring your toes closer to you. A partner should provide resistance by pushing down on your toes. 10 to 20 repeats with 2 to 4 sets.

Quadriceps, Calf, Buttocks

There are a whole series of exercises for the quadriceps:

1) With your back against a wall, sit down on an imaginary chair and hold this position for 15 to 60 seconds. Your back should be pressed flat against the wall and your arms should hang down at your sides.

2) Jump as high as you can over a bench with both legs together 10 to 30 times (back and forth), depending on fitness. 2-4 sets.

3) End jumps: Jump into the air with both legs together and your back straight. After landing with your feet flat on the ground, or, better yet, on the balls of your feet, do not bend your knees further than 80° and initiate another jump as soon as possible. 8 to 20 repeats with 3 to 5 sets. This exercise is especially useful to improve hill climbing and sprinting performances. Serious athletes can increase the difficulty by jumping onto small crates.

4) Almost all jumping exercises are ideal for leg strength training, but one-legged jumps should only be attempted after a high strength level has been reached.

The jumping exercises, especially exercises 2) and 3), improve speed-strength. Skipping rope combines strength and endurance exercises and is perfect for improving strength-endurance. A program for the legs should always include a combination of several exercises.

Back, Stomach, Arms and Shoulders

Exercises for these muscle groups are found at the end of the "Stretching" chapter. A medicine ball is ideal for training arm and shoulder muscles. Two athletes toss a medicine ball (3-6 kg) back and forth using different throwing and blocking techniques in multiple sets of exercises. A program for strengthening back and arm muscles should be done daily to prevent overuse injury.

On the Bike

Strength training on the bike was already discussed at length in chapter 3.3 (strength-endurance and speed-strength training). A training program for improving the different strength abilities and anaerobic metabolism is given here: after a thorough warm-up (min. of 30 min), do 6 to 10, over 30 second-long, jumps in the saddle using sprint-appropriate (in each case, almost maximum) gearing and reaching the highest possible speed without shifting. Rest 3 to 5 minutes in between the efforts while riding easy. Junior 15-16 riders can decrease the time from 30 to 20 seconds and reduce the number of repeats to six.

3.9 Stretching

The following chapter provides cyclists with exercises for loosening up while on the bicycle, but these can also be done at home before or after training or competition.

What Is Stretching?

Stretching is a type of gymnastics that has a strong influence on flexibility. As a rule, every athlete should have a daily stretching routine, which is best combined with several strengthening exercises. One restriction must, however, be mentioned: parts of the body that are injured or have been operated on should not be stretched, unless specifically advised by a physician. Especially for cyclists, stretching is mandatory for preserving flexibility, since the legs are very active, while the rest of the body is ignored. Unused muscles can shorten with time, reducing flexibility and the quality of movement.

What Does Stretching Accomplish?

First of all, it increases muscle blood flow and metabolism, preparing muscles and tendons for exercise and decreasing regeneration times after exercise (training and races). Stretching as part of a warm up reduces the risk of injury, improves muscle coordination, and allows muscles to work more efficiently. A regular stretching program frees attachments between muscles, tendons, and connective tissue, improving muscle functioning. The elasticity of the muscles and the range of motion of the joints noticeably improves. Even bothersome tightness (back) can be managed through a specialized stretching program. One more vital point should be added: stretching improves body awareness and body monitoring, and being more familiar with your body lets you detect the smallest changes faster. This long list of convincing arguments should suffice to motivate anyone to start a stretching program.

How Do You Stretch?

Several points are important for proper stretching: the most important rule is to concentrate during the exercise on the body part being stretched to perceive stretching and relaxation. During each 10-30 second (per exercise) stretch, the muscles should feel pleasantly tense, and this feeling should subside somewhat near the end of the stretch. Thereafter, the tension can be increased once again. When first starting a stretching workout, the stretch time can be counted silently, but with experience, this becomes unnecessary.

Stretching does not involve pain or teeth-gritting. If the tension in the muscles is too great, adjust the joint angles to reduce it. Stretching should never involve bouncing or pulling, which unfortunately happens quite frequently. Bouncing only leads to further tightening of the muscles due to the stretch reflex. The **stretch reflex** is a reflex that opposes extreme stretching of the muscles to protect them from being over-stretched or even torn.

Warming up, by running in place or riding the rollers with no resistance (5 min), should take place prior to the stretching routine. Breathing during the exercises is slow, regular, and controlled. Do not hold your breath, since this leads to undesirable force-breathing. Stretch in comfortable clothes (jogging suit), on a soft surface in a room that is at a comfortable temperature. Stretching on the bike should be done on sparsely-traveled roads or a bicycle path and requires good bike-handling skills, since body contortions are carried out while riding. These suggested exercises can be combined to create a program that suits your needs, but you should always start at your head and work your way down to your legs. An almost endless number of other stretching exercises are possible, as long as they adhere to the maxim that stretching should not be painful. There is more in-depth literature on this topic that contains a wealth of exercise suggestions. This first set of loosening and relaxing exercises is carried out while riding the bicycle.

Exercises on the Bike
1) Throat and Neck
Over-extending the cervical (neck) spine while riding often results in muscle tightening, which can be painful. Tilt your head for 5 seconds to the left and then to the right; use your hand to help increase the pressure. In the same way, arch your back and touch your chin to your chest, helping out with your hand.

2) Vertebral Column/Back
Sit up and ride with no hands, stretch, and finally extend your body as far as possible with raised arms.

3) Shoulder Girdle
While holding onto the handlebars close to the stem with extended arms, raise both shoulders up to ear-level (5 sec) and then depress them. Afterwards, let go of the handlebar with one hand, let this arm dangle loosely at your side, and move your shoulder or your whole arm several times in forward and backward circles.

4) Upper Arm and Shoulder

With your right hand holding onto the handlebars, place your left hand on your right shoulder. Now push this hand as far as possible towards the center of your back. This exercise stretches both the triceps (the extensors of the elbow) as well as the shoulder.

5) Hands and Arms

While steering with one hand, push the other, with your fingers and back of your hand pointing up, for 10 seconds into your waist so hard that you can feel a stretch. The stretch should be felt in your hand, forearm, and shoulder. Hands that are tired from gripping the handlebars can be stretched through this exercise. This exercise also improves circulation through the wrist.

6) Back

The back is often tight and sore, so it must also be stretched thoroughly.

a) While holding onto the handlebars in a normal position, arch your back (like a cat) and then extend it the other way. Both parts of this exercise should be repeated in an alternating fashion several times.

b) While your left hand holds onto the handlebars, your other arm is passed underneath your left arm, so that your upper body is twisted, stretching some of the back muscles (each side 5-10 sec).

7) Hamstrings

The flexors can easily be stretched while riding. To do this stretch, rise out of the saddle and bring your left pedal forward to the 9 o'clock position. While the balls of your feet rest on the pedals, lower your heels, keeping your legs straight, and drop your upper body forward (5-10 sec). Next, stretch the other leg by bringing your right leg forward.

8) Quadriceps

The extensors can also be stretched while riding, but this stretch requires a little bit more riding skill and good balance. Take one foot off the pedal and grab that ankle with the same-side hand. Now move your knee back until you feel the muscles stretch.

9) Calves and Achilles Tendon

Rise out of the saddle with the cranks horizontal and push down with the back leg. While doing this, press the heel of the back leg down until a stretch is discernable. To transfer this stretch to the achilles tendon, slightly bend the knee of the leg being stretched.

The last three exercises (7, 8, 9) are also useful for putting an end to bothersome cramps; especially calf cramps can be helped in this manner.

Exercises before or after Training or Competition

1) Neck

As on the bike, the stretching program on the "ground" begins with the head-neck region. Bend your head for a few seconds each to the front, the left, and the right. The shoulder axis should not change its position parallel to the ground during this exercise. Afterwards, turn your head as far as possible to the left and hold this position; then do the same to the right.

2) Shoulder

To loosen up the shoulders, you can move your arms or shoulders in circles. Stretch your shoulder girdle by raising one elbow above your head and placing your hand between your shoulder blades. Hold this position for about 10-20 sec for each side. This exercise increases the flexibility of the shoulder joint tremendously, which is extremely advantageous during crashes.

3) Upper Arm and Shoulder

Cross one hand underneath your chin and place it on the opposite shoulder. Use your other hand to press your elbow towards your shoulder.

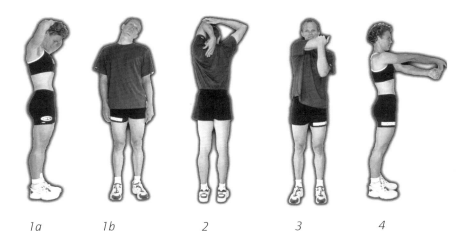

1a   1b   2   3   4

4) Forearms and Wrists

From a kneeling position, place your hands palm-down with your fingers pointing towards your knees. Now move your body backwards (in the direction of your heels) to increase the tension in your forearms and wrists. A similar effect is achieved by over-extending the wrist while the arm is held straight. During this exercise, your palm should face away from your body and your fingertips should point down.

5) Back

With feet shoulder-width apart, bend your upper body sideways; bend one arm over your head towards this side, while you use the other to press an imaginary object into the ground.

6) Back and Legs

Stand stiff as a board and stretch out as far as possible with raised arms, then hang your arms at your sides and begin to slowly bend your head toward your chest. This exercise arches your back, first in the chest area and then also in the lower back region, until your torso finally dangles completely relaxed while your legs are straight.

5

Your hands should now almost touch your toes. Straighten out again equally slowly, until you are completely stretched out once again. During this exercise, as in the preceding ones too, you must tune out your environment and focus completely on your body. This task is easier with closed eyes. "Dangling" is an excellent exercise for the back. Hang from a bar or branch with one or both arms for as long as you can sustain this position.

7) Hip and Lower Back
While lying on your back, pull one knee up to your chest and hold it there, as the other leg is extended. To stretch your hamstrings from this position, grab this leg behind the knee and straighten the leg out vertically.

8) Hamstrings (flexors) and Calves
a) In a walking stance (feet facing forward), bend forward with a straight back and the toes of the front leg pointing up. With this exercise, you should feel your hamstrings and calf stretch.
b) Bend forward with crossed, straightened legs and a rigid back. Afterwards, cross your legs the other way.

9) Quadriceps (extensors)
To maintain balance more easily, you can hold onto a wall while stretching the most important "cycling muscle", the quadriceps. Grab the instep of the raised leg with your same-side hand and slowly pull it towards your buttocks until you feel a good amount of stretch. The hips should be tilted slightly forward, but the quadriceps sould remain parallel to each other and the upper body should be kept upright; duration: 20-30 sec per leg.

6   8a   8b   9

10) Adductors

In a wide straddle position with parallel, forward-facing feet, bend one knee so far that you can feel the stretch on the inside of the other leg's thigh almost down to its knee. This stretching maneuver can be carried out in a similar way by taking a step forward.

10

11) Quadriceps and Shin Muscles

Sit down on your feet with your knees on the ground; after about 15 seconds, raise one knee with one hand, so that the front shin muscles get stretched.

11

12) Gluteal Muscles

Stretch out on your back on the ground. Then bend one knee and lay the ankle of the other leg on the knee of the bent leg. Now grasp the knee of the bent leg, and slowly pull it towards you, keeping your pelvis on the ground, however. If the stretch is not enough, you can pull the knee a little to the outside.

12

13) Hamstrings, Calves and Back

Sit down and place one ankle on the opposite thigh slightly above the knee. Now bend forward keeping your back straight; in addition, you can pull the toes of your stretched-out leg towards yourself.

Exercises to Strengthen the Trunk Muscles

To conclude this chapter, a few effective exercises for strengthening the trunk musculature (back, stomach, shoulders, lower back) and ultimately improving posture will be introduced. These exercise can easily be integrated into a stretching program.

1) Stomach Muscle Exercises

a) Crunches: Lie on your back with your legs propped up and slowly curl your body toward your legs, beginning with your head; repeat this exercise 10-20 times (straight abdominal muscles).

b) Diagonal crunches: Using the same position as above, fold your hands behind your neck and curl your body toward your legs once again, but this time attempt to touch each elbow to the opposite knee; repeat 10-20 times (oblique abdominal muscles).

2) Back Muscle Exercises

While lying on your stomach and looking at the ground, raise your extended feet a little off the ground. Now slowly move your arms up and down as if you are doing pull-ups. You can also move your arms reciprocally back and forth close to your body as fast as you can; 15-30 repeats.

3) Push-ups

Properly done push-ups are an excellent exercise for the back and stomach as well as for arms and shoulders. A high amount of body tension is important during this

crunches   *diagonal crunches*

exercise: your body should be straight as a board. Many variations are possible: with arms close together or far apart, fast or slow, or with an emphasis on height. The number of repetitions depends completely on individual ability. Do three sets with a certain number of repetitions.

push ups

3.10 The Training Diary

Recording your workouts in a training diary is called training documentation in sports science. Based on these entries, the coach, but also the rider himself, can draw useful conclusions about the structure of the training program, avoid mistakes, and repeat positive outcomes.

For the hobby cyclist, who must not reach his personal peak fitness level, a pocket calendar is more than sufficient for recording mileage and some additional useful information such as route, weight, resting pulse, or weather; this log provides a brief overview of the training year.

This form of documentation is not enough for serious athletes, who need to record significantly more information. The daily recording of resting pulse and weight and the categorization of training zones and body aches and pains only represents a fraction of the important information that must be recorded in a clearly organized manner. The xeroxed training diary sheets, which can be kept in a binder, are ideal for keeping track of this information. These sheets provide a clear overview of all important training data and competition results. Two sheets are needed for every month (cross out any days that do not exist for that month). Not only bicycle training, but any form of athletic activity is recorded on these sheets (see Table 3.5).

Training documentation is more than the simple collection of data, however. Subsequent evaluation, the so-called training analysis, is even more important. Several different analysis approaches are possible: the weekly and monthly mileage data can be graphically presented. Going a step further, race results can be incorporated into the graph, yielding important observations for the next year. In addition, the results can be tied to resting pulse values, fitness test results, and illnesses. All this data and information creates a complex graph.

Table 3.5: Trainning diary (sample)

Cycling training diary		Name:		Month:			Category:		
Date	training route/ race lacation, additional training	type of training type of race	Number of riders	daily mileage	time	monthly mileage	weight	resting pulse	comments
1./16									
2./17									
3./18.									
4./19.									
5./20.									
6./21.									
7./22.									
8./23.									
9./24									
10./25.									
11./26.									
12./27.									
13./28.									
14./29.									
15./30.									
31.									
Number of workouts on the bike: Numer of cross-training workouts		Training hours: (total/bike/other):		Race mileage: (Month)		Monthly mileage:		Yearly mileage: carried over:	

In the elite ranks, the individual training zones are differentiated on the graph as well, making the whole thing even more complicated. Time intervals other than the calendar year or the training year, for example the special preparation for a race or a multiple-year overview, can also be represented. These time-consuming analysis procedures are only important beginning with Juniors 17-18; before this, an analysis of only the fundamental training aspects with no graphic representation is more than sufficient. Unfortunately, many cyclists do not keep a training diary, let alone evaluate their training, or if they do, this important data often lands in the trash at the end of the season and is lost. Therefore, young cyclists should get used to keeping a simplified training diary at an early age.

Training Programs

The coaches who create their riders' training programs, as well as the riders who take this task upon themselves, need an easily-visualized plan that enables them to control their training within the target range. The blank sample training program given here has a space for recording planned training distances and intensities and another for filling in the actual training. The proximity of these values enables a direct comparison of "should" and "did". Especially Juniors 15-16 will be tempted to inflate their mileage, even when training little or not at all, in order to put themselves in a good light. These young athletes should be told that they will only cheat themselves if they do this. If the coach/rider relationship is relaxed and friendly, problems of this nature should not occur.

Table 3.6: Sample training plan

Week				Name	
Day	Date	km	Content Workout training zones	Additional factors nutrition, Gymnastics	Actual km content
Mon					
Tues					
Wed					
Thurs					
Fri					
Sat					
Sun					

4 Fitness Diagnosis and Testing

4.1 Laboratory Diagnostic Test

Regular laboratory fitness diagnosis has become indispensable for the performance analysis and training regulation of professional and other elite cyclists. Four to six fitness tests are done each year: at the beginning and middle of the preparation period, as well as at the beginning and middle of the competition period. During the direct preparation period for a season peak, the fitness diagnostic test is used to detect weaknesses that can then possibly be corrected.

However, as often occurs, too much emphasis should not be placed on the results of such a test, since peak performance can also be achieved without complicated tests through proper training and experience. In addition, the test results are influenced by many factors, which explains why occasionally completely false training deductions are made, especially when the coach has only limited experience with fitness tests. A single test cannot provide much training information; to get the maximum benefit out of fitness testing, regular tests must be performed. The fitness test is supposed to shape the training program so that training stress is optimal. The heart rate and lactic acid concentration, not the riding speed, are intensity control measures.

The step test, normally carried out on a bicycle ergometer, is ideal for cyclists, who are accustomed to the pedaling motion. For a runner, the bicycle ergometer test would be less useful, since the unaccustomed pedaling motion on the bike would not allow him to give his maximum effort. The bicycle ergometer should be adjusted exactly like the cyclist's own bicycle and he should use his own shoes and pedals, so that he can carry out his usual pedal stroke.

Step-wise increases in workload stresses the athlete until he is unable to continue. Depending on the coach's opinion and test objectives, the step-lengths vary between two and six minutes with workload increases between 20 and 50 Watts per step. Lately, tests performed on elite athletes have longer workload steps of about six minutes to give the metabolism time to adjust and reach a "steady state" (balance). Because of the delayed lactic acid distribution in the bloodstream, shorter step-lengths would predict training intensity zones that are too high; the training goals would not be met.

To enable comparison, the tests should be done under standardized conditions, since, for example, the type of nutrition, the previous day's training intensity, and the method of measuring lactic acid all have considerable influence on the test results. All tests in a training year must use the same method with the same step-lengths and workload increases to permit the comparison of the individual tests to each other. During the tests, physiological and biomechanical parameters such as heart rate, electrocardiogram (ECG), pedal cadence, performance, oxygen uptake, breathing volume, and lactic acid, urea, and creatine kinase concentrations can be measured.

However, the determination of oxygen uptake (spiroergometry) requires considerably more equipment, which greatly increases the cost of such a procedure. The determination of maximum oxygen uptake is, nevertheless, useful and should be done whenever going through the trouble of doing a fitness test. There exists, a simple, but nevertheless dependable, formula for calculating the oxygen uptake: VO_2 (ml/min) = approx. 350 + 12 x load (Watts). The athlete should keep a pedal cadence of 80 to 100 revolutions per minute for the duration of the entire test.

This section does not go into the precise details of performing the step test, since such a test cannot be self-administered anyway. The most important parameters, which should eventually be related to one another, are performance, heart rate, and the corresponding lactic acid values. A graphical representation of these parameters yields the so-called **lactic acid performance curve**, from which the aerobic and anaerobic thresholds can be determined.

The aerobic threshold for an endurance athlete is about 2 mmol lactic acid/L blood, and the anaerobic one is about 4 mmol/L; however, the opinions of sports scientists with respect to these values vary substantially. The interpretation of such a graph involves correlating certain lactic acid values with the corresponding heart rates. For example, the aerobic threshold (lactic acid 2 mmol) may lie around a heart rate of 150, which means that this heart rate should not be exceeded by much during basic endurance 1 training. The other training zones can be determined through the same process, although this method does not always accurately differentiate the individual zones.

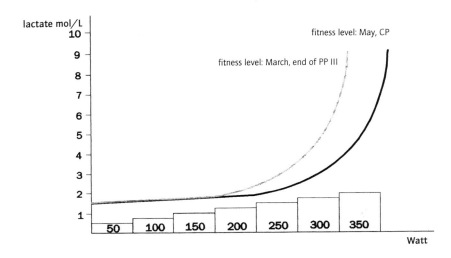

Figure 4.1:
On the basis of two lactic acid curves, the fitness improvement over the course off a training segment can be represented.

Using several lactic acid curves, the fitness improvement or general fitness development can be traced. Laboratory diagnostic tests are very important in the areas of preventative and rehabilitative health-conscious athletics, since these tests enable the physician to precisely diagnose performance ability and allow the physical therapist to design exercise programs with the right amount of stress; in this athletic area, the ECG and blood pressure are more important measurements than the lactic acid values. Aside from the influence that some factors can have on the test results, the laboratory diagnostic test is the most precise method for determining the training zones. Furthermore, this test is the only way to determine and quantify maximum performance ability.

By now, many cyclists have been fitness tested, and this data has been used by sports scientists to construct fairly accurate rules or principles that are more than sufficient for determining many cyclists' training zones. Naturally, there are always exceptions to the norm: athletes with atypical heart rate behavior, for whom fitness testing is almost indispensable. In general, as the performance level of a cyclist increases, determining the precise training zones via a fitness test becomes necessary, since the margin between effective and ineffective, or even harmful, training gets progressively smaller.

Other Laboratory Tests

Complex cycling-specific fitness diagnosis encompasses the determination not only of the total fitness on the bike but also of the individual components of the total fitness by using specific tests. The following enumeration illustrates once again the diversity of the possible tests: maximum power, maximum pedal cadence, anaerobic capacity, strength to pull back on the pedals with respect to the cadence, power generated at different loads, etc.

4.2 Road Step Test

Before this chapter goes into the simple fitness tests, it should introduce the road step test as a compromise between the pure laboratory diagnostic test and the highly simplified time trial test. The road step test is a test (of increasing workload steps) that is not performed under standardized and idealized conditions in the laboratory but rather "on the open road", that is, on the street or track with one's own bicycle. The advantage of this test is that it approximates actual riding conditions, but, in exchange, it also has greater sources of error. Due to various external factors (wind, route, temperature, equipment, tire pressure, etc.), comparing several tests performed on one athlete or simultaneous tests done on different athletes becomes very difficult. If possible, such a road test should be performed under the homogeneous range of conditions that exist on the track (consistent lap distance, predictable wind, easy feasibility), or for road cyclists, on a trainer.

Normally only two or three parameters, namely heart rate and lactic acid values and their relation to speed, are specified during a road test. The intensity during the test is controlled by either speed or heart rate. Choose step-lengths between 2.4 and 6 km. These longer steps are more suitable for determining the training intensities for very fit riders than are the occasionally suggested short steps (under 1 km).

For example, start at a speed of 28 km/hr and increase this speed by 2 km/hr every 2.5 km (on a 250 m track: 10 laps).

The heart rate is stored (i.e. in the Vantage NV) during the test and the lactic acid values are determined at the end of each step. The riders have an obligation to adhere to the speed specifications as closely as possible with the help of their computers until exhaustion sets in and they cannot continue. The POLAR Vantage NV and higher models (Accurex Plus and XTrainer Plus) have programming and computer download capabilities that make them highly suitable for performing a road test. The choice of gearing becomes problematic during the road step test, since a cadence of 100 revolutions per minute should be maintained during all steps. Therefore, a computer that measures cadence becomes necessary as well. At low speeds, small gears are used, and at high speeds, large gears are used; however, matching up the correct cadence with the proper speed is not an easy task.

4.3 Quick and Easy Tests of Fitness

Since both the precise and expensive laboratory diagnostic test as well as the road step test are reserved mainly for the few elite athletes, simple, inexpensive fitness tests are also available. These tests should be performed during the preparation and competition periods, most appropriately after the individual training cycles, to evaluate fitness based on time trialing ability and to possibly modify training for the following cycle.

Fitness testing is also useful for documenting the fitness development of cycling new-comers, especially Juniors 13-14 and 15-16, but also more experienced cyclists. This form of fitness test is recommended not only for bicycle racers, but also for bicycle tour riders (BTR). So that the results of fitness tests can be objectively evaluated and compared, the time trials should be done under similar weather conditions (wind). The time trial gives the coach an indication of the effective-ness of his training advice, and it also highly motivates beginning cyclists, whose performance improves so much in the first year that it is visibly obvious from the fitness test.

The first time trial should be done at the beginning of the preparation period, at the beginning of the first training cycle. A good warm-up (at least 30 min) is advisable to prevent overuse injuries; moreover, the largest gears should be avoided, since the muscles are not well-developed enough to push them – pedal them in circles –

anyway. Those who do not wish to stress themselves with large gears at the beginning of the preparation period can do the first three to four fitness tests entirely in the small chain ring, with a gearing of 42 x 16-14, but this demands a very high cadence.

To allow for the possibility of comparison, it is not enough to perform the test only once in very small gears. Choice of gearing can be set free when the legs have accumulated enough base miles; however, the category-appropriate gearing must never be exceeded.

What Does the Course Look Like?

The fitness test should be done on a sparsely-traveled road without dangerous curves or descents. A loop has several organizational advantages over a straight stretch from point A to point B. The course distance should be between 5 km and 15 km: for Juniors 13-14 and 15-16, the distance should not exceed 10 km, but Juniors 17-18 and Amateurs can extend the course to up to 20 km. Once the desired route has been found, write it down and create a table in which all the times can be recorded. This table may even allow you to follow the development of your performance over the course of many years of training. A coach can derive valuable comparison data from such a log that will enable him to classify his "new" rider.

With starts at one minute intervals and only one stop-watch, any one rider's time can be calculated by subtracting the time difference between his start and that of the first rider from the total elapsed time. The space for comments is for recording such things as whether the rider had mechanical problems. How the rider feels – from 1 to 10 (1 = very bad; 10 = excellent) – should be recorded before the time trial.

Having two different time trial courses is recommended:
  a) a flat or slightly hilly course and
  b) a mountain climb, to enable evaluation of climbing fitness.

When Should the Fitness Tests Be Performed?

From the beginning of the training year to the start of the racing season, the fitness test can be performed anywhere within the microcycle (week); it can even be a race-substitute on the weekend. Once the season (competition period) has begun, though, a suitable weekday must be chosen. Monday, the day of regeneration,

Table 4.1: Form for recording time trials

Fitness test: time trial:				Date:
Course: Weather: Participant number:				
Starter: (age category)	Time	Average speed: (dist/time)	Comments:	Subjective feeling: (1-10)
1.				
2.	- 1 min			
3.	- 2 min			
4.	- 3 min			
5.	- 4 min			
6.	- 5 min			
7.	- 6 min			
8.	- 7 min			
9.	- 8 min			
10.	- 9 min			

and Friday, the day before a race, are out of the question. Since Tuesday is usually reserved for strength and sprint training, only Wednesday and Thursday are left. Of these two days, choose the one that best fits into your training schedule. If there is no race on the weekend, the time trial can be done on that Saturday or Sunday, as a form of race-substitute. Don't underestimate the stress load of a 10 to 30 minute time trial, which falls into the category of long-distance endurance type I and places very high demands on the aerobic and anaerobic capacities.

How Should the Time Trial Be Done?
A thorough warm-up (30 min) should precede the time trial and a basic endurance workout can follow it. Time trials are best done as a group, since the presence of

training partners increases motivation and ambition. Especially for younger cyclists, who usually avoid extreme exertion, time trialing offers a rare occasion to put forth their best effort.

Regular time trial workouts benefit riders by allowing them to develop a good feeling for pace, which makes them better able to estimate their own endurance performance ability. Coaches normally let weaker riders start before stronger ones, but should change this order, particularly for Junior 15-16 riders, to prevent frustration and disappointment. An example would be to start two or three equally strong riders right after one another and then to leave a somewhat larger gap. Start order could also be drawn at random. Time gaps of one minute are most often used. The person timing, as a rule the coach or assistant, stays at the start/finish and records the exact start order (see form).

Evaluation of the Results

Based on the times taken over the course of a season, a meaningful season performance profile can be constructed that can be compared to the race results and/or the training log (see training documentation); certainly elite athletes are not the only ones who will find this profile interesting.

5 Nutrition

At a time when, at least in the highest performance categories, training has reached a near optimum level, nutrition is one of the few aspects with which performance can still be improved. Even the recreational cyclist can increase his performance, improve his health, and, therefore, better his quality of life, with good nutrition. Cycling history is fraught with athletes, coaches, and assistants' attempts to find secret foodstuffs or nutritional supplements to give them an edge over the competition. Hardly any other sport has as many nutritional myths as cycling. This chapter provides nutrition facts and explains how simple it is to eat like an athlete.

5.1 Fundamentals of Nutrition for Endurance Athletes

"Those who take their sport seriously, should also nourish themselves appropriately." Unfortunately, only very few cyclists take this guiding principle to heart, even though sensible nutrition not only improves performance but also promotes health. The recreational cyclist, in particular, can improve the effect of his training through an athletically-suitable and healthy diet, which can also taste good. Nutrition and exercise often make you more aware of a healthy and athletically-appropriate lifestyle. Not uncommonly, other family members also change their eating habits and, in this way, benefit from the athlete in the family.

Performance-conscious and elite athletes must pay special attention to their nutrition and employ diets for performance enhancement (carbohydrate loading) that a recreational cyclist can ignore without a second thought. First, though, a little nutritional theory, without which a fundamental understanding of these diets would be difficult, will be provided.

You are what you eat.

Purposes of Nutrition

- to provide energy (for bodily activity and vital functions)
- to build-up and maintain the body (cells, tissues)
- to control metabolism and protect health (to keep the negative effects of environment and strenuous exercise on the body to a minimum)

Four nutritional groups are differentiated:

1. Energy Suppliers (combustible materials)

Carbohydrates (starch, sugar) and fats are energy suppliers. During long endurance performances with a paucity of carbohydrates, proteins can also be used to supply energy. (A long-distance race may require 10-15% of the energy to come from protein metabolism.) The body may also attack the blood's immune defense proteins (globulin, albumin), which is the reason for the higher susceptibility of cyclists to infection during and after stage races.

The list of energy suppliers also includes alcohol (with 7 kcal/g), which often represents an unfortunately high proportion of the total energy amount.

2. Building Substances

Proteins belong to the building substances of the body; they participate in building muscles, tendons, ligaments, cartilage, etc. One of the most important building substances of the body is water, which comprises about 60% of the human body. The bones contain minerals as building substances. However, even fats are used for building cell membranes and ensheathing nerve cell axons.

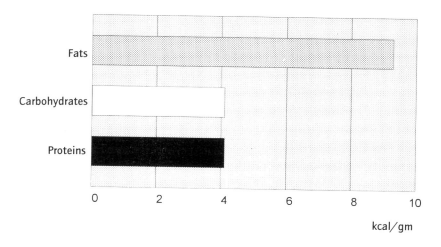

Figure 5.1: The calorie value of nutrients

3. Regulatory and Protective Substances
Vitamins, minerals, and trace elements are included in this group, but so is water, since it is responsible, for example, for body warmth regulation.

4. Function-promoting Food Substances
Fibre belongs in this category, since it stimulates digestion and increases the feeling of satiety. Enjoyment of food is dependant to a large degree on the smell, taste, and color of food, since what use would visually appealing food be if it lacked taste and smell. Next, the **energy suppliers** – the cyclist's fuel – will be introduced and discussed:

Carbohydrates
Carbohydrates are the main component of an athletic diet, since they provide energy during intense exercise, are easily digestible, and are, in most cases, healthy. Two advantages distinguish them from other energy suppliers: they are an oxygen-sparing energy supplier (they deliver 10% more energy than fats per liter of oxygen intake) and they provide a quick source of energy. Complex sugars should comprise 2/3 of the energy provided by carbohydrates: sucrose (table sugar), lactose (milk sugar), maltose (malt sugar), and starch. All four of these sugars are complex sugars whose molecules are composed of at least two simple sugars; starch molecules are constructed of as many as a thousand glucose molecules linked together. At most 1/3 of the carbohydrate energy should come from simple sugars (monosaccharides); glucose (dextrose), fructose (fruit sugar), and galactose are examples.

Our diets are composed of about 35-60% carbohydrates; in a 1988 survey of the German people, this value was barely 40%, which represents too small a proportion not only for athletes but also for non-athletes. The percentage of carbohydrates in the diet should be at least 60% of the total caloric intake.

Which Foods Contain a Lot of Carbohydrates?
Pasta, rice, bread, grain products, potatoes, honey, jams, fruit, etc. Since complex carbohydrates (complex sugars) must be cleaved to simple sugars before being absorbed into the bloodstream, it may appear that the direct intake of simple sugars, such as dextrose or fruit sugar, would be most advantageous to save time during digestion. However, this method has two drawbacks: 1. simple sugar (rapid absorption) causes an immediate rise in blood sugar, but this rise is followed by an

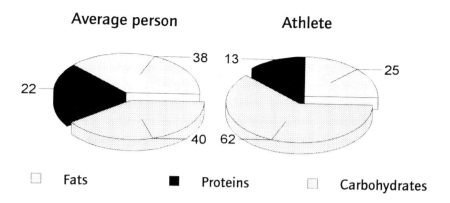

Figure 5.2: The fuel distribution in a cyclist's diet

equally fast drop in blood sugar levels (insulin promotes the rapid absorption of sugar into cells), with a consequent drop, or even collapse, in performance. Therefore, simple sugars should not be ingested before a tour or race, but rather during the last few kilometers in an attempt to boost declining performance. 2. Simple sugar has more particles (molecules) than the same energy-yielding amount of complex sugar; therefore, its osmotic concentration is higher. Since the amount of time food spends in the stomach is determined by its concentration, less concentrated foodstuffs (i.e. complex sugars such as dextrose) pass through the stomach faster and can be absorbed into the bloodstream from the small intestine after being cleaved to simple sugars.

Therefore, you must find the right balance between the time the food spends in the stomach (depends on concentration) and the speed with which it is absorbed into the bloodstream (depends on the type of carbohydrate). For this reason, energy drinks are a mix of different "sugars". In the ideal situation, complex carbohydrates should be ingested before and during exercise, while simple sugars can be eaten near the end of the exercise period. Simple sugars should be avoided if possible during training and tours.

The storage form of carbohydrates in the body is called glycogen (see chapter 2.2). Glycogen, in turn, is a molecule composed of many simple sugars (glucose). During exercise, the glycogen reserves in liver and muscle are activated.

Fats

The "average" Central European and American ingests too much fat. While fat should account for approximately 25-30% of the total energy intake, a Central European or American typically takes in over 40% of his calories in fat. This diet creates the following problem: unused, excess energy is stored by the body in the form of fat pockets. In addition, certain health risks are promoted by a high fat diet: for example, high amounts of fat accelerate atherosclerosis. For these reasons, fat intake should be reduced.

95% of the fats eaten by humans belong to the family of triglycerides that supply energy; about 5% are phospholipids and cholesterol, which are used as building substances. Triglycerides are broken down to glycerin and free fatty acids, absorbed by specialized cells in the small intestine, and distributed to the circulation via the lymph system. Whatever is not used immediately for energy is reassembled to triglycerides and stored. If the glycogen reserves are being depleted, the fat storage depots can be mobilized again and used to generate energy. However, fats can only be burned in "the fire of carbohydrates"; if the carbohydrate stores are extremely depleted, fat metabolism also runs on pilot light and performance sinks. Fatty foods increase the transit time in the stomach and, in this way, postpone the absorption of nutrients. They slow down the replenishing of the glycogen stores, which are so important for recovery, after an exercise bout.

Which Foods Contain too much Fat?

First, there is the group of foods that obviously contains a lot of fat, such as fatty meat, butter, cream, and fried foods. In addition, there is a whole series of foods, including such good-tasting things as cakes, sweets, ice cream, gravy, milk products, sausage, etc., whose high fat content is not readily visible. The goal of an athletic diet is not, however, to forbid all good-tasting things. Instead, making intelligent choices and refraining from certain sweets can reduce the total fat content of the diet considerably. More on this topic below.

Proteins

Proteins also belong to the group of energy suppliers; their proportion of the total energy requirements should be between 10 and 15%. The importance of protein for athletic performance in cycling was overestimated for a long time.

Many cyclists and people in general used to, and some still do, believe that eating a steak daily is fundamental to an athletically-suitable and performance-enhancing diet. In reality, aside from their main function in structure and transportation, proteins are only of minimal value as an energy source inside cells.

Proteins are chains of amino acids. 20 different amino acids are known, but humans only have to supply ten of these through the diet, since the rest can be synthesized by the body. Proteins are cleaved by enzymes in the stomach and small intestine and are absorbed into the bloodstream as amino acids. If the specific amino acid requirement of the cell has been met, the amino acids can also be used for energy by being converted to fat and glycogen. The recommended protein intake for endurance athletes is between 1.2-1.5 grams per kg body weight, which is equivalent to the amount of protein that is ingested by the average person in Germany. Supplementing the diet with additional protein is, therefore, completely unnecessary. Extra protein in the diet is not automatically all converted to muscle mass. Instead, as already mentioned, the extra portion is used as a fuel of third choice and is excreted as urea, making the kidneys work especially hard. To prevent dehydration (desiccation) of the body, you must drink more whenever you eat more protein. The other portion of the extra protein calories is stored as fat. From what was said above, it becomes clear that what matters is the percentage of fat and the amount of high-quality protein in food. Therefore, you should pay attention to the protein-fat-relationship.

Which Foods Contain High-quality Protein in Combination with Little Fat?

Low-fat or fat-free milk products, whole grain products, rice, and pasta, as well as almost all types of fish, fowl, and lean cuts of beef, pork, and lamb are ideal protein sources of this type. A less well-known fact is that legumes are also a very good source of low-fat protein. A well-balanced diet eliminates the need for protein supplements, especially for endurance cyclists. Specific supplementation of certain amino acids should only be done under a physician's supervision and should only be used to correct an imbalance.

Water

The proportion of total body weight comprised of water is about 60% for adults, a little more for children, and a little less for elderly persons. Almost all metabolic processes require water as a medium, and without water, the body would not be able to function. The body loses a lot of water in endurance sports, such as

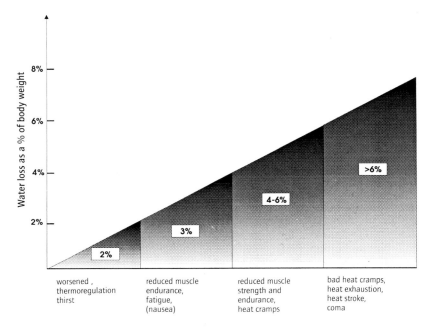

Figure 5.3: The consequences of water loss (dehydration) through exercise

cycling, through the expired air and as perspiration. Because of this loss of water (dehydration), metabolic processes can no longer function at their usual rate, and metabolism increasingly slows down as **dehydration** progresses, resulting in a drop in performance.

During strenuous exercise, for example cycling, the body loses between one and two liters of water per hour, depending on the weather conditions. During a training ride, the water loss is between one-half and one liter per hour. A several hour-long training ride can, therefore, severely deplete the water stores of a cyclist. Body temperature may increase when perspiration is decreased during dehydration.

Lack of water is the nutrient deficiency whose effects on performance are quickest and most severe. Therefore, the "water level" (hydration condition) of the body should be sufficiently high before the workout to provide a reserve to draw upon during the workout. Water loss can be replenished through plain water alone, as was customary a few years ago, with a homemade drink, or with one of the many expensive sports drinks advertised on the market. The advantage of the last method is that it replaces the necessary water as well as carbohydrates, minerals, and vitamins, whose importance should not be ignored, considering that not water alone but also minerals are lost with perspiration.

The sports drink manufacturer's challenge is to determine how high the drink can be concentrated so that, on the one hand, it gets absorbed rapidly but, on the other hand, still contains enough carbohydrates to prevent a drop in performance. For most cyclists, a concentration of 5 to 8% carbohydrate is most effective. So, 5-8 gm of carbohydrates can be added to 100 ml of water (500 ml bottle: 25-40 gm). A higher concentration (greater than 10%) may cause intolerance and stomach cramps. Some athletes, however, can tolerate up to 25% carbohydrate solutions, although such a high concentration seems useless from the scientific standpoint. The choice of concentration depends most on personal tolerance and individually different effects. Fruit juices, which usually have a concentration of over 10%, can be diluted one-to-one with a good magnesium-, calcium-, and potassium-rich mineral water with low carbonation levels. This old-fashioned fruit juice-mineral water mixture is an excellent, good-tasting, and still relatively in expensive sports drink.

New research has shown that during endurance exercise up to three hours long, the mineral deficit can be completely replenished by the minerals present in mineral water and that this fluid is absorbed even faster from the intestine when combined with the carbohydrates in fruit juice. Normal mineral water alone is completely sufficient for short training rides (90 min).

Beverages Suitable for the Athletic Diet

- mineral water (a lot of Mg, Ca, K; relatively little Na)
- fruit juices (especially, freshly squeezed), no fruit juice drinks
- juices with mineral water
- milk, milk shakes (1.5% fat)
- tea
- malt beer
- vegetable juices (if possible, without added sugar)

After exercise, fruit juice with mineral water is especially recommended for replenishing the glycogen stores, since it has a relatively high carbohydrate and mineral content.

How Should You Drink during Exercise?

- slowly, in small swallows
- 150 ml about every 15 minutes, not the whole bottle at once
- under no circumstances, start a workout with a water deficit (thirst)

You should drink regularly during workouts and races before you feel the first sign of thirst, since after the onset of thirst, the fluid deficit is already too great. When it is very hot outside, you can take along a bottle of frozen water and drink the melting cool water. In cold weather, on the other hand, you can fill a bottle (thermos bottle) with hot tea, which will not be ice-cold even after an hour.

Vitamins, Regulatory and Protective substances

Vitamins are organic, essential nutrients that influence metabolism in many different ways, although they are present only in very low concentrations. Vitamins are not a combustible body fuel: they provide no energy. In general, the importance of vitamins for improving athletic performance is over-rated; the actual effect does not warrant the indiscriminate use of vitamin preparations. A diagnosed vitamin deficiency, however, does require taking extra vitamins. A performance improvement should only be expected when a deficit was actually present before the vitamins were taken. Vitamins are divided into fat-soluble and water-soluble types.

• **fat-soluble vitamins**	A (retinol), D (calciferol), E (tocopherol), K (phylloquinone)
• **water-soluble vitamins**	B_1 (thiamine), B_2 (riboflavin, niacin), B_6 (pyridoxine, pantothenic acid, biotin, folicacid), B_{12} (cobalamin), C (ascorbic acid)

Endurance athletes require a higher concentration of vitamins, but this increased requirement is usually covered through the larger food intake and should pose no problems provided nutritionally balanced meals are eaten.

At the highest performance levels (pros), vitamin supplements probably do not enhance performance but, rather, protect athletes from the extreme stress of their sport, since their bodies are pushed to their absolute stress limits; this does not hold true for recreational sports. During a weight loss program, a vitamin deficit may occur because of the reduced food intake; however, the conscious choice of vitamin-rich foodstuffs (fruits, vegetables, milk products) and the use of multi–vitamins will usually remedy this problem.

Be careful when taking extra vitamin supplements in addition to multivitamins or juice, since almost all vitamins can be harmful if taken in over-doses; the same probably even applies to vitamin C. A competent physician should always be consulted before initiating any form of vitamin therapy. Supplementing the vitamins B_1, B_2, E, and C is of particular interest for endurance athletes. Vitamins E and C have an antioxidant effect (prevent cell death by oxidation).

Minerals

Minerals are inorganic elements and their bonds. They are very important building and regulating substances in the human body. Even the trace elements (iron, zinc, chromium, selenium, copper, iodine, molybdenum, cobalt, manganese, etc.) are counted as minerals. In the following section, the most important minerals and trace elements are discussed briefly:

Sodium (Na)

Sodium is essential for maintaining water balance and activating enzymes. It is found mostly in the form of sodium chloride, commonly known as table salt, of which the body contains about 100 grams in dissolved form. Although a sodium intake of 5-7 grams per day is completely sufficient, the average Central European or American takes in over eleven grams a day. Although salt is excreted in large amounts and sweat also contains a high concentration of salt, deficits in salt, and consequently sodium, almost never occur, since too much salt is ingested in the first place. Well-trained endurance cyclists' bodies adjust to higher levels of perspiration by producing sweat that has a greatly reduced sodium content. However, magnesium and potassium are still present in the same concentrations in perspiration.

Magnesium (Mg)

Magnesium is the crucial mineral of metabolism, since it activates nearly all metabolic enzymes, which number over 300 different types. In contrast to sodium, it is found almost exclusively inside cells, similar to potassium. Cyclists lose fairly large quantities of magnesium in perspiration (Mg is several times more concentrated in sweat than in blood) and may have to replace (replenish) this mineral through magnesium supplements. Magnesium deficiency can result in a whole series of symptoms: headache, fatigue, and muscle cramps are especially prevalent.

Since cyclists must prevent a magnesium deficiency, a diet rich in magnesium is recommended: magnesium-rich mineral water alone (over 120 mg/L) supplies the recommended daily amount of magnesium (daily need: 600-800 mg/day). However, only about 35-55% of the magnesium ingested is actually absorbed. Simultaneous high intake of fat, protein, alcohol, calcium, or phosphorous negatively influences magnesium absorption (i.e. even less magnesium is absorbed).

Calcium (Ca)

Calcium plays an important role in muscle contraction and in the nervous system, so one of the most obvious symptoms of a calcium deficit is muscle cramps. Only one percent of the body's calcium is in its free form; the greatest percentage (99%) is stored in the skeleton (about 1,000 grams) and can be mobilized to a small degree if necessary. The calcium requirements (1.5-2.5 gm/day) are largely met through milk products, so a strict vegetarian who refuses to eat all milk products has great difficulty supplying his body with enough calcium through diet alone. Children and pregnant women need higher amounts of calcium than adults to facilitate bone growth.

Potassium (K)

During extreme perspiration, the body also loses a great deal of potassium, which, like calcium, is important for muscle contraction. Since potassium is particularly necessary for glycogen synthesis, cyclists should eat foods rich in potassium. Humans need between 3 and 6 grams of potassium every day. Potassium deficits result in muscles that have a "contraction weakness" and a prolonged recovery time; severe cases can result in functional abnormalities of the heart.

Alex Zulle and Abraham Olano – two all-around cyclists

Phosphate

Phosphate is found predominantly bound to calcium in the skeleton. Phosphate is also an important element for cyclists, since, aside from being a structural element, it plays an important role in metabolism (forming adenosine triphosphate, ATP). Endurance sports greatly increase the phosphate requirements of the body.

Iron (Fe)

Iron has many different associations in the body and is especially important for oxidative metabolism and for binding oxygen to red blood cells (hemoglobin) and to muscle cells (myoglobin). In order to maintain a body iron concentration of four to five grams, men need a daily intake of 10 mg iron; women need more iron due to menstrual blood-loss (15 mg). Because of the relatively poor iron absorption of only ten percent, female athletes in particular frequently become iron deficient. Iron deficiency anemia, which can only be diagnosed with certainty through a blood test, manifests symptoms ranging from reduced performance ability, fatigue, and concentration difficulties, all the way up to circulation disturbances. If iron deficiency is detected, therapy must follow at once. Athletes are assumed to have a higher iron requirement of about 25 mg. Vegetarians, in particular, must pay attention to their iron intake, since the iron found in meats is absorbed better than the iron found in the vegetarian's diet.

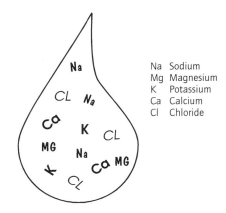

Na Sodium
Mg Magnesium
K   Potassium
Ca Calcium
Cl Chloride

Figure 5.4: Mineral losses (electrolytes) through perspiration

Trace Elements
Zinc (Zn)

Zinc is an activator of over 100 different metabolic enzymes. To avoid a zinc deficiency (possible symptoms: inflammatory disease of the skin and mucus membrane), you should ingest 15 milligrams of zinc per day. Fish, meat, and milk, as well as whole grain products are especially rich in zinc.

Selenium (Se)

Selenium is also an activator of several enzymes. At 50 to 200 micrograms per day, the body requires only the tiniest amounts (traces) of this nevertheless extremely important element. Evidence is accumulating that a selenium deficit may be linked to sudden heart attack deaths in athletes. Selenium is essential (without substitute) for the immune system and certain organs and tissues (liver, muscles, heart, joints); a deficiency first affects these structures. Experiments have shown that the selenium concentration that usually lies in the low or deficient range in performance athletes can be raised through additional selenium supplements, and the danger of deficiency symptoms can be eliminated. Additional selenium intake must be supervised by a physician, since selenium is toxic in over-doses. In general, scientific knowledge about trace elements and their effects is still very primitive. This area of sports nutrition will surely yield a number of interesting discoveries in the future.

Chromium (Cr)

The element chromium, previously only recognized as the material used to plate metal parts, is an equally essential trace element that influences carbohydrate metabolism to a very small degree. However, too little is known about this element to provide tips for athletic nutrition or to give recommended doses.

5.2 Food Staples of Training

All the foods that are part of a good athletic diet also reduce the risk of artereosclerosis, high blood pressure, and cancer – all more or less diseases of civilization.

In brief, athletic diets are low in fat, high in carbohydrates and proteins, and devoid of alcohol and nicotine. This section discusses the basic daily diet only in general terms; further questions are addressed in the subsequent sections.

How Can you Eat a Carbohydrate-rich Diet?

Pasta, rice (both also as whole grain products), whole grain products (whole grain bread, crackers, and cereal), potatoes, legumes (beans, peas), vegetables and fruits, as well as fruit juices are all excellent *carbohydrate sources* that – in contrast to refined products – also contain a number of other valuable nutrients. White sugar, for example, is made up of only "empty" calories, since, aside from the sugar molecule, it contains no other nutrients, such as vitamins, fibres, or minerals. Whenever possible, eat natural foods and avoid processed foods or products and ready-made meals that are almost always prepared with additives (artificial flavors and colors, preservatives, emulsifiers, etc.). The section on carbohydrates goes into greater detail on the benefits of different carbohydrates.

What Should You Watch for when on a Low-fat Diet?

On the one hand, you should consciously reduce your consumption of visible fats, such as oil, butter, margarine, and meat fat, and on the other, you must also learn to recognize and avoid hidden sources of fat. Hidden fats are found in fatty sausages and cheeses, eggs, sweets, gravy, and fried foods. The goal of a low-fat diet is not to eliminate all fat consumption, but rather to make wise food choices and avoid unhealthy high-fat items. It is important to distinguish between saturated and unsaturated fatty acids, the latter being healthier. Essential polyunsaturated fatty acids, such as linoleic acid, can, in contrast to saturated fatty acids, lower cholesterol levels. Fats that are liquid at room temperature (oils) are healthier than solid fats (lard).

Which Proteins Are Healthy?

As was finally recognized, eating a steak daily is not necessary to insure sufficient protein intake for a cyclist. Meat should merely garnish a plate filled with high carbohydrate foods, and not the other way around. The goal is to reduce the excessive proportion of meat proteins and replace them with plant proteins derived from rice, pasta, rye, legumes, soy, potatoes, and oats. A higher consumption of plant proteins reduces the fat and increases the fibre, vitamin, and complex carbohydrate content of the diet. Other healthy protein sources are low-fat milk products and fish.

In general, the diet of a serious athlete should be nutritious, but somewhat limited to achieve a slight weight reduction. Cyclists do not have to consciously limit their food intake during high training intensity or heavy periods of competition. A more limited diet is important during the winter months, however, while training less, to avoid gaining too much weight.

5.3 Eating before Competition

Although the following sections use the term "competition" or "race", the same principles can easily be applied to long tours or rallies during which performance is also important. Do not experiment with different foods before or during the competition. New products or foods should always be tested first during training rides, where the consequences of incompatible foods are less severe. Here are some tips:

- eat a high carbohydrate diet (65%) in the days before the competition;
- possibly carbo-load (see below);
- eat an easily digestible, high carbohydrate, low-fat meal the night before the competition;
- make sure you drink enough (no alcohol);
- the last solid carbohydrate-rich meal before the competition should be eaten at least 3-4 hours prior and should be easily digestible;
- do not eat too much, but drink plentifully.

Carbo-loading

Carbo-loading is just the filling up of glycogen stores before a stressful competition to help maintain high riding speeds for a longer period of time. Even cyclists, who, through a high carbohydrate diet, already have an elevated glycogen level compared to other athletes, can further increase their glycogen stores. To accomplish this "loading", do a hard, glycogen-depleting training ride (without food), and for the next two to three days, train at lower intensities while eating a high carbohydrate diet, which helps fill the glycogen stores, in particular in the legs, to a higher level than before (super-compensation). For a weekend race, the hard training ride is best done on a Wednesday or Thursday.

Before experimenting with carbo-loading prior to a big race, try it out while preparing for less important races, since its effect on individuals varies. High glycogen concentrations also cause muscles to store more water, often resulting in legs that initially feel heavy and swollen, but this feeling disappears soon after exercise begins. Carbo-loading is recommended only for especially fit athletes, since unconditioned athletes do not experience the expected glycogen super-compensation and the larger amounts of carbohydrates may even cause a gain in weight.

5.4 Eating during Competition

Only races and training rides lasting over 60 min require nutrient intake, and carbohydrates should definitely be ingested during exercise periods lasting over 90 min to prevent a drop in performance. In cycling, the state of complete depletion of carbohydrate stores is called the **bonk**. The bonk is characterized by symptoms such as food hallucinations, dizziness, concentration difficulties, disorientation, and drastically reduced performance levels – a condition that can cause problems and even be dangerous for a cyclist riding in traffic. To raise the very low blood sugar level typical of the bonk, it is usually sufficient to eat a few cubes of sugar. Although performance does not improve significantly thereafter, you should feel much better and can think clearly again while searching for food or finding your way home. Cyclists usually bonk in the spring during the first longer workouts in the still cold weather. Bonking can be prevented and performance maintained by eating carbohydrate-rich snacks. Especially granola bars, fruit (bananas, apples, pears, dried fruit), rice cakes, sandwiches (low-fat ingredients), crackers, and energy bars are good solid foods to eat while riding.

A basic principle of the athletic diet is that it must taste good; this principle applies especially for food eaten during a ride. Fluid replacement is described in the section "Water". On longer rides, the complex carbohydrates are eaten first, and the simple sugars (glucose) are only eaten near the end of the ride. To boost energy near the end of a contested race, many cyclists drink some coffee with lots of sugar 30 min prior to the finish. However, since a high concentration of caffeine is on the list of prohibited substances, this practice is not recommended. Eating while riding is something that you need to get used to and frequently beginners are unable to do so due to stomach problems. The ability to eat while exercising is an often overlooked but nevertheless important detail, since, especially during longer tours or stage races, huge quantities of food must be consumed on the bike. During the last 15-30 min of a race, eating solid food may cause nausea.

When preparing for a race or long tour, you should tear open the packaging of the energy bars before the start and store them in your jersey to avoid having to ride free-handed during the race. Fruit and sandwiches can be wrapped in aluminum foil.

5.5 Eating after Competition

Food intake after exercise plays a critical role in recovery. The activity of the enzyme glycogen synthase increases due to the depleted glycogen stores. Glycogen synthase promotes glycogen formation and storage in the cells. Since the concentration of this enzyme is highest between two and four hours after the end of the workout and then drops to normal levels again within 24 hours, cyclists must eat enough carbohydrates after a training ride or race to refill their glycogen stores. If this replacement does not take place, the next day's workout will drain the stores, which were not filled up, even further; thus, glycogen stores can be depleted not only through a long, strenuous ride, but also through several days of short workouts if glycogen is not regularly and sufficiently replaced.

During the first 24 hours after a tiring race or workout, there is no difference between the body's use of complex and simple carbohydrates; however, after 24 hours, complex carbohydrates are more effective than simple ones at increasing glycogen synthesis. Moreover, the complex carbohydrates are healthier, since they are found in foods that contain numerous other nutrients and roughage. After exercising, you should eat foods such as pasta, rice, whole grain products, or fruit.

High carbohydrate drinks (fruit juices, not too acidic) can be used to promote recovery during the period (about 2 hrs) immediately after a race that is often characterized by a lack of appetite. Normally, special energy drinks are not necessary, unless you are doing a several-day tour or a stage race, during which the body is stressed to its limits and the recovery times are very brief. The fluid deficit is gradually, not immediately, replenished. Ice-cold drinks should be avoided because of the increased sensitivity of the digestive tract. Fruit juices (potassium rich, increase glycogen storage) diluted with a good mineral water can replace lost fluids, as well as minerals and carbohydrates.

5.6 Weight Problems – Being Overweight

Energy balance is the key to understanding obesity. If a person ingests a certain number of calories beyond that which he can use, part of the excess will be excreted but most will be stored in the body in the form of fat. Over time, this person will gain weight. If, on the other hand, he eats less than he uses, he will lose weight, since energy is derived by the break-down of stored fat. Fat depots are depleted, however, less than one would predict, since the body adjusts to the reduced caloric intake and lowers its basal metabolic rate. These two simplified examples show the two deciding factors in energy balance: a) the caloric intake; b) the caloric expenditure, which depends on activity (more exercise yields higher expenditure).

To effectively lose weight, reducing food ingestion and consequently caloric intake is not sufficient; rather, the body must burn more calories than it receives and this objective can only be accomplished through exercise, especially through classical endurance sports, such as cycling (also running and swimming). If body weight stays constant over a long period of time, caloric intake equals caloric expenditure: the energy balance is in a steady state. Having a constant weight does not mean that you have an ideal weight. Only strenuous exercise with its accompanying high caloric expenditure allows cyclists to eat relatively large amount of food without gaining weight – over the course of a season, many even lose weight.

The consumption of excess and unhealthy foods coupled with a chronic lack of exercise is a major problem in our society. Losing weight should be a gradual process; a radical diet of not eating at all only harms the body. Considering the amount of time it took to gain the bothersome excess weight, a weight reduction of, for example, 10 kg in two weeks, as advertised by countless diet programs, is hardly feasible.

A hypothetical calculation dealing with fat cushions: An approximately 20 kg overweight man could use his 20 kg of fat (180,000 kcal) to ride, at a rate that burns 12 kcal (at 30 km/hr) per minute, for about 250 hours; the total distance covered amounts to about 7,500 km, and this feat can be accomplished using only his excess body fat. This highly simplified, theoretical calculation shows how energy-rich fat tissue is and how long it takes, due to the above mentioned reasons, to lose excess weight. If caloric intake is reduced and exercise is increased, the energy balance tilts into the negative zone and the fat cushions disappear. The reduced caloric intake is facilitated by a decrease in appetite that occurs because of hormonal changes brought about by high amounts of exercise. Just as important as the above mentioned points is changing one's eating habits. Eating well-balanced and nutritious meals is especially important when undertaking a low-calorie diet.

What seems so simple theoretically, may be difficult to accomplish in actuality, since psychological factors play a large role. Laziness and habit, as well as food cravings, often prevent successful weight loss.

How Should You Train to Lose Weight?

Since fat comprises the largest part of the excess weight, training that burns the most fat is most effective. Relatively long distances at low intensity, and not the well-known "training time trials" at 33 km/hr, are appropriate. Riders that do such short training rides, mostly on a fixed route, have a tendency to attempt to break the old record every time; the intensity level is very high, the energy supply comes mainly from glycogen metabolism, and weight loss is practically out of the question. The proper training plan depends on the fitness of the athlete; for an average tour rider, a training time of about two to four hours at an average speed under 28 km/hr (in the summer time) is recommended. These numbers are strongly dependant on the weather, the route, and the training group size. A simple criterion to determine the right training stress is that you should be able to talk without problems during the entire ride. The user of a heart rate monitor should also find it easy to train in his fat burning zone: the optimum training heart rate is normally in the range of 180 minus your age. The 50 year-old would therefore do his endurance training around a heart rate of about 130. However, even here, the individual fitness level must be considered, since for the unconditioned rider, 130 beats per minute could be too high. There are still many cyclists who believe that the faster they ride, the more fat they burn. If you heed the principles "slower is better" and "ride without wheezing", you'll usually train in the right zone.

The Food Diary

Keeping a food diary helps a lot when you are trying to change your diet, since it makes you aware of small and large eating "sins". Record everything that you eat during the course of a day in your diary; if you look back the next day at your previous day's entry, you'll be surprised at how many different things you ate. Simply by keeping track of what you ate over the course of several weeks, you'll become more conscious (as you should be) of what you eat. A simple food diary could look like this:

Date	Time	What/How much?	Place	Comments

5.7 Making Your Weight

Normally the phrase "making your weight" is used only in combat sports, where athletes starve themselves to shed excess water shortly before the competition in order to qualify to compete in a certain weight class. Luckily, this is not necessary in cycling, where the phrase is used to describe an athlete's ideal racing weight. The process of attaining your ideal weight is not a short-term one beginning a few days before the competition, but rather a long-term process of weight reduction stretching over the course of months.

Every racer knows the relationship between fitness and weight: the more fit you are, the lower your weight. The weight described here is race weight, which varies individually (depending on body type) and lies between two and eight kilograms below "winter weight"; in general, your weight during the winter, the time of reduced training, should not deviate too much from your race weight.

Often, a cyclist's performance will jump after a weight reduction. The best example of this phenomenon is Miguel Indurain, who took the advice of his coach and lost a few kilograms and became nearly unbeatable. His already high performance level increased even more due to his weight loss, although certainly other factors played a role, too. This practice really only makes sense for elite athletes, since the well-trained, ideal-weighted recreational athlete is not dependant on his performance ability as much as a bicycle racer and must not put forth the same effort.

A reduction in body weight increases the relative maximum oxygen uptake, which is seen as the determining criterion for performance ability. The relative maximum oxygen uptake is dependant on body weight. When the athlete's weight is reduced, while his performance stays the same or even increases, he is able to ride faster. Even if you think you are very slim, your physique, especially your fat tissue, is still markedly different from that of a cycling professional. Cycling pros are athletes with the lowest percentage of fat tissue; their skin, especially on their legs, is only paper-thin, witness to their excellent, but almost extreme, conditioning. The goal should not be to develop a similar physique but rather to merely lose a few additional kilograms; even a very well-conditioned amateur still has some fat that he can shed to enhance performance. Several pounds can easily be lost through long, fat-burning rides, especially during the preparation period, when coupled with a slightly calorie-reduced diet. The diet should be particularly low in fat, but still provide plenty of protein to prevent the use of muscle proteins in metabolic energy production. The carbohydrate intake must also be sufficient, at least after hard workouts, to prevent glycogen depletion.

5.8 Vegetarianism and Cycling

In the last few years, endurance sports in particular have experienced a vegetarian boom, which has generated much food for thought and has changed the athletic diet in a positive way. However, this food revolution is not yet very wide-spread in cycling. There are three different forms of vegetarianism:

1. the pure vegetarian, who eats only plant products;
2. the lacto-vegetarian, who eats milk products as well;
3. the ovo-lacto-vegetarian, who also includes eggs and egg-containing foods in his diet.

Performance-conscious cyclists should at least avoid the strict vegetarian diet; the ovo-lacto-vegetarian diet, on the other hand, can meet all athletic nutritional demands as long as the food is wholesome and diverse and follows certain ground rules (above all, providing enough high-quality proteins). This diet supplies an especially high percentage of carbohydrates. Meeting iron requirements can, however, become a problem with all three vegetarian diets, since meat has a relatively high iron content and animal-derived iron is also more easily absorbed than plant-derived iron; iron deficiency, in general, is more prevalent among athletes, in particular female athletes, than non-athletes.

5.9 Alcohol

Alcohol is a hotly contested topic in sports nutrition. "A few beers never hurt anyone" or "One beer a day is healthy" are frequently heard statements that may contain some truth, but have only limited application in the areas of recreational and performance cycling.

A few facts: One liter of beer contains, depending on type, 400-450 kcal, and strong beers may contain up to 600 kcal (1 gm alcohol = 7 kcal). This additional caloric supply should not be underestimated and often tips the balance on the scales; the higher caloric intake leads to a positive energy balance (weight gain), and to make matters worse, alcohol consumption also stimulates the appetite. The performance athlete who rides many miles can tolerate the extra calories without problems, but the recreational athlete may wind up with a beer belly. Beer also depletes the tissues of water, since it contains very little salt. The consequence of drinking beer after exercise is a delay in the rehydration process (the replacement of lost water).

Beer consumed the evening before a workout depletes the body's water stores: the athlete becomes water-deprived faster and performance drops. In addition, every form of alcohol consumption as a rule increases magnesium excretion in the urine and therefore worsens glycogen synthesis during the recovery phase. In light of these drawbacks, alcohol consumption should be avoided at least immediately before and after competition. At other times, alcohol should be enjoyed only in moderation.

6 Medical Aspects of Cycling

6.1 Introduction

Cycling belongs to a group of sports that has the lowest injury rates, if traffic accidents involving cyclists are not counted. Although cycling has low injury rates relative to other sports, sometimes injuries and overuse damage sustained during crashes and accidents (although rare) can lead to very serious consequences. In general, cycling has an unequivocal health-promoting effect on the human body. This chapter introduces and explains the different cycling-specific injuries.

Injuries

Often, injuries sustained while cycling do not require medical attention, since they are not serious. Most injuries are caused by defective tires or other equipment defects, as well as by collisions with other cyclists. Most of these injuries are small abrasions, bruises, and minor twists (sprains). An American study (Bohlmann, 1981) showed that 98% of injured cyclists resume riding and training less than a week after their accident. Within a month at the latest, they participated in bicycle races again.

Overuse Injuries/Sports Injuries

Overuse injuries occur when the effects of repetitive stresses on certain anatomical structures exceed tolerance limits. These injuries mostly affect the musculoskeletal system (muscles, tendons, bones, ligaments, and joints).

Overuse injuries to joints and tendons may result from training too much and too intensely at the beginning of the build-up period, because muscle, a very vascular tissue, adapts functionally much faster to training stress than do tissues, such as cartilage, tendons, and ligaments, that have a weak blood supply. Therefore, muscles may quickly become too powerful for the poorly vascularized tissues and may damage them. The lack of blood supply in these tissues is also the reason that injuries to these structures heal slowly; once again, this phenomenon is the result of the extremely slow metabolic rate of tendons, ligaments, and cartilage.

The tolerance limits for mechanical stress are influenced by many factors and are individually extremely variable; a smart, gradual build-up in training stress, but also genetic factors, appear to play a role. Unfortunately, it seems as if cyclists can tolerate overuse injuries and the associated pain for much longer than other comparatively minor injuries. Another American study (Vetter, 1985) showed that cyclists wait an average of 4.8 months from the appearance of the first overuse injury symptoms until they seek a medical specialist's help. This inattention to pain probably leads to a worsening of the injury, which then becomes more difficult and time-consuming to heal, the longer it persists. Overuse injuries are often caused by improper bicycle position or defective pedals or cranks (i.e. unnoticed damage to pedals and cranks during a crash).

The next sections will describe sport injuries and the damage that these cause to the individual structures. The knee joint, a cyclist's most important joint, will be used to illustrate how complex and difficult the prognosis for an overuse injury can be.

6.2 Orthopedic Problems

Most of the medical problems in cycling are in the area of orthopedic medicine: they affect the structures of the musculoskeletal system. Because the seated position transfers the burden of the body weight to the bicycle, the stresses on the musculoskeletal system are relatively low and constant. There are countless examples of athletes, even elite ones, who had to switch sports due to joint problems and chose cycling as a joint-sparing sport. Joint problems in cyclists usually originate from injuries and overuse damage sustained outside of cycling. Next, injuries and overuse damage to the leg will be described.

Hip
Hip joint problems are extremely rare in cycling, since the hip joint is only very minimally stressed during cycling, in contrast to running or standing. Pain that emanates from the hip usually originates from a slipped intervertebral disk or a pinched nerve. When hip pain occurs, it is often the consequence of an incorrect sitting or pedal position.

Knee
The knee joints are undoubtedly the structures that cause the most problems for cyclists, since they must tolerate large amounts of push and pull stress and are

exposed to the cold riding wind. Even so, cyclists have very few knee problems when compared to "running" athletes, and degenerative diseases (arthritis) are much less commonly caused by cycling than by running. The knee joints must not cushion road shock, as in running, and are also not subjected to twisting or bruising as in many other sports.

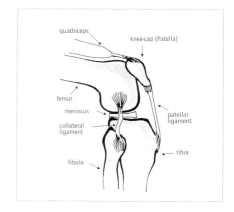

In cycling, the knee is most vulnerable during falls directly onto this body part. Ligament

Figure 6.1: The anatomy of the knee joint

injuries, caused by the rotation of the lower leg in relation to the thigh, are only sustained during crashes in which the foot is fixed in the pedal. Falling onto the knee can cause deep cuts and bruises over the kneecap that may injure a patellar bursa. This injury often is a chronic situation and should be treated by a doctor. Leg fractures occur rarely during crashes, which have declined in the last years thanks in part to the clipless pedal.

Now a little about the specific **anatomy of the knee joint**: The knee joint, the largest joint in the body, is formed by three bones (femur, tibia, and kneecap) and is not a simple hinge joint, like an automobile door, but rather a modified hinge joint: in addition to extension and flexion, it also allows the lower leg to rotate with respect to the thigh when the knee is flexed. The end of the femur, the head of the tibia, and the back side of the kneecap form the knee's joint surface, which is covered with a thick sheet of bluish-white shimmering cartilage. Since the cartilage surfaces do not fit together precisely, mother nature thought of something special to match up the joint surfaces with each other: the well-known menisci. A meniscus is a wedge-like, half-moon-shaped piece of cartilage that fits the two convex joint surfaces of the femur and tibia together and acts as a cushion between these two bones. The menisci also distribute the pressure to a larger cartilage surface (thereby reducing wear) and stabilize the joint (2 menisci per knee). Together with the cruciate ligaments (anterior and posterior) found in the knee and the two collateral ligaments, these structures help form a stabile articulation. The muscles that attach to the knee joint contribute to a further stabilization; the stronger the upper and lower leg muscles are, the better they protect the knee and foot joint from injuries.

The knee joint is actually composed of two joints: in addition to the already discussed joint between femur and tibia, the articulation between the kneecap and femur forms a second joint, which is also the one that occasionally causes cyclists problems. The kneecap – patella in latin – is imbedded in the tendon of the four-headed quadriceps femoris muscle and moves in a groove on the femur; both joint surfaces are normally covered with sufficient cartilage. The patella serves as a "pulley" for the quadriceps tendon and acts like a lever to increase this muscle's power.

When the extensor muscles are used to stretch out the leg, – for example, while pedaling – the kneecap glides in the groove on the femur. If the pressure on the cartilage is too high and unevenly distributed over a long period of time, the cartilage may change its structure and a type of inflammation occurs, causing pain; the cartilage itself, however, does not perceive pain.

The flexor muscles attach to the tibia and fibula on the back side of the knee joint – near the hollow of the knee. Even they occasionally cause cyclists pain at their tendons' sites of attachment to bone. Bursae generally lie below tendons, muscles, and sometimes even skin overlying bony prominences to protect the sensitive structure of these tissues. The knee contains numerous bursae, which are cold-sensitive and, therefore, can easily become inflamed. The knee joint is enclosed by a two-layered capsule: an outer, tough capsule that provides additional protection, as well as an inner capsule that supplies the joint with "synovial fluid" (synovia), the joint lubricant. The synovial fluid contains nutrients that reach the joint cartilage by diffusion (spontaneous distribution). The knee's long lifetime, unmatched by synthetic joints, is a biological miracle. Furthermore, a biological joint can regenerate to a certain extent following damage or injury, and this repair is not yet possible with synthetic joints or joint surfaces.

When the Knee Hurts!

Describing the clinical picture is impossible without using medical terms, but these will be clearly defined and explained. What may appear obvious and clear in the following explanation, is in reality much more complicated; it is often very difficult to make a precise diagnosis and administer the proper therapy due to the multitude of possible factors.

1. One of the most common clinical presentations of cyclists' knees is **chondromalacia patellae**, a cartilage degeneration on the back side of the kneecap. *"Chondro-"* means cartilage and *"-malacia"* is the degenerative softening of a tissue; as already mentioned, *"patella"* is the kneecap. This cartilage softening results from microstructural changes coupled with a nutrient undersupply of the cartilage. In this "starving state", the cartilage is unprotected as it is exposed to mechanical friction. The consequences are pain under the kneecap during exercise and in serious cases, pain lingering after exercise or even at rest. An audible grinding is also frequently a sign of chondromalacia. *Chondromalacia patellae* results from a combination of many factors, a number of which can be avoided, as will be discussed. Above all, too much stress on the knees, improper bicycle fit, and cold all promote the formation of *chondromalacia.*

Once this condition has developed, the three factors mentioned must be eliminated to provide a chance for successful medical therapy. A slightly higher saddle position can provide immediate relief by reducing the pressure of the kneecap rubbing against the femur and thereby allow the cartilage to repair itself. Another cause for *chondromalacia patellae* is a difference in strength (muscular imbalance) between two heads of the quadriceps (*musculus vastus lateralis and musculus vastus medialis*). Since cycling does not develop the m. vastus medialis as much as the m. vastus lateralis, the outer head pulls the kneecap to the outside, generating a significant stress on the cartilage under the kneecap. Inflammation and degenerative conditions can result from this stress. Treatment consists of physical therapy to strengthen the m. vastus medialis and restore the balance of strength between the two muscles.

2. **Tendonitis** is at least as common as *chondromalacia patellae. "Tendon-"*, the first part of the word, combined with *"-itis"*, an inflammatory process, describes this disease that is a tendon inflammation at the attachment sites to bones and the tendon/muscle transition zone. Predisposed to such *tendonitis* is a) the patellar ligament at its attachment site to the tibia and where it "originates" below the kneecap; b) the quadriceps tendon; c) the head of the fibula as well as d) the

tendons of those flexors attaching to the inside of the knee hollow. If the latter are affected, a slightly lowered saddle position can often provide relief, since it reduces the tension on the muscles and tendons. The top border of the kneecap, where the quadriceps attaches, also frequently exhibits *tendonitis*. Tendonitis manifests itself as pain at the affected site during both rest and exercise. *Tendonitis* is also caused by cold and too much stress, as well as incorrect cleat alignment and an occasional intolerance to "fixed" clipless pedal systems. Stretching helps keep muscles and tendons flexible and pliant. More importantly, it prevents an irritation of the tendons and muscles around the knee from establishing itself.

All clinical pictures may also be caused by factors unrelated to cycling. A leg-length discrepancy (should be compensated for by shoe adjustments) or a tilted pelvis, bow-legs or knock-knees, flat feet, and previously damaged knee or foot joints can all cause the same sports injuries and damages that may result from the negligence factors already discussed. If pain develops – pain is the body's first warning signal – first investigate the contributing factors, but if "self treatment" is not effective, consult an experienced sports medicine doctor.

3. A third knee problem, caused mainly by cold weather, is **bursitis**, a bursal inflammation that can become extremely painful if left untreated. The bursa in front of the kneecap, normally not palpable, is most frequently affected; it swells up and makes every pedal revolution painful.

This next section lists the principal mistakes responsible for musculoskeletal, in particular knee, pain that you should review before consulting a physician.

1. Pedal Easy Gears
Although cycling is gentle on the knees, famous cycling stars such as Bernard Hinault and Stephen Roche had to cut short their careers because of extreme knee pain. How does this happen, when cycling is supposed to be so kind to joints? The reason for these professionals' knee problems is probably the many years of riding in excessively large gears (53 x 12 or greater) and under too much stress. Therefore, easy to medium gears should be used if possible, especially during the preparation period. The consequences of misusing "big" gears are unavoidable pain around tendon and muscle insertions, and if these gears are used over many years, irreparable joint damage can develop – can develop, but must not, since many amateurs and pros can handle these stresses. Individuals whose bodies are sensitive to being over-stressed should, however, exercise caution.

2. Staying Warm Is Important

The second mistake that hobby cyclists, but also experienced cyclists, frequently commit is not protecting their muscles and joints enough from the cold, for example, by riding in shorts in cold weather. Aside from the higher risk of straining a muscle that has cooled down or catching a cold, this practice also harms knee joints tremendously. The knee cools down particularly fast, since it is only sparsely covered by subcutaneous fat and the bones, tendons, ligaments, and muscles lie directly underneath the skin. These structures often react to cold during the days following with inflammations that are often long-lasting, especially since the bursae can be affected. The cartilage cools down too, its nutrient supply diminishes even further, and the knee's whole metabolism slows down; through this process, the cartilage loses its elasticity. Frequently-repeated cold-shocks, especially if the training intensity is high as well, can cause microscopically small transformations in the cartilage, resulting in a loss of surface smoothness. A joint with cartilage defects does not function "frictionless" anymore and degeneration is inevitable.

Therefore, especially the legs of a cyclist must be kept warm, and shorts should only be worn when the temperature is at least 18-20'C. During races, most riders foolishly wear shorts, regardless of the weather. In recent years, there has been a change in this type of thinking, since now more and more cyclists use knee warmers and two-thirds length tights during cold, wet weather to keep their most important joint warm. Those incorrigible riders who nevertheless wish to race with naked knees can protect their joints at least a little from the cold with a thick coat of oil (see "Massage"). The widely recommended warming creams are not nearly as effective as knee warmers and can even be detrimental, since they only increase blood flow to the skin. On long daytours, wear knee warmers on chilly mornings; later on, you can easily remove them, even while riding. By following these guidelines, even cyclists with cold-sensitive knees should be able to pursue their sport during the winter.

3. Saddle Height

Saddle height is another factor that must be checked, since a position that is too low or too high affects the amount of work done while pedaling. The knee is bent more when the saddle height is too low, and the pressure on the joint structures, especially on the kneecap, is therefore significantly higher than it would be if correctly adjusted. A saddle that is too high, where the legs are completely stretched out at the bottom of the pedal stroke, can cause problems, especially for the knee flexors. However, a slightly higher saddle position is recommended for riders with patella problems to remove pressure from the sensitive structures.

4. Pedal System

Finally, the pedal system should be evaluated, since an incorrectly adjusted cleat can cause much damage to joints and muscles in the legs. Once you picture how often a leg must flex and extend on only a 60 km ride (about 10,000 times), the importance of correctly adjusted cleats becomes obvious. The feet normally pedal parallel to the cranks; however, the joints should never feel uncomfortable while riding. Those unable to tolerate the fixed clipless pedal system, which does not allow the foot any side-to-side motion, should try the floating system, for example the one made by TIME. This system does not suppress the natural rotation of the lower leg, and the foot can rotate freely by several degrees before clipping out of the pedal.

There is one solution to alleviate pain generated by the inward rotation of the lower leg (during leg extension), which is caused by a dropping of the arch of the foot during larger stress loads: by supporting the arch with a custom-made orthopedic insole, it no longer drops during leg extension and, therefore, does not lead to the painful rotation described.

5. Bent Equipment

After a bicycle wreck, it is not uncommon for cranks and pedals to be bent; the feet are thrown out of their ideal plane of motion and are thereby exposed to stresses that they cannot withstand over long periods of time. However, the body can tolerate this maladjustment for a short period of time. The maladjustment is transferred from foot joint to knee and hip and can ultimately even be the cause of back pain.

Foot

In the foot, inflammations of the achilles tendon are most common. The achilles tendon attaches the calf muscles to the heel; its exposed location on the heel subjects it to cold weather. Incorrect saddle height, cold weather (no booties), or too much stress (gears that are too large) often lead to an irritation, from which an inflammation can develop. All these factors must considered when a **tendonitis** of the achilles heel occurs. **Insertion tendonitis** is the inflammation of the attachment sites of the tendon to muscle or bone.

Therapy: Changing the above mentioned contributing factors, as well as physical therapy.

The tendon of the muscle in front of the shin can cause cyclists pain, especially after cold, rainy races. With respect to therapy, the same as said above applies.

Burning soles of the feet can have many causes: straps or shoe laces that are closed too tightly limit blood circulation in the foot and very hard insoles can also promote this burning sensation; a thin, soft insole can bring relief. The cycling shoe's sole should also be anatomically designed, since a flat sole promotes dropping of the arch of the foot, which can lead to pain in the sole of the foot (plantar pain) and also in the knee.

Back

The back muscles, although not directly involved in pedaling, allow the cyclist to generate a powerful pedal stroke. These muscles stabilize the body and improve the strength transfer from the legs to the pedals. The term *back pain* is a general term for a whole series of clinical pictures and symptoms; thus, muscles, ligaments, and joints, as well as joint capsules and tendons can be affected and cause pain. About 55% of all bicycle racers complain of back pain or claim to have suffered from it at some time during their career. This percentage equals that of the non-bicycle-riding populace.

Local pain, which does not radiate to other areas, is differentiated from the so-called **pseudo-radiating pain**. The latter radiates outward, for example, to the leg or to the head; perception distortions can occur in the worst cases. Slipped disks happen only rarely during cycling, but their formation can be promoted by riding.

Especially when pushing big gears (i.e. 52 x 13), the pressure on the lower back vertebrae, as well as on joints and other structures of the lower back, is very high – so high that degenerative changes (attrition) can result if there is enough of a predisposition. Especially for beginners, there may be other causes of back pain. A poor bike fit, for example, can cause pain within a very short time span; once it is adjusted properly, the pain usually subsides quickly. Racers as well as beginners often complain of back pain at the beginning of a season; this results from poor muscle flexibility and conditioning. During the winter, but also in the summer, letting the skin, and therefore also the muscles, become cold can be another cause of pain that is, however, avoidable with the appropriate clothing.

An inequality between stomach and back musculature (muscular imbalance) changes the position of the spine and this frequently creates problems; as a rule, cyclists only have weakly-developed stomach muscles. Even an unequal distribution of strength between left and right leg can cause pain. The problem with back pain is that it can perpetuate a vicious circle in which one muscle strain leads to another. To put an end to this vicious circle, you must recognize and eliminate primary causes, not just treat the symptoms. In addition, countless other causes of back pain that did not originate from cycling must be considered.

Therapy

For every case of back pain, back gymnastics, exercises for strengthening the back musculature in general (see chapter 3.8 and 3.9 and general athletic conditioning), and physical and massage therapy can all help. A stretching program, as introduced in chapter 3.9, improves symptoms within a few days. However, the following are also important: wearing weather-appropriate clothing, riding in smaller gears, and checking the saddle position, since large differences in saddle and stem height promote back pain. Athletes who have serious lower back problems should try to adjust their saddles and handlebars to the same height to remove the pressure on their backs; this position is easily accomplished by a mountain bike stem with a slight rise or through spacers in a threadless headset. Tires with more shock-absorbing abilities (at least 22 mm thickness, do not pump up too much) should be used. Athletes who have already sustained a serious back injury (i.e. slipped disk) should be extremely cautious and should consult a sports medicine doctor about their exercise program.

Landing on your back during crashes can bruise ribs and muscles, cause skin abrasions, especially on the spinous processes of the vertebral column, and may even result in slipped disks, whose treatment should be handled by a physician or chiropractor.

Neck

Neck pain is fairly common among cyclists. The position on the road bike increases the natural hyperextension (lordosis) of the cervical vertebral column, especially when riding in the drops. If the stem is too long or the saddle/stem height difference too large, the neck must be extended even further to look at the road ahead. This posture frequently results in pain, generally of muscular origin, in the neck and upper back. Especially at the start of the training year and in beginners, the neck muscles (trapezius, small neck muscles) cramp up due to their poor conditioning and cause pain, which, however, subsides after several weeks of training. The type of work performed by the muscles supporting the 7 kg average-weight head is primarily static (isometric), which means that they do not cause movement, but rather provide support. Through the isometric contraction, the blood vessels in the muscle tissue are compressed, decreasing the blood supply. The consequence is a cramp-like, painful condition. In addition, muscles have a hard time getting rid of metabolic wastes, causing even more pain.

Relief can only be provided through increasing blood circulation by moving the affected parts, for example with regular stretching and position changes. The same holds true for the back. In addition to specific back and neck exercises, there are also other measures that can prevent or alleviate neck pain: a light helmet (250 gm) puts less strain on the neck musculature than an old, heavy one does. Undershirts with turtle-necks and jerseys with high collars protect the neck from the cold riding wind. While riding, the elbows should always be slightly bent, and never locked, to cushion bumps in the road like shock-absorbers.

Head

Headaches can be caused by a constantly cold head, the result of fast descents or riding during the winter. To prevent such a cold draft, cyclists wear caps, which also protect them from catching a cold and getting sunburned. Not wearing high-quality sunglasses with UV protection when riding in sunny, bright weather (in the mountains or along the coast) may lead to head and neck pain originating in face muscles cramped from squinting.

Characteristik of professional cyclists: darkly tanned arms and legs and pale and, therefore, very sun-sensitive upper body

Happiness and satisfaction after victory: the training efforts have paid off.

The head and neck are especially vulnerable during falls and collisions. Concussions of all severities are often a consequence of a fall on the head. In the worst cases, a fall may cause a fracture of the base of the skull, which is one of the most serious injuries that a cyclist can sustain.

However, according to an American study, 80% of fractures of the base of the skull could have been avoided if riders had been wearing a hard-shell helmet. A fall on the head can also cause a neck fracture, an injury whose risk is increased by wearing styrofoam helmets without shells. This type of helmet acts like a rubber eraser and slows the head down as it slides across the pavement. Since the rest of the body does not experience this braking to the same extent, a broken neck may result.

Fortunately, neck and skull fractures are absolute exceptions to the rule. More frequently, strained necks, broken noses, strained and broken jaws, or skin abrasions occur. Rarely, degenerative changes to the joints of the neck may occur.

Shoulder/Arm

A fractured collar bone is the most common injury to the shoulder area. The collar bone connects the shoulder joint (upper arm, scapula, collar bone) to the sternum and by way of the ribs to the vertebral column. Therefore, it is practically the only attachment of the arm to the trunk. During a crash on the shoulder, hand, or elbow, the collar bone is exposed to enormous pressure, which it often cannot withstand, so it breaks. The tough ligaments attached to the collar bone can also tear. Since the healing process often takes about 5 weeks, professional riders often chose to have surgery to speed up this process, so they miss as few important races as possible. Aside from possible crashes and the consequences thereof, the shoulder area creates relatively few problems for cyclists. Shoulder strains can occur, however, and may be caused by cramped neck muscles.

Once again, do special gymnastics and check to make sure the saddle position is correct. Again: the whole arm should be bent slightly at the elbow to act like a shock absorber.

Hands

Holding onto the handlebars while riding, especially when gripping the bars too tightly, heavily uses the forearm muscles, and the tension in the tendons of the forearm muscles may lead to "tennis elbow" in both arms.

Usually, the only effective treatment plan is not riding, resting the arms, and undergoing physical therapy. The grip on the handlebars should be loosened up once in a while, the hand position should be varied, and the hands should occasionally be removed from the handlebars and moved around. This advice will also help prevent nerve compression symptoms in the hand that can range in severity from numb fingers to paralysis. These symptoms are the result of the compression of the nerve that runs through the carpal tunnel (tunnel in the wrist).

The wrists and the arm are extremely vulnerable body parts, since a falling rider almost always reflexively attempts to break his fall with outstretched hands. Despite gloves, many of these falls result in injuries to the palms of the hands. More serious than such skin abrasions are wrist, forearm, and upper arm fractures that may result from falling onto the upper extremity.

6.3 Injuries and Skin Abrasions

Skin Abrasions Due to Crashes

Injuries to the skin following crashes are usually in the form of skin abrasions. Unfortunately, skin abrasions are almost part of being a bike racer. They mostly occur on the hip (thigh), shoulder, knee (lower leg), or elbow. These wounds often affect areas on which you sleep or that constantly have to be flexed and extended. If large areas are affected, it may be wise to build a device (i.e. a type of cage for the leg) that will keep the blanket away from the wounded area while you sleep. All cyclists should be immunized against tetanus, since they frequently come into contact with tetanus-causing agents during falls (even when the skin abrasions are minor). Despite many rumors, a tetanus injection does not reduce performance. Having shaved legs is just as self-evident, because wounds containing hairs heal slower and are more painful, since the hairs act like tactile hairs; in addition, wounds can be cared for more easily when legs are shaved. The dirt that inevitably gets into a wound during a fall must be removed when cleaning the wound. If the wounds are not too deep, they can be cleaned with antibacterial soap and a clean brush; if they are deeper, a physician should treat them.

It is always wise to apply a thin layer of a wound disinfecting agent to a clean wound. Smaller wounds do not have to be bandaged, while larger wounds should be treated further. An antibacterial ointment, such as Neosporin, is applied to the clean surface, which is then covered with a non-stick bandage. A little bit of sterile gauze is applied on top and the whole bandage is held in place with a "fish-net" sleeve.

However, if a hard scab has already formed over the wound, it is best left uncovered. Deep cuts must be treated by a doctor.

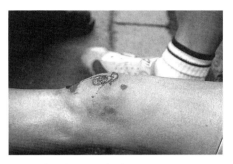

Deep abrasion on the kneecap

Groin Area

In this area, pain stems from the chaffing of the skin as well as from the pressure to which the skin and the underlying structures are exposed. However, other reasons for painful saddle sores are a poor-quality, hard chamois, a saddle that is not anatomically shaped, bad road conditions, and a lack of hygiene. Boils and even carbuncles (clusters of boils) may occur easily, since sweat and skin-surface bacteria get massaged into the skin that has become sensitive from the rubbing, and the roots of delicate hairs may become inflamed (hair follicle inflammation).

This illustrates the importance of groin area hygiene, which includes a clean and daily fresh chamois and, if necessary, the use of a special chamois cream before riding. Once an inflammation has developed in this area, take a bath with a soothing bath oil and then apply a good quality commercially available anti-inflammatory, or better yet, antibacterial agent. Any number of anti-bacterial ointments are excellent for wound healing and the formation of new skin following skin abrasions. Boils can be effectively treated with numerous commercially available salves. Timely treatment, as discussed, is very important for the prevention of abscesses and other inflammations.

Sunburn

A cyclist's skin is exposed to the sun's strong rays especially during the summer months. Often, people forget that riding for several hours in shorts and a short-sleeve jersey can burn your skin just as badly as sunbathing at the beach.

Especially in the mountains, the UV radiation is significantly higher than in the plains (per 1,000 m, 20-100% more UV rays), which can lead to serious burns. Aside from sunburn, UV radiation can also have the following negative effects on the skin:
1. skin aging,
2. carcinoma (skin cancer),
3. allergic and toxic reactions (sun allergies).

For these reasons, you should apply sun screen before riding in the summer, especially since the UV radiation has increased over the last few years because of the thinning of the ozone layer. If a sunburn has already occurred, this skin area should be protected even more, possibly even by covering it up with clothing. In particular during the spring training camps (Feb/Mar) in the south, riders' skin is especially sensitive to the sun and may even respond to the unaccustomed exposure with a sun allergy. Such sensitive riders can take calcium compounds as a prophylactic measure to prevent a possible allergy during training camp (physician's approval needed).

Cyclists must be especially careful when exposing their upper bodies to the sun in the summer: the skin on their arms and legs is already used to the sun and tanned, while the normally clothing-covered skin on their upper bodies can burn after only a brief period of sunbathing; bad sunburns can lead to a feeling of sickness and even fever, and these symptoms can lead to a drop in performance.

6.4 Various Medical Topics

Prostate Problems
Probably every male cyclist is familiar with the genital problems that may occur after long rides. The high pressure in combination with numerous bumps and jolts (poor road surface) can cause a swelling of the prostate, a pressure lesion of the urethra, and/or a pinched nerve that can lead to numbness in the penis, pain while urinating (urethra), and possibly even blood in the urine or, in rare cases, even temporary impotence.

A few days of mandatory rest will usually allow even the most stubborn symptoms of this cycling-typical clinical picture to disappear quickly. A special, anatomically-shaped, soft saddle that can perhaps even be tilted slightly nose-down (if necessary, a women's saddle may even be used); wide, well-cushioning tires; and a slightly higher handlebar position can bring relief. In addition, getting out of the saddle regularly during the ride to take the pressure off the groin area and the sensitive tissues beneath it (prostate, urethra, nerves, spermatic duct) is effective. If there is no improvement, visit a physician to rule out prostate cancer or other diseases. Under unfortunate conditions, cycling may lead to a temporary impotence. Regular and not too excessive cycling should, however, have a positive effect on sexual performance. Nevertheless, it is also certain that strenuous endurance exercise causes a clear drop in testosterone (male sex hormone) levels, which could be another possible cause of sexual problems.

Performance and Menstruation

For some women, performance varies over the course of the menstrual cycle. A drop in performance during menstruation is especially noticeable in endurance sports. Taking birth control pills often helps stabilize performance, although there may be side-effects (i.e. weight gain, loss of speed, psychological complications). Regular endurance exercise over the course of years can lead to missed periods and irregular bleeding. Top female cyclists may have these irregular periods for many years. An exercise-induced shift in hormones, which is however reversible, is held responsible for these symptoms. With normal menstrual cycles, the monthly blood loss and the high physical stress often causes iron deficiency, which can be countered through a sensible diet and, if necessary, iron supplements.

Medications that Affect Performance

There are a whole series of medications that can negatively influence the performance ability of a cyclist. When taking medication, you should always consult your physician about the advisability of exercising while suffering from your particular illness and taking the prescribed medication. In many cases, you should not ride until your health has been restored. Here are some medications that can decrease performance: sleeping pills, high blood pressure medication, medication for colds, allergy drugs, and muscle relaxants.

Colds and Cycling

Cyclists are at a higher risk of catching colds because of their exposure to wind and bad weather. Especially during the preparation period or at the beginning of the competition period in April, when the weather is often bad, athletes who wish to protect themselves from colds and infections must take great precautions.

Very high training and race stresses can attack the immune system and increase susceptibility to infection. Training with a bad cold or even a fever is forbidden, since organs could be damaged (myocarditis). Once you are well again, you should begin training slowly, since increasing training stress too quickly often leads to an overtrained state. After having a bad cold for one week, it takes at least two to three weeks to reach the same level of fitness as before the illness. A cold that is ignored may develop into a chronic sinusitis affecting the maxillary or even frontal sinuses that must be drained before training can resume, since such an accumulation of pus carries a risk of heart damage. To guard against respiratory infections, wear sensible, weather-appropriate cycling clothing, which should be removed immediately after riding. A warm winter cap can protect the head from cooling down too much after a race. A vitamin- and mineral-rich wholesome diet contributes to a strong immune system as much as regular visits to the sauna. During the training camp, when the immune system is usually somewhat low, avoid sharing water bottles to prevent the spread of germs through body fluid contact. It has happened that an illness (stomach flu or cold) has put a whole training group out of commission.

Allergies (hay fever)

For many cyclists, the spring is one long torture, since they suffer from allergies. At this time of year, the air is particularly thick with different pollens, making training, not to mention racing, impossible for some allergic cyclists. A prominent example is Tony Rominger, who had to struggle with allergies. When serious allergies are present, a desensitization treatment is recommended, during which "pollen injections" are given to attempt to desensitize the patient to these allergens. In general, there is a noticeable improvement in allergy symptoms after one year of treatment. In addition to desensitization, medications, so-called antihistamines, may also be taken, but these are often very potent and stress the body so much that performance drops noticeably. Some cyclists have had their careers ended by allergies that developed suddenly from one year to the next.

6.5 Overtraining

Overtraining is an over-burdening of the body that manifests itself as chronic fatigue symptoms. In contrast to the acute fatigue following a workout, this condition is protracted and can be characterized by a number of symptoms.

The exact mechanism by which it occurs, especially in cycling, is not precisely known. It is certain, though, that recovery in an overtrained state no longer functions normally but is disturbed. There are two forms of overtraining, both of with have relatively complicated names: **parasympathetic overtraining**, which frequently occurs in endurance sports, especially in cycling, and **sympathetic overtraining**. These names originate from the two divisions of the autonomic nervous system (see 2.1). From the standpoint of excitability, parasympathetic overtraining exhibits more of an inhibited excitability, while sympathetic overtraining is defined as an over-excitable state. The parasympathetic overtraining that is so common in cycling is hard to diagnose, since it develops insidiously and manifests primarily symptoms that are also present with normal exhaustion. It requires much experience to recognize the smooth transitions and make a precise diagnosis. A blood test on the athlete can confirm a suspicion of overtraining if the results show elevated urea and creatine kinase (an enzyme) concentrations at rest and lactic acid concentrations that only reach low values during exercise, a finding that could be falsely interpreted as an improved fitness level. Table 6.1 lists the symptoms of the two states of overtraining.

parasympathetic overtraining	sympathetic overtraining
• easily fatigued	• easily fatigued
• diminished performance ability	• diminished performance ability
• inhibition	• excitement
• lower resting pulse	• higher resting pulse
• reduced maximum heart rate	• prolonged heart rate recovery time following stress
• normal or increased sleep require ment	• sleep disturbances
• bad mood, depression	• restlessness, irritability
• normal appetite	• loss of appetite
• constant body weight	• weight loss
• drop in performance causes increased training	• no training desire
• higher susceptibility to infection	• higher susceptibility to infection
• glycogen depletion	• heart palpitations

Table 6.1: Overtraining

Overtraining is in most cases a consequence of excessively high training or competition stress or a completely wrong training program. Parasympathetic overtraining is more often the result of excessively high training intensity rather than high mileage.

The first priority is to reduce intensity. Even psychological stress can lead to a state of overtraining, especially when the psychological stress is related to cycling, and it becomes impossible to find a release.

Treating Overtraining

The treatment for overtraining depends on its severity, since a few days without training are often sufficient to allow the body to recover from mild cases with only weakly expressed symptoms. More serious cases may require a modified training schedule for several weeks or even months following a training break of at least one week. After the rest break, you should only train with reduced intensity and lowered mileage; participating in races is naturally prohibited and training should be increased only slowly following a steady improvement. A mental break from cycling is also necessary. The measures that promote recovery, such as sauna, massage, stretching, and also mental recovery and relaxation, are critically important in treating a state of overtraining. Since this state is frequently accompanied by a glycogen depletion of the muscles, a well-balance, carbohydrate-rich diet is important as well. In any case, consulting a sports medicine doctor specializing in endurance sports may be helpful.

6.6 Doping

Doping is the attempt to improve performance by using substances and methods that are prohibited. The practice of attempting to raise performance with mysterious substances is almost as ancient as mankind itself. Even Greek and Roman athletes used "magical drinks" and precious substances that were supposed to endow them with greater strength. In another example, the Incas in South America were able to run about 600 km in three days under the influence of cocaine; this unbelievable accomplishment cannot be attributed solely to the use of cocaine, but also stemmed from pure religious fanaticism. Back then, as today, superstitious beliefs in certain substances played a large role, since most substances do not have any physical benefits and may even harm the athlete. If a benefit is observed, it is commonly a placebo effect.

From its first beginnings, cycling proved to be a classical "doping discipline", and so it is no wonder that for a long time, and to some extent even today, many bicycle racers regarded doping as the norm. Fortunately, doping is seen as immoral today and is widely despised. Even so, cycling is one of the sports in which the most doping violations are discovered, although these figures only represent the tip of the iceberg, since the actual numbers are no doubt significantly higher. The first recorded doping death occurred in the year 1886 during long Bordeaux-Paris road race.

The most prominent doping victim was surely the Englishman Tom Simpson, who collapsed in the Tour de France on July 13, 1967, shortly before reaching the top of the famous climb to Mont Ventoux and died shortly thereafter. Especially those sports that showed an early tendency to professionalize (cycling, boxing) and in which relatively large sums of money are at stake were, and unfortunately still are, especially plagued by the doping phenomenon.

What Leads to Doping?

Doping substance propaganda is passed along by word of mouth, since there are few studies about the effects of substances on the doping list. Often, riders are encouraged by coaches or assistants to take a certain substance that will "definitely improve performance". The problem herein is that almost no one, whether rider or coach, has the necessary knowledge to predict the substance's immediate effect, let alone possible side-effects or later consequences. Often, the substance does not even lead to the intended performance enhancement. Such short-sighted attitudes that focus only on immediate success and completely ignore the future (later consequences) are unfortunately difficult to eradicate.

Doping Controls

In cycling, only large road races and stage races have doping controls; small circuit races, which frequently sport high prize lists, are lost in a gray zone in which doping can be done with little risk of discovery. The problem with doping control is that testing is time-consuming and expensive; monitoring all athletes at every point in time is impossible and sporadic testing is performed only at top competitive levels. Infrequently, recreational and hobby cyclists may also take substances to enhance their performance.

The following section briefly addresses the different doping substance classes without going into detail about specific drugs to avoid fostering possible imitation.

Substance Abuse Classes

Most substances abused in cycling are supposed to prolong performance time and thereby reduce the associated pain. Substances used to pep up athletes are called **stimulants**; cyclists most often abuse amphetamines and may even become addicted to them. Aside from amphetamines, caffeine is also a commonly-used stimulant, which is relatively harmless in low amounts, but may have side-effects at higher doses.

Pain is masked with **narcotics**, of which there are many different types on the market that are all readily accessible and are, therefore, quite frequently used. Aside from their not entirely insignificant side-effects, the danger of taking stimulants and narcotics is that they enhance performance by enabling the athlete to tap into reserves that are normally unavailable; this may over-stress the body and place him in danger by causing significantly diminished alertness, coordination, and reflexes.

The third class of substances abused by cyclists are **anabolic steroids**, or simply steroids. These drugs are similar to the male sex hormone testosterone. The anabolic steroids are supposed to improve an athlete's strength by promoting muscle hypertrophy. The list of side-effects for these drugs ranges from a greater injury risk, to kidney and liver damage and higher blood lipid levels, all the way to infertility.

Another forbidden method to raise performance is **blood doping**.

Some illnesses are treated with medications (i.e. cough syrup) that contain ingredients on the doping control list. To be fair and protect your own health, you should refrain from participating in races under such circumstances. Often, how-ever, an illness is used as an excuse to take prohibited substances.

What Can You Do to Prevent Doping in Cycling?

Education is the most effective tool for decreasing the incidence of doping, especially in a sport such as cycling that has traditionally been affected by doping. Only after athletes, coaches, and assistants are aware of the health risks and moral obligations of doping, can this problem be solved from the inside. If you know of riders who occasionally take drugs, you should talk to them about it and, if necessary, even threaten to report them. Nevertheless, there will probably always be athletes in every sport who attempt to gain an edge over their opponents by using prohibited substances.

6.7 Massage

The massage is an ancient technique for soothing stiff and painful muscles; it is known as the oldest of the healing professions. Since the beginning of cycling, the masseur has been an irreplaceable assistant, particularly in the professional and elite amateur ranks, since he not only provides massage therapy but often also takes care of the riders in many other ways. Moreover, he functions as a psychologist, who listens to athletes and directs their attention away from problems. Based on what was just said, massage clearly has, aside from its physiological-mechanical value, an extremely important psychologically relaxing effect on the athlete. A good masseur can determine an athlete's fitness from the feel of his legs, since skin thickness, amount of connective tissue, and suppleness of the muscles are characteristic for certain fitness levels and types of riders.

In cycling, there are three different types of massage classified according to when and how they are applied:

Massage is one of the daily routines of the 6-day professional (Etienne de Wilde).

1. The post-training massage, which takes place after a strenuous workout, usually during the week.
2. The pre-race massage, part of the warm-up program before a race that serves to loosen up and increase blood flow to the muscles.
3. The recovery massage, following a race for rapid recovery and relaxation.

Before more is said about massages and particularly self-massage, first a few details about their mechanisms of action.

- The physical kneading of the body promotes an **increase in blood flow** to the skin as well as to the muscles, which in no way means that massage can replace the warm-up, as some still occasionally falsely claim.
- **Strains and knots** can be loosened through massage. Massage stimulates nerve endings, relaxing the nervous system, and to some extent promotes organ function.
- **Heart and breathing rates** decrease.
- New research has questioned and, in part, even disputed that the **elimination of metabolic wastes** (especially lactic acid) improves.
- One of the most important effects of massage is the **psychological effect**, since it is pleasant-feeling, stimulates a sense of well-being, increases psychological preparedness (for future efforts), and, in addition, promotes relaxation and recovery.

What Is Important in a "Cycling Massage"?

First of all, to allow the athlete to relax as much as possible, massage should be done in a room that is at a comfortable temperature, draft-free, and not too bright. Massage technique will not be described in detail here, since that is best left to professionals with much experience. Nevertheless, several tips are given to help a masseur who is inexperienced with cyclists to provide the best massage for his riders. It is important to massage not only the legs, the cyclist's most important body part, but also the back, neck, and shoulders to relieve stiffness in these areas. The leg muscles are normally exquisitely sensitive, so the massage should be fairly gentle and consist mainly of rubbing, soft kneading, and shaking. The normal massage technique is too rough for the cyclists' thin-skinned legs. With a few exceptions (knots), pain should be avoided. Too much pressure and the use of finger tips can cause muscle soreness in the athlete's legs.

Shaved legs, a necessity for road racers, make the masseur's task significantly easier, prevent him from pulling leg hairs, and also protect the athlete against painful hair follicle infections. There are many massage oils on the market, but simple baby oil is sufficient. After the massage, the oil should be removed with rubbing alcohol so that the pores (which allow the skin to breathe) do not remain clogged.

The masseur should allow the athlete to initiate the conversation and respect the athlete's wishes if he prefers not to talk. If a conversation takes place, the masseur should attempt to steer it away from cycling, especially after a race, to let the rider think about other things.

Self-massage

Self-massage is an excellent method to loosen up muscles with little expenditure in time or money, especially when you cannot afford the relatively expensive professional massage. However, the psychological relaxation benefits of self-massage are less, since you must do the work yourself. Due to the limited reach of the arms, self-massage is restricted primarily to arms and legs. Self-massage can be used both before and after training as well as competition. Before doing a recovery massage after a hard effort, first stretch as described in chapter 3.9 to relax both physically and mentally. You should familiarize yourself with the following massage techniques and use them after hard efforts; a brief form of massage is also very effective to loosen up muscles before competition. Massaging both legs requires about 10 to 15 minutes.

Where?

Self-massage is best done while sitting on a towel spread out on the ground. Before a race, you can sit in the car or on a curb.

What Do You Need?

For a massage, you need one or more towels, massage oil, and rubbing alcohol to subsequently remove the oil. Baby oil is an ideal massage medium that is inexpensive. Naturally, you can also use special massage oils, which can, on the other hand, be quite expensive. When preparing your legs for a race, your choice of massage oil should depend on the weather conditions. If it is cold, you should apply a thick layer of warming oil; if it is also raining, you may first wish to rub your legs with a special warming cream on top of which a layer of oil can be applied. The warming effect of the cream should not be so great, though, that it shunts the blood from the muscles to the skin. Because of their lack of deep penetration, the use of warming creams or oils is controversial. In hot, dry weather, you should not rub your legs with oil, since this could impede the necessary heat loss through the skin.

How?
Prior to the massage, you should stretch a little bit. Then, you can prop your legs up against a wall for several minutes to increase venous return. Once you are ready to begin the massage, relax and sit down on the towel with bare legs and feet. The following points briefly describe the sequence of the individual massage strokes.

1. Feet and Ankle Joints
As a rule, you should start the massage in the extremities furthest from the heart and work your way toward the heart. While you massage one leg, you should cover the other with a towel to protect it from the cold. Apply a little oil to your thigh and calf; the oil that sticks to your hands is then more than sufficient for massaging your foot. First rest your foot and ankle on top of your other thigh and rub it vigorously to warm it up. Then firmly stroke the sole of your foot with your knuckles or another hard object to stimulate the reflex nerve endings found on the bottoms of your feet. Kneed each individual toe with your fingers and pull the arch of your foot out in both length and width. Next, concentrate on massaging the ankle joint, using your finger tips in a circular motion. Subsequently, rub both hands up your lower leg, starting at your ankle and going past your knee.

2. Achilles Tendon
With your foot propped up, massage your achilles tendon with a gentle rubbing and kneading motion. Stretching the tendon during the massage is particularly beneficial.

3. Calf
Begin the calf massage by rubbing up your calf several times in the direction of your heart. Next, slowly loosen up your calf muscles with smaller strokes that are always towards you, and then kneed your calf a bit. Intermittently, rub up your leg and use your hands to shake your calf.

4. Shin Muscles

Use the back of your hand to rub over the shin muscles, which are located on the outside of the lower leg. You should not massage the edge of the tibia on the inside of the lower leg, since this procedure is not only painful, but can, over time, also result in an inflammation.

5. Knee

You should only lightly rub the knee with your fingers; apply very little pressure.

6. Front of the Thigh

After rubbing and shaking your calf several times, begin with your thigh massage. Here, too, you should start with firm, two-handed rubbing and shaking, and should repeat this type of massage intermittently as well. With your leg stretched out, massage the individual muscle heads of the quadriceps from their insertion at the knee to their origin at the hip. Loosen up the muscle insertions in particular with many small, gentle kneading movements.

7. Back of the Thigh

The back of the thigh is not readily accessible for self-massage, but you can easily shake it. You prop up your leg or bend your knee to enable you to lightly kneed and use the palm of your hand to rub the muscle groups in this area.

Several stretching exercises can also enhance the massage's effectiveness. Before beginning with the other leg, cover the finished leg with a towel. Your massage should take 5-8 minutes per leg. Stiff spots or knots in the muscles should not be kneaded with brute force until they are soft. You should take your time when massaging these stiff areas, since they can often be resolved through careful kneading and rubbing.

After the massage, remove the oil from both legs and then elevate them for several more minutes. Following a recovery massage, you should not subject your legs to large stresses, such as standing for a long time. After you are fairly experienced in self-massage, you can also carefully give a training partner, for example during training camp, a massage; as long as you heed the maxim that the massage should not be painful and should feel pleasant, you can do no harm.

7 Psychology

7.1 Introduction

"Sports psychology" is a relatively new science that deals with the identification, explanation, and use of those psychological factors that affect performance. However, this book is less concerned with the scientific/theoretical side of cyclists' minds and more with the practical application of psychological techniques. This chapter provides a brief insight into this very interesting topic and complements it with several suggested mental exercises to help in preparing psychologically for competition.

Several years ago, people still generally believed that a winning spirit would naturally follow a fit body; today, it is known that exactly the opposite holds true. Willpower is what drives you to continue sprinting, long after the pain in your legs would have caused you to stop. In a competition between two physically equal riders using the same equipment, the mentally superior one will always win. Once elite athletes have reached nearly perfect physical (bodily) fitness, psychological training is one of the few possibilities if doping is eliminated to further enhance or at least stabilize performance. Many sports already have male and female athletes who achieve phenomenal performances with the help of mental training programs.

In cycling, mental training is still in its infancy and is used only by a vanishingly small number of cyclists and coaches. Psychological training programs are of interest, however, not just to the elite rider who can further improve his performance only in this way. Hobby and recreational cyclists can also achieve stunning successes with the help of this type of training, since they, too, can develop optimal psychological attitudes and performance preparedness. Moreover, tactical and technical sequences can be learned more easily and, in this way, mistakes can be remedied. The different relaxation techniques serve the recreational athlete as stress-release mechanisms and help the serious athlete find a beneficial mind-set before the start of a race.

The "Training World Champion"
This type of athlete is especially common in cycling; these are riders who perform very well in training or in fitness diagnostic tests, but cannot prove themselves

under pressure, as in a race. Thus, supposedly stronger riders often leave the race course as losers. The presumptive strength of these athletes applies only to their physical conditioning, since mentally they are far from peak form.

For peak performance, as required to win a difficult race or finish a long tour, not only physical factors such as endurance, strength, etc. play a role, but also intellectual and psychological performance components help the athlete to excel; the role of these contributing factors, however, may often go unnoticed. Those who possess the proper mental attitude and instinctively handle situations correctly are fortunate; those lacking this ability, however, will have problems if they don't change their mental outlook. Although our training world champion is physically in peak shape, he is psychologically unprepared for racing.

Mental Attitude

"As soon as self-doubts surface, you can no longer be a successful bicycle racer." This somewhat exaggerated statement illustrates the importance of mental attitude. Mental attitude has a strong influence on both physical and mental performance readiness, as well as on physical, mental, technical, and tactical performance ability. "Winning types" have a very high level of self-confidence, something that "losers" often lack. The first victory, the first placing, or the first 100 km tour are all crucial steps on the way to athletic self-confidence; you yourself are suddenly the winner, and this realization not infrequently allows you to break through the shackles that previously prevented success. Following a victory, you must, however, not put too much pressure on yourself to succeed or allow others to do so, since you may not be able to live up to those expectations. Positive thinking and a high level of self-worth and self-confidence are mandatory attributes of the successful rider.

Winning Occurs in Your Head

Mentally, you must be prepared to perform your best, since winning first occurs in your head, not with your legs or with a negative attitude: you first lose in your head, which means that only after you think the race or situation is lost, do your legs give up. Not until you are mentally prepared to give it your best, will success come, unless you have entered an unchallenging race in the first place.

The success of athletes who do not seem physically capable of such performances can be explained only by an optimal mental attitude. In such success situations, you may enter a "flow state" in which body and spirit are in harmony. In retrospect, racers often describe this "flow state" as one in which they no longer perceived extreme stress (pain) during a race situation (breakaway attempt) or a tour, but rather were able to ride relatively easily and relaxed at a pace that they otherwise would never have been able to maintain. Although humans are usually able to use only a certain percentage of their absolute performance ability, they can tap into their performance reserves under certain conditions. Mental training can decrease the discrepancy between actual and absolute performance ability.

The mental strength that leads to success is not easy to acquire and requires a good coach or assistant. From race to race, you should gradually work on and improve your mental performance. The following paragraphs illustrate how such a "training ladder" could be constructed.

Pick Medium-hard Races
To foster development of your mental performance ability, you should choose performance tests or races that are neither too easy nor too difficult, but rather ones that are appropriate to your physical and mental fitness. A very easy race against weak opponents would inflate your assessment of your physical and mental performance abilities, while a very difficult race would accomplish just the opposite.

Set Realistic Goals
Just as in choosing your races, you should also be careful when selecting your goals, which are absolutely necessary to guide your training. If you set goals that are several years away (i.e. becoming world champion) and unrealistic as well, you will easily lose sight of them and will once again be goal-less. On the other hand, goals that are too easily attainable will keep both motivation and personal effort low. Both hobby and serious athletes can benefit from recording their athletic goals in writing; relatively distant, yet realistic, goals, such as becoming part of a certain racing team or completing a 200 km tour, should be preceded by several smaller, more quickly attainable goals (i.e. to be in the lead group in a certain race, to ride 200 km in two days). You should be conscious of (possibly, even write down) the obstacles you need to overcome to reach your smaller goals and focus your training (i.e. cornering, sprinting, eliminating mental weaknesses) on surmounting them.

Take a Break from Cycling

Only those who can take a break from cycling after they get off the bicycle, can mentally relax and preserve their motivation for training and races. Athletes who think about cycling every day for the whole year often show mental blocks and put themselves under too much pressure. In order to reserve enough motivation for the season, you should take a mental break from cycling during the transition and preparation periods in particular, but nevertheless you should not fail to follow through with your training program.

Motivation

The high level of motivation required in cycling for training and racing becomes obvious when you consider the many kilometers cyclists ride in bad weather or

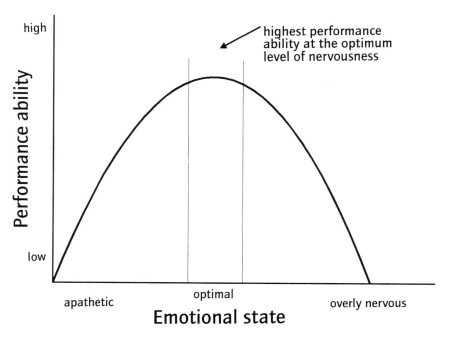

Figure 7.1: Emotional state: the highest performance ability can only be delivered at he optimum level of nervousness. The figure is highly simplified, since the optimum emotional state differs form person to person.

the frequent moments when continuing to ride is associated with great pain and only willpower and motivation enable riders to continue. Motivation is highly dependant on self-assessment of performance, since a consistent over- or under-assessment precludes success.

Talking with acquaintances (coach, parents, friends) can change your self-assessment. Through mental training, you attempt to discover and harness motivational reserves. Simple ways to enhance motivation are changing the surroundings in which you train (training camp), planning a break (of several days) from training, or participating in other sports in the winter. You can also grant yourself small "rewards" for reaching certain goals.

Emotional State

Many riders are overly nervous before the start of a race and, therefore, cannot concentrate properly on the forthcoming competition. On the other hand, an apathetic rider is understandably just as unlikely to perform at his best. Thus, there is an optimum emotional state somewhere between these two extremes (see figure 7.1). An important goal of mental training is to teach riders to control their emotional states before and during competition through relaxation techniques for the nervous athlete and by heightening the excitement (mobilization) of the athlete who is too calm.

7.2 Relaxation Techniques

You should resort to relaxation techniques whenever you are in an emotionally strained state. Tension due to fear, stress, pressure to succeed, or uncertainty is classified as negative tension, while tension that stems from pleasure, eagerness to perform, or self-confidence is termed positive tension. Before a race, use relaxation techniques to reduce negative tension and, in this way, create an optimum level of nervousness. Even excessive positive tension can be controlled with relaxation techniques. You must determine your individual optimum level of nervousness through experimentation.

Progressive Muscle Relaxation

The progressive (advancing) muscle relaxation technique, developed in 1934 by G. Jacobsen, is well-suited for athletes, since it is easy to learn and effective.

Individual muscle groups are alternately isometrically contracted (producing tension without joint movement) to get the sensation of advancing muscular relaxation, which also leads to a calming of the mind.

Practice daily for about 10 minutes, for example before going to bed or in bed when you have trouble sleeping. You should not perform this relaxation technique within the last 30 minutes prior to a race, since you might start the race too relaxed. An abbreviated program can be used as a lead-in to visualization. Although the recumbent position is more comfortable, progressive muscle relaxation can also be performed while sitting up. When first practicing this technique, you may find it easier to have a partner give you the relaxation directions in a calm voice. The technique that is repeated with every muscle group is as follows:

1. Concentrate on the muscle group or body part.

2. Maximally contract the desired muscles; hold for 5-8 sec.

3. When given the signal, relax for about 30 sec, while concentrating on that region.

Cyclists should begin the relaxation sequence with their legs, on which they may repeat it at the end if necessary. The following is a sample program:

1. left thigh	8. back
2. left calf	9. left upper arm
3. left foot	10. left hand & forearm
4. right thigh	11. right upper arm
5. right calf	12. right hand & forearm
6. right foot	13. neck and throat
7. stomach	14. face

Both sides of the body can be done at once to save time. Modifications to the program, such as treating the individual muscles, especially in the legs, differently, are possible at any time.

Breathing Exercises

Breathing exercises are employed while preparing for visualization. Concentrating on breathing and exhaling more slowly leads to a rapid relaxation that, with a little bit of practice, can be attained nearly everywhere, such as before the start of a race or in other stressful situations. The exercise duration is between one and three to five minutes.

Autonomic Training

Autonomic training is a form of psychological training that should only be learned under the supervision of an experienced expert and that requires, in relation to the other techniques presented here, a lot of practice.

This section only provided a brief overview of sports psychology; there are, however, a series of more in-depth books on this topic published by the Meyer & Meyer Verlag, i.e. *Psychologie im Sport* by Sigurd Baumann. The important points, again, are an open-minded attitude to psychological training, the courage to try new approaches, and a little bit of perseverance.

7.3 Mental Training

Visualization

Visualization (thinking in pictures, imagining) is a technique that is used more and more frequently, is relatively simple to learn, and can yield excellent results.

Think in Pictures

When visualizing, free yourself from using words by thinking in pictures and supporting these images with imagined sounds, smells, and feelings. Watch a movement or a reflex flash like a movie before your eyes. The imagination of an action is often so intense that the electrical activity (electromyograph) of the muscle groups normally used for that action noticeably increases due to the visualization alone. Since the muscles as well as the nervous system "memorize" these movements, they can be carried out more easily later on. It is possible to visualize different riding techniques (jumping, cornering, drafting, braking, etc.), great performances, various emotional situations (calmness, performance desire), and, after some practice, even tactical situations. Start with simple movements, and, only after they have been successfully carried out, progress to harder situations. Mental training novices in particular should practice often (several minutes a day) if possible. Just as with mental training, not every athlete immediately succeeds with visualization, and it is even possible that you may not find this training technique useful.

How Do You Do It?

Before you begin visualizing, describe the technique or tactic in words and write it down (in detail, about one page). The next day, read what you wrote several times, attempt to picture the situation in your mind's eye, and change the text if necessary. Use one of the relaxation techniques described in the previous section to loosen up and calm down before beginning with the exercises that precede visualization. Once you have almost completely memorized the text, begin by closing your eyes and attempting to see the situation; support your imagination with silent words if necessary. Recording your text onto audio cassette so you can listen to it while visualizing may be helpful. The final step is to actually visualize the movement, either by observing yourself as in a movie (by-stander's point of view) or, better yet, by seeing the situation through your own eyes. Actions should take place in the present, never in the past, and should always remain realistic. Avoid visualizing incorrectly carried out movements or reflex actions, since these will also be memorized. As you become more experienced with visualization over time, you will develop individual techniques and methods most suited to your personal needs.

Before Riding

In the training period, it is useful to train not only the body, but also the mind, by visualizing technical, tactical, and mental abilities. The day before or immediately prior to a race you should visualize the specific tactical and mental performance required for the race.

While Riding

On the bike, use a visualization program with no preceding relaxation phase. Short tactical advice (ride near the front, watch a certain rider), technical movement sequences (follow the back wheel of the rider in front of you and do not brake in the turn), as well as motivational advice (persevere, give it your best, ride relaxed, pedal smoothly) can easily be recalled and carried out with the help of the previously imagined pictures.

Imagine a Motivational Picture
In cycling, as in other endurance sports, you eventually reach a stress level at which continuing becomes a struggle between body and mind. In such a situation, where you are close to giving up, you should imagine a personally pleasing" picture" that helps your mental desire prevail and makes the task seem easier than it is. You must individually chose your pleasant images, such as a beach, a sun-draped field of flowers, or a rope that pulls you towards the finish line. Imagining something pleasant can often work wonders and allow you to use your last reserves. Also, projecting the already described "flow state", in which everything appears playfully easy, onto the extremely demanding situation can enhance performance.

After the Ride
After a race or training ride, you should think about the mistakes you made and then visualize the proper sequence of actions, but never the mistake. Your image should always suggest the playful easiness of the action sequence. The visualization technique can be used just about everywhere and especially during forced periods of rest due to injury.

Example: The Smooth Pedal Stroke
The smooth pedal stroke is used as an example for a visualization program.

1. Relaxation
While lying on your back, close your eyes and rest, concentrate completely on your breathing, which comes and goes like the ocean's waves. After about a minute, start prolonging exhalation until inhalation is initiated by itself. Maintain this breathing rhythm throughout the visualization. The wording for relaxation could be as follows:

I am completely quiet and calm,
completely quiet and calm,
I am quiet, calm, relaxed.

My breathing is quiet and regular, it comes and goes like the ocean's waves.
Now I am prolonging my exhalation, until inhalation is initiated by itself.
I am quiet, calm, relaxed.
I will now concentrate completely on my athletic performance.

The requests should be repeated two to three times.

2. Visualization Task

The text for visualizing a smooth pedal stroke could be as follows. Translating the words into pictures and feelings is the important thing.

I am sitting on my bicycle and riding relaxed and smoothly, my legs feel good, and I feel well. I pedal, I pull, and I push.
During the whole pedal revolution, I deliver power to the pedal.
The incline I am riding up now does not bother me, and I ride smoothly further. I pedal, pull, and push. (repeat) I concentrate on my pedaling. I pedal, pull, and push. (repeat)
The bicycle rolls playfully easily. I ride up the mountain just as easily in a bigger gear, since I feel good.
I pedal, pull, and push. (repeat)

3. Withdrawal

After the visualization, withdraw the relaxation, open your eyes, and stretch and move about.

A visualization program's wording, which is converted into pictures, should be as above or similar to it. The person who has no experience with mental training may think it to be somewhat ridiculous, but already after several attempts, he will notice that there is more behind such a program than there appears at first sight.

Only regular practice leads to an improvement in visualization technique and, consequently, to an improvement in movement. Once on the bicycle, you only have to think about your picture of the smooth pedal stroke to help you pedal in circles. Due to space restrictions, it is unfortunately not possible to go into more detail about other movement sequences or tactical situations; visualization programs for other situations can be modified from this sample.

Fear Compensation

Many riders are always afraid in certain situations, and this fear can prevent them from performing at their best. Fear can take a number of many different forms and have various causes. Crashes, for example, can generate such an intense fear of high cornering speeds or fast descents that the pack rides away from you.

What is fear? Fear is comparable to an emotional strain and is very often the anticipatory thought of a threatening situation, which could occur under certain circumstances or has already occurred in the past. In this way, fear represents your reflection on uncertainty. In addition to the specific fears already mentioned, primarily of crashes and their consequences, there are also more complex fears in cycling, such as the fear of defeat or victory, or the fear of self-blame. In order to combat your particular anxiety, you have to recognize and be able to put into words the fear-triggering factors, since this process alone is occasionally sufficient to control your fears. Talking with a trusted person or your coach can help you concretely state these factors.

How is fear expressed? For a stranger, diagnosing fear before or during certain situations is difficult; several outward manifestations can, however, be provided:
Physical symptoms: trembling, upset stomach, paleness, increase in pulse rate.
Motor symptoms: poor coordination, cramps, poor performance.
Behavior: abnormal behavior, such as aggressiveness or passivity.

How should you combat fear? Only the self-control methods that you can carry out on your own will be briefly discussed here.

Physical Techniques

On the one hand, fear, as an emotional state, can be dissipated through physical activity, such as a thorough warm-up. On the other hand, the relaxation techniques described in the following section can also help you to control your anxiety, since relaxation is the basis for controlling fear.

Mental Techniques

Mental techniques involve giving a new value and interpretation to fear-triggering negative thoughts by attempting to think realistically and in positive terms. Revaluating and placing into perspective the real significance of a race greatly decreases pressure and allows relaxed participation.

Common crash fears can usually be vastly reduced by visualizing correct, completely harmless, and smoothly executed techniques, such as cornering, riding in a pack, or descending. This visualization should, however, not lead to an increased willingness to take risks, such as in downhill mountain bike racing. Incorrect techniques and the crash scene itself must be kept completely out of the visualization program.

7.4 Mental Training before a Race or a Long Tour

The following sequence can be used the night before and/or on the day of the race to prepare for the imminent performance. This exercise should be completed at least 30 minutes prior to the race start (it is best done at home, before you drive to the race). Find a comfortable place, where you will be undisturbed for about 20 minutes, and sit or, better yet, lie down and relax: your legs should lie loosely together without touching; your feet will angle slightly outward.

1. Progressive Muscle Relaxation
With closed eyes, relax your body by using your own muscle relaxation program or the one provided. Pay special attention to your legs.

2. Positive Thoughts
Transfer yourself in your thoughts to a place that is suggestive of peacefulness, security, and relaxation; this can be a field, a beach, a forest, or something similar. You should focus only on this place and concentrate on positive thoughts.

Exhaustion and happiness: the victory

3. Visualization

After successful physical and mental relaxation, you should begin visualizing the imminent race or tour. Picture yourself on the course, carrying out your positive, success-promising tactics. Any foreseen difficulties (i.e. mountains) should be overcome with playful easiness. You should attempt to adopt a positive, performance-eager attitude toward the upcoming effort; the race should be fun.

4. Withdrawal

After you have achieved a personal success (whatever that may be) in the race you are visualizing, you have to energetically withdraw from your relaxed state by stretching. On the day of the race, you should now begin with your warm-up. The night before a race, you do not have to force yourself back into reality as abruptly, especially if you are ready to lie down and go to sleep.

8 Riding Technique

This chapter first discusses the proper position on a racing bicycle and then introduces and explains different riding techniques and tricks.

8.1 Adjusting Your Position

The person who wants to perform at his best on a bicycle can only adjust to his equipment to a very limited extent. If man and machine are to function together optimally, the bicycle must be made to fit the rider and not the other way around. Therefore, you must carefully chose the proper frame size and make the correct adjustments to your bicycle. The cycling world is full of tips and formulas for adjusting bicycle position that are probably more confusing than helpful in finding the correct position. Newcomers to the sport or those with new bicycles must unquestionably adjust their bicycles properly to perform at their best without discomfort. There are several rules that must be heeded for finding the correct sitting position on the bicycle, but even so, you may have to deviate from them to find your individual position. Orthopedic problems, such as back pain (lower back vertebrae) or knee problems, require different sitting positions that will also be described in detail here.

After you have found your position, record the individual position measurements on a measurement card to make it fairly easy to "tailor" a new or borrowed bicycle to your body and to prevent bothersome experimentation and possible musculoskeletal discomfort.

Saddle Height

The saddle height is the most important adjustment to the bicycle. Choose a frame that fits your height, since frames that are much too large or small are difficult to adjust properly. Assuming you have a correct frame size, the only way to adjust the saddle height is by moving the seat post. The method that was used to adjust the saddle height for the older style of toe-strap pedals has only limited application to the new clipless pedals due to the significant variation in construction. Sit on the bike and hold onto a fence or a wall; when pedaling backwards with the heels of your feet on the undersides of the pedals, your legs should be completely extended without requiring you to slide from side to side on the saddle.

If you are clipped into your pedals, your leg extension should be about 155 to 165 degrees at the bottom of the pedal stroke. Therefore, your legs are almost completely extended.

Saddle height preference depends on the discipline and the type of rider; the track sprinter or the time trialist has a very high saddle position to extend his legs as far as possible, while the points rider or criterium specialist chooses a lower saddle position to maintain a high cadence over long periods of time and to be able to react faster to changes in pace. In summary, a lower saddle height, and therefore less leg extension, is advantageous for high pedal cadences, while the higher position is better for lower cadences with a higher use of strength. Road racers choose an intermediate position, since the demands placed on them are relatively variable.

The saddle height can be precisely adjusted to this intermediate position using a formula (Hueggi-Method) that has been around for a long time. First, you must determine your leg length by standing barefoot against a wall with slightly spread legs and using the spine of a book that is held up to your crotch (perpendicular to the wall) to make a mark on the wall, which can then be measured. This value is multiplied by the factor 0.893 to get the saddle height (center of the bottom bracket – top of the saddle).

Despite all formulas and advice, your "riding feeling" must guide saddle height adjustment, since no theoretical value derived from a formula can take into account individual variation and, therefore, such values must remain only a starting point.

With clipless pedals, stick to the manufacturer's advice for adjusting saddle height. When buying new shoes and before switching pedal systems, measure the distance from the inside sole of the shoe (over the pedal axis) to the top of the saddle (with the cranks parallel to the seat tube) to make the saddle height adjustment for the new shoes or pedals precise. *The proper saddle height*

Recreational riders in particular often have too low a saddle position that does not allow them to deliver full power to their pedals and also places greater pressure on their knees. New saddles lose height after a certain amount of use, necessitating an adjustment of saddle height. Knee problems also require saddle height adjustment and, depending on the type of injury, this adjustment will be up or down, as was described in more detail in chapter 6 ("Medical Aspects of Cycling"). If your saddle height is too low, raise it slowly (only about half a centimeter every two weeks) to avoid joint problems. No one, not even occasional cyclists, should ever raise their saddle several centimeters from one day to the next.

Saddle Tilt

In addition to saddle height, saddle tilt must also be adjusted. A racing saddle is positioned precisely parallel to the ground to distribute the pressure, so that saddle sores and pressure points can be avoided. If the nose of the saddle points down, your arms have to bear too much weight, and you constantly slide forward. A saddle that points up eliminates the danger of "sliding forward", but places too much pressure on the urethra and may lead to unwelcome pain (chapter 6). Moreover, such a position may tilt the pelvis back, putting more pressure on the joints in the lower back and possibly leading to pain in this area and, in the worst cases, even to degenerative changes in the vertebrae (over the course of years).

Saddle Position

The saddle position is the position of the saddle on the seat post clamp; the saddle can slide several centimeters forward and backward on its rails. Before adjusting the saddle position, make sure the saddle is parallel to the ground, so the rider is sitting normally on the saddle. The cleats should already be adjusted correctly. Starting from an intermediate saddle position, begin with the fine adjustments. A plumb line hanging from the nose of the saddle should hit the chain stay 2-5 cm behind the center of the bottom bracket. Riders with extremely long or short thighs must modify this position accordingly.

Within this range, the saddle should be positioned so that a plumb line dropped from the front of the kneecap intersects the middle of the pedal axis when the cranks are in their horizontal position. If the plumb line does not intersect the pedal axis, move the saddle so that it at least comes close. Road riders prefer a position behind the pedal axis (1 cm), which allows them to sit further back and gives them more power to push large gears.

Pedal Adjustment

The cleats must be adjusted with much care to avoid future joint injuries (knee, foot, hip). Often cyclists, out of laziness, continue to ride with a slightly maladjusted cleat that only causes them minor discomfort while pedaling but certainly may cause knee damage over the course of a year. Even if the cleat position after adjustment causes only minimal discomfort while pedaling, it must be adjusted a millimeter at a time until it is perfect.

The foot should normally be parallel to the cranks. Lengthwise, the cleats should be adjusted so that the balls of the feet (toe joints) are directly over the pedal axes, since power is transferred by the balls of the feet just like in running, and therefore, only this position will deliver power effectively. There is no helpful formula for this adjustment; simply feel through your shoe for your toe joint and position it over the pedal axis. Many pedal manufacturers offer helpful cleat adjustment templates or brochures, without which optimal adjustment of the occasionally fairly complicated pedal systems would scarcely be possible. Several pedal systems, such as those made by TIME, only require lengthwise adjustment of the cleat, since lateral adjustment is unnecessary due to the 5 degree side-to-side range of motion (for all cleat adjustments, an assistant is extremely useful).

Handlebar Height

The handlebar height is limited by the stem length, which is normally not longer than 13 cm. The handlebar height should be chosen so that the height difference between the top of the saddle and the top of the handlebars is at most six to eight centimeters. The recreational cyclist will adjust his saddle and handlebars to about the same height. Large height differences strain the back and can lead to degenerative changes in the spine, especially in young athletes. Lumbar and thoracic vertebral columns are flexed too much, and this low position also results in a cervical vertebral column that is over-extended. If the arms are very long, however, a larger height difference is sometimes necessary.

If you feel pain in your lumbar or cervical spine, you must change your position. Height differences of over 10 or 12 cm are fairly common. If you have injured your back in the past (slipped disk) or you feel pain, you should adjust your handlebars so that the height difference between them and the saddle is minimal or non-existent. Spacers in the stem shaft can increase handlebar height up to three centimeters. Frames with longer head tubes are also ideal. The strain that beginning cyclists or experienced riders starting their season feel is usually short-lived and disappears when the back musculature's flexibility and performance ability increases.

Reach Length

The reach length is the distance from the nose of the saddle to the center of the handlebars. This distance is determined by the frame's top tube length, the stem length, and the saddle position. Mass-production frames have standard top tube lengths corresponding to their seat tube lengths; you have limited influence on the length of the top tube.

In general, you should pick a frame that is as small, and therefore as short, as possible with a stem that is as long as possible. A six or eight centimeter-long stem on a large frame would be out of place, since a significantly smaller frame should have been chosen. If possible, do not change your saddle position to adjust your reach length, since this position was already adjusted with respect to your legs. Therefore, only the stem length can be varied to adjust the reach length. Feeling is crucial in adjusting the reach length, since you should feel comfortable on your bicycle.

There is a simple method to check the correct reach length: lean on a wall or have an assistant hold you, put your hands in the bends of the drops, and place one pedal parallel to your down tube. In this position, your elbows and knees should only be a few centimeters (1-4 cm) apart. Another rule of thumb is that your view of the front hub should be obscured by the handlebar when you are in the drops (holding onto the bend) with your elbows slightly bent. Your position can be neither too stretched out and flat, nor too upright. You should be able to ride in the drops with your hands near the brakes for long periods of time without back pain. Once your bike is properly adjusted, you may feel very uncomfortable and stretched out, but this feeling will subside after the first 1,000 km, since your body will quickly adjust to this new position.

Crank Arm Length

Road bicycle cranks are sold in lengths of 165 to 180 mm. The normal length is 170 mm, from which you can deviate as necessary depending on body size or discipline. Time trialists and climbers prefer somewhat longer cranks (175 mm), while circuit racers and track riders use shorter cranks (170 mm, or even shorter on the track). It would be difficult to provide crank length rules for certain body sizes or leg lengths. Shorter cranks permit a higher cadence, while longer cranks allow better power transfer (longer lever arm) at the expense of cadence and cornering clearance. A criterium specialist may use somewhat shorter cranks to enable him to pedal through turns that would cause him to clip his pedal if he had longer cranks. Every racer swears by his optimum crank arm length. Even so, as a rule children should use shorter (165 mm) and tall athletes, longer (175 or 180 mm) cranks.

Measurement Card

Once you have found your ideal position, it is worthwhile to record all important adjustment positions on a measurement card, which enables you to quickly adjust a new bicycle to your position. The following measurements should be recorded: *seat tube length* (center of the bottom bracket – top of the seat tube), *top tube length* (center of the head tube – center of the seat tube), *saddle height* (center of the bottom bracket – top of the saddle), *reach length* (nose of the saddle – center of the handlebars), *stem length* (center of the stem bolt – center of the handlebars), *crank arm length* (center of the bottom bracket – middle of the pedal axis), and *handlebar width and type*.

Name:	Date:
seat tube length:	top tube length:
saddle height :	reach length:
stem length:	crank arm length:
handlebar width:	pedal system:
chain rings:	cog rations:
seat tube angle:	saddle:

Table 8.1: Record all your bicycle measurement on this measurement card (sample). Either copy this card or enter the values directly here.

8.2 The Smooth Pedal Stroke

The smooth pedal stroke is the even distribution of power to the pedals during the course of the entire pedal revolution. An even power distribution during every movement phase is, however, possible only in theory due to the variable strengths of the muscle groups in the legs (flexors, extensors). The extensors are responsible for most of the muscle work propelling you forward. The smooth pedal stroke, nevertheless, differentiates the bicycle racer from the hobby cyclist. The use of racing pedals that attach the foot firmly to the pedal enables not only generating power from top to bottom, but also pushing, pressing, and pulling, all of which the hobby cyclist cannot do with his normal pedals.

The term "pedal cycle" is a bit confusing and does not describe the actual situation, since you do more than just pedal; "crank cycle" or "crank revolution cycle" would be more neutral terms. If you pedal only from top to bottom, you ignore important muscle groups in the legs, namely the knee and hip flexors. You should attempt to use all leg and hip muscle groups, if possible, to reduce the demand on the highly used extensors and permit more efficient forward motion. New studies have shown that only a small proportion of racers master the smooth pedal stroke. Therefore, juniors must be taught pedaling technique early on, but even serious older athletes should regularly incorporate pedaling technique exercises into their training program. How this is done is described later. The smooth pedal stroke is part of spinning.

Spinning is supposed to be the fluid and smooth application of the correct technique that is actually, as already mentioned, much more than just pushing down on the pedals. During a fluid pedal stroke, the legs should pass close to the frame: a good riding style does not include broad-legged stomping. Upper body and head should be held still if possible to avoid wasting energy through unnecessary muscle movements. The strength for pedaling is derived primarily from the leg muscles and cannot be augmented by rocking the head or body back and forth. Even so, body and arm muscles perform work while pedaling; they form a counteracting support structure for the unilateral pedaling motion. The hand, arm, shoulder, stomach, and back form a muscular sling, which rhythmically moves back and forth, supporting the trunk and the pelvis. The function of this muscular sling is illustrated when rocking the bike back and forth while standing up: the same-side arm and the other structures provide the support that counteracts the force of the leg extension. The former East Germans even conducted experiments using a string that was supposed to provide additional support and allow more power to be generated by fixing the upper body to the bicycle frame.

What was just said illustrates the necessity of general athletic conditioning to develop performance-capable, yet not bulky, arm and trunk musculature. The upper body should only be moved during a sprint or a difficult climb. Leg strength measurements on athletes have shown that only rarely are both legs equally strong. Even in cycling, there are only a few riders who can generate the same forward-propulsive power with both legs. However, this leg-equality is a requirement for a perfect smooth pedal stroke. If you have the opportunity to get your leg strengths measured and the result indicates a muscular imbalance (different leg strengths), you should attempt to equal out the difference with a focussed strength program under a physical therapist's supervision.

The **crank cycle** can be broken down into three separate parts:
1. The down-stroke phase, in which the extensors push the pedal down.
2. The pulling phase, which encompasses the part of the cycle from the bottom dead center until shortly before the top dead center and whose work is done by the hip and knee flexors.
3. The pushing phase, in which the foot is pushed forward at the top dead center.

The three main phases just described overlap in their beginning and end zones. A more precise division follows in figure 8.1, in which the cycle is divided into 8 segments of each 45 degrees.

1st Segment
In the first segment of the cycle, the down-stroke or pressure phase begins at about 10 degrees. Near the end of this segment, the thrusting phase stops.

2nd and 3rd Segment
During these two segments, the leg extensor muscles (quadriceps, gluteal muscles, calf muscles) supply most of the pedaling power, and the greatest percentage of forward motion-producing power is generated. The point of maximum power is usually (depending on the rider) between 90 degrees and 110 degrees.

4th Segment
The pulling phase starts here, even though the down-stroke phase still persists and still generates high power output.

5th Segment

Between the 4th and 5th segments, lies the so-called **bottom dead** center of the crank cycle. The dead center is characterized by poor leverage: neither the flexors nor the extensors can act effectively at this point. The bottom dead center must be overcome using the momentum generated by the early initiation of the flexors, and thus of the pulling phase. The other leg assists with a strong pushing phase at the top dead center. In the 5th segment starting at 200 degrees, the pedal can be pulled more strongly back and up due to the improved leverage.

6th and 7th Segments

The main work phase in the 6th and 7th segments is the pulling phase; hip flexors, knee flexors, and shin muscles pull the pedal back and up.

8th Segment

The pushing phase begins at 320 degrees in the 8th segment. The top dead center of the crank cycle is overcome with the help of the knee extensors.

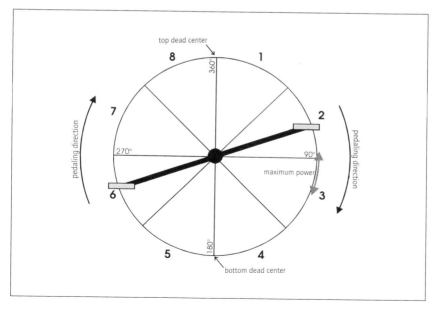

Figure 8.1: The crank cycle

The simple pedal of a normal bicycle does not allow for pulling power. One leg's weight is lifted solely by the pedaling power of the other leg, representing an enormous waste of energy. An efficient pedal stroke has smooth transitions between down-stroke, pulling, and pushing phases and both crank sides have the same cyclic power output. Figure 8.1 shows how the power output of both legs depends on the crank arm angle.

The foot position in the crank cycle varies according to the pedal cadence:

At **low pedal cadences** (up to 85 revolutions/min), you can concentrate particularly on the individual phases. Low pedal cadences are usually combined with a high to very high strength requirement. The slow motion allows more power to be applied to the pedals in the pushing and pulling phases than is possible at higher cadences. During pushing, the heel is lowered and the toes point slightly upward, while during pulling, the toes point strongly downward.

Intermediate pedal cadences (from 85-105 revolutions/min) necessitate less movement from the ankle joint, resulting in a more or less horizontal foot position. The foot movements described above are still recognizable, but with less range of motion.

High pedal cadences (over 105 revolutions/min) place high demands on the motor coordination of the individual muscles involved. Since the high movement speed results in a shortened contraction time, the muscle contraction distance must be abbreviated by raising the heel throughout the whole crank cycle. The ankle joint is almost immobile in this position.

Studies have shown that conditioned cyclists prefer a flatter foot position than do occasional cyclists. Their heels may even drop below their toes during the down-stroke, while occasional cyclists prefer a foot position in which the heel is slightly raised.

Ways to Improve the Smooth Pedal Stroke
The smooth pedal stroke, or at least something close to it, is essential for a high performance level. There are many possibilities for improving a smooth, even stroke. To get a feel for what it means to apply constant pressure to the pedals, ride for 100 meters using only one leg. In order to propel yourself forward, you must concentrate on down-stroke, pulling, and pushing phases.

Large gears, as used in strength training, paired with low pedal cadences, enable conscious coordination and variation of each of the individual cycle phases.

Even **high pedal cadences** help shape a smooth pedal stroke, since they demand a pulling phase in order to be efficient. A long-used method for this type of training is riding a **fixed gear** bike during the winter, since coasting is impossible, preventing you from stopping to pedal. To efficiently propel yourself forward in a fixed gear, your muscles must more or less pedal in circles. Choose gear ratios of 42 x 16-20 and ride about 500 to 1000 km on relatively flat roads during the first phase of the preparation period. The smaller the gear, the more useful the fixed-gear training.

There are two other methods for learning the smooth pedal stroke that begin not with the leg movement itself, but in the head, where the movement is created and planned. One way is to imagine the perfect execution of the smooth pedal stroke; you can do this motionless training in your living room or integrate it into indoor training.

This **visualization** was described in more detail in chapter 7 ("Psychology"). Ultimately, this conceptualization will also improve actual pedaling technique.

Another method is to write down on a piece of paper: *smooth pedal stroke: pushing – down-stroke – pulling, especially pulling on the back-stroke and pushing at the top*. This note should then be attached to your handlebar or stem to serve as a constant reminder to work on your pedal stroke. Technique training is best incorporated into short basic endurance or compensatory training workouts; you can also work on other techniques, such as bunny hopping or cornering. The difficulty with a smooth pedal stroke is not the down-stroke, but the pushing and pulling. Therefore, a reminder note with these two words alone is generally sufficient. What may seem somewhat simplistic here, is actually an effective aid for learning and improving the smooth pedal stroke. In the same way, you can also remind yourself repeatedly to pull and push. A combination of these mental techniques used in conjunction with a torque-measuring pedal, which indicates (also acoustically) the force generated throughout the pedal stroke, is ideal. This special pedal is, however, available to only a few and is technologically not fully developed.

8.3 Hand Position on the Handlebars

The road handlebar's bent shape offers a number of different hand positions. Depending on the situation, you can grip the handlebars in the drops or assume a more relaxed position on the top of the bar. While riding in a group or training alone, the ideal grip is the **top handlebar position**, which relaxes your body and enables you to ride comfortably for hours. Your hands can grip the top of the bars up to the brake hoods in many different positions.

Brake hood position

This position is not, however, appropriate for aggressive riding in races, since it is aerodynamically not very efficient. It is also very unstable, and therefore not recommended, for standing up while riding.

The **brake hood position** is a position that is very often used even in races. Compared to the top position, this position is more aerodynamic and, above all, safer, since the brakes can be used and difficult steering maneuvers can be performed. Since your body is not as flat as in the drops, you can observe the traffic or race situation better, and the brake hoods allow you to pull strongly on the handlebars while climbing or sprinting. The brake hood and top handlebar positions are, therefore, the ideal training positions.

In a race and while doing intervals, the **drops** are the ideal position, since they are very aerodynamic. This position is far too uncomfortable to be used over long distances in everyday training. Hold onto the handlebar in the bend, at the end, or somewhere in between. When riding very fast, flatten your body over the frame, so that your forearms are parallel to the road. This position is also possible in the brake hoods. If the traffic situation is difficult to survey or dangerous, riding in the drops with your fingers close to your brakes is the safest hand position, since this enables both the most braking power as well as the best steering ability.

8.4 Climbing Position

Climbing requires a special technique to conquer the mountain with the most efficiency. Aerodynamics do not play a large roll at such low speeds. Generally, your grip on the top of the handlebars should be wide and your back and shoulders should be relaxed to restrict breathing the least. Holding onto the brake hoods while climbing in the saddle is a matter of personal preference that is individually extremely variable, since some riders feel too stretched out and believe that it restricts their breathing. The brake hood grip is, however, ideal for climbing out of the saddle. While climbing, you should only use the drops during breakaway attempts and on flat sections.

During steep, long inclines, alternating between sitting down and standing up is a helpful technique that interchanges the use of different muscle groups. Flatter sections should be ridden at a steady pace primarily in the saddle, since more energy is expended when standing.

When riding in the saddle, your own rhythm and individual gear preference is most important, although the smooth, high-cadence style using small gears is usually more efficient than powerful stomping in large gears.

Rocking the bike is a useful technique that beginners in particular must practice. **Bike rocking** is used primarily during sudden tempo increases and very steep inclines. This technique requires the body weight to be shifted to the extended leg while the same-side arm is used to tip the bicycle to the opposite side. Importantly, the body should not move over the bicycle, but rather the bicycle should be tipped from side to side underneath the body. The full body weight is used to power the downward motion of the cranks, and this motion is supported by the pull of the same-side arm and the push of the opposite arm. When high pedaling power is

Climbing position

required (starting from a stand-still, riding up a hill), both arms alternate pulling and pushing on the handlebars; on the other hand, the work done by the arms during low power but high pedal cadence work is limited to the pushing (down) with the opposite arm. The arms' pushing and pulling should not produce unnecessary handlebar movement, which can lead to zigzaging. Young junior riders often sprint in this zigzag style, which is ineffective due to the extra distance covered, although it looks impressive. While sprinting and climbing, all your energy should be used for forward propulsion.

While **descending**, an aerodynamic position is important to reduce wind resistance. Riders assume very different, and sometimes even risky and dangerous, positions; however, a position with horizontal cranks, knees pressed tightly to the top tube, close-together arms, and an extremely low upper body is sufficient in most cases and enables you to overlook the road to react quickly. From this position, you can also slide off the saddle a bit or even put one arm behind your back.

Even if you prefer a position in which your nose almost touches your front wheel, your head must still be tilted back until you can see the road. Your speed during descents is often so high that pedaling is no longer necessary or possible. To allow your legs to recover, you should nevertheless pedal lightly, shake your muscles, and stretch a bit. Descending requires a high amount of concentration, and dangerous situations come up, especially during races; therefore, you should attempt to work your way up to the top third during the climb, so that you do not get gapped after the descent. It is best to be one of the first to start the descent.

8.5 Correct Braking

First a little about the physics of braking: the slowing down caused by the rubbing of the brake pads on the rims can be explained through physics. The rotational speed of the wheels decreases during braking, and the energy of the forward motion is almost entirely converted into heat (through friction); on long descents, heavy braking may cause the rim temperature to rise so much that the tubular tire glue softens, and eventually, the tire may come off the rim or the valve stem may tear off. Front and rear brakes have different strengths: the front brake has one-third more braking power than the rear one, since braking transfers most of the weight to the front wheel, significantly increasing the front wheel's contact with the road surface. The back wheel locks up much easier than the front one because of its decreased road contact.

You should learn to apply the brakes in such a way that your wheels do not lock up, causing you to skid or be thrown over the handlebars. You should practice slamming on the brakes several times to prepare yourself for a dangerous situation in a race or in traffic. As a rule, you should brake with both levers and attempt to control your braking with the right amount of pressure. If you suddenly have to brake heavily, slam on the brakes briefly, but immediately loosen up your grip a bit to maintain control over your bicycle. Slamming on your brakes without subsequently releasing them has dire consequences. However, when you are unfamiliar with your brakes, this reaction is the normal startle reflex. Repeatedly squeezing and releasing the brakes, as when driving a car, is not safe for cycling in a group, since you will endanger those behind you. Unfortunately, an anti-lock brake has not yet been manufactured for the bicycle.

When coming to an emergency stop, braking hard before a turn, or during a descent, you should shift your center of gravity back by stretching out your arms and sliding back on your saddle. Braking works less well in the rain than on dry rims; therefore, you must brake earlier before a turn to shake the water off the rims so the brake pads can grip better. During descents or when riding in traffic, you should squeeze the brake levers slightly, but not enough to feel a braking effect.

The new brake models have improved braking and offer noticeably better control in all situations, but especially in the rain.

8.6 The Proper Cornering Technique

The proper cornering technique is of fundamental importance both for traffic safety, as well as for successful racing. Beginners, especially, often have a lot of trouble with cornering, which places them in dangerous situations that should have been avoidable. Often, poor cornering ability is the cause of their inability to finish races, even though they have sufficient fitness. Of particular importance is incorporating the teaching of proper cornering into the cycling-specific technique exercises for juniors 15-16.

During a turn, centrifugal force acts on the cyclist and his bicycle. Centrifugal force pulls the rider toward the outside of the turn and is determined by the mass of the system (rider and bicycle), the cornering speed, and the cornering radius. Simply stated, the heavier the system, the higher the speed, and the tighter the turn, the larger is the centrifugal force and the harder it is to successfully negotiate the turn. Since mass and turn radius are unalterable,

During the proper cornering technique, the athlete and his bicycle are lined up (Roman Joerdens).

the centrifugal force can only be limited by the cornering speed. If the centrifugal force exceeds the tires' traction on the road, the rider's bicycle will slide.

Cornering Tips

Reduce your speed before the turn enough to avoid sliding; only experience can tell you how far you can go. You should complete all your braking before the turn, so that you only have to tap your brakes in the turn. During races and descents, the drops are the best position for safe cornering, since they maintain a low center of gravity, thereby increasing the system's stability. The faster the cornering speed, the greater is the lean angle of the cyclist and his bike; when cornering, you should be on the same plane as your bicycle, rather than leaning either your bike or your body more into the turn. Your knees should lie close to your frame, but you may have to stick out your inside knee in an emergency situation to put more weight in the direction of the turn without leaning into it more. The inside pedal should be in the top position to avoid scraping it. Your outer, extended leg exerts some pressure on the pedal.

If you want to pedal through the turns (criteriums), you need a lot of experience and a special pedal with a high amount of cornering clearance. Take the ideal line through the turn, which begins wide, cuts to the vertex of the turn, and ends wide again. This turn path increases the turning radius, thereby reducing the centrifugal force. This technique should never be used in traffic and should only be used on completely blocked off race courses, since road race courses may have obstacles that you will hardly be able to avoid if you have committed yourself to this cornering technique. In a race at high cornering speeds, you should ride on the inside and leave about half a meter of room between yourself and the curb for other riders (who may get squeezed out); the inside line is best, since the risk of being involved in a crash as riders slide out is significantly lower. It is smart to take the turns near the front of the field where riders do not brake a lot. In the middle or in the back of the pack, riders brake frequently and subsequently must sprint out of the turn.

If you suddenly notice dirt or sand in a turn, straighten out your bicycle, ride upright over the dirt spot while braking, and then lean into the turn again, making sure that you can still make it around the bend. Riding over dirt while leaning, especially if you brake as well, usually leads to the tires sliding out.

In the rain, as mentioned in the section on braking, completely different rules apply than on dry streets, with the consequence that turns must be executed much more carefully and, therefore, more slowly. During the first few kilometers of a rain race, the riders gradually increase their speed until they have reached the highest possible cornering speed for those conditions. Crashes are most common when it starts raining during a race, since the high cornering speeds on dry streets become excessive once it begins to rain. Manhole covers (whether small or large) and road lane markers, which have given some riders trouble not only during races, are particularly dangerous in the rain. Reduce your tire pressure a little when riding in the rain to increase your contact surface area. More about improving your cornering technique follows in the section on technique training.

8.7 Correct Shifting

Shifting has become progressively easier in the last few years due to the enormous, but long overdue, technological progress. Proper shifting technique for modern shifters is limited to moving a lever or, for the electronic models, to just pressing a button. This technology cannot, however, replace the rider's judgement of when to shift. To avoid putting too much stress on the chain rings and cogs, you should reduce the pressure on your pedals while shifting. At low pedal cadences, even modern shifters work poorly. The new brake lever shifters are conducive to frequent shifting, which is beneficial during a race but not necessary during training. Shift promptly as the terrain demands: before a turn, a road that is difficult to overlook, or an incline. Riders often fall over on sudden, steep inclines, since the low pedal cadence and high amount of pressure they must apply to the pedals no longer permits them to shift on the hill. In such a situation, you should turn around, shift, and then resume riding in the proper direction. You should avoid crossing your chain, i.e. riding in the big chain ring in the front and a big cog in the back, because this mistake will produce a greater amount of friction and waste energy.

The Right Gearing
Choosing the right gear depends largely on the situation and is usually determined by the pedal cadence. Your choice of gears matches your individual fitness (performance) to the terrain, situation, and wind conditions. During races, as well as in training (with the exception of certain training exercises), the pedal cadence should be about 90 revolutions/minute and sometimes higher during training. The pedal cadences for track racing are between 110 and 150 revolutions/minute, clearly higher than those for road racing. Therefore, your choice of gears that will cause your cadence to fall somewhere between the above-mentioned revolutions will be determined by your speed, fitness, and training goals, as well as by the terrain.

There are, however, riders who prefer to ride in very big gears at low cadences; these riders usually have an unusually high strength level. A frequent mistake committed by cycling newcomers and recreational cyclists is to use gears that are too large; by training almost completely in the big chain ring, they not only significantly reduce training effectiveness, but also place a lot of stress on their joints.

The following **development table** provides common cycling gear ratios with their respective developments in meters. The distance given for each ratio is that traveled by the bicycle during one full revolution of the cranks.

You can calculate the development by using the following simple formula: wheel circumference (C in meters) x the ratio of the front chain ring teeth (tF) to the back cog teeth (tB).

$$\text{Development} = C \times tF/tB$$
Example: 2.10 m x 53/15 = 7.42 m

front →

rear	54	53	52	51	50	49	48	47	46	45	44	43	42	41	40	39	38	37	36
12	9.62	9.44	9.26	9.08	8.90	8.73	8.55	8.37	8.19	8.01	7.84	7.66	7.48	7.30	7.12	6.95	6.77	6.59	6.41
13	8.88	8.71	8.55	8.38	8.22	8.05	7.89	7.73	7.56	7.40	7.23	7.07	6.90	6.74	6.58	6.41	6.25	6.08	5.92
14	8.24	8.09	7.94	7.78	7.63	7.48	7.33	7.17	7.02	6.87	6.72	6.56	6.41	6.26	6.11	5.95	5.80	5.65	5.50
15	7.69	7.55	7.41	7.27	7.12	6.98	6.84	6.70	6.55	6.41	6.27	6.13	5.98	5.84	5.70	5.56	5.41	5.27	5.13
16	7.21	7.08	6.95	6.81	6.68	6.54	6.41	6.28	6.14	6.01	5.88	5.74	5.61	5.48	5.34	5.21	5.08	4.94	4.81
17	6.79	6.66	6.54	6.41	6.29	6.16	6.03	5.91	5.78	5.66	5.53	5.41	5.28	5.15	5.03	4.90	4.78	4.65	4.53
18	6.41	6.29	6.17	6.05	5.94	5.82	5.70	5.58	5.46	5.34	5.22	5.11	4.99	4.87	4.75	4.63	4.51	4.39	4.27
19	6.07	5.96	5.85	5.74	5.62	5.51	5.40	5.29	5.17	5.06	4.95	4.84	4.72	4.61	4.50	4.39	4.27	4.16	4.05
20	5.77	5.66	5.56	5.45	5.34	5.24	5.13	5.02	4.92	4.81	4.70	4.59	4.49	4.38	4.27	4.17	4.06	3.95	3.85
21	5.50	5.39	5.29	5.19	5.09	4.99	4.88	4.78	4.68	4.58	4.48	4.38	4.27	4.17	4.07	3.97	3.87	3.77	3.66
22	5.25	5.15	5.05	4.95	4.86	4.76	4.66	4.57	4.47	4.37	4.27	4.18	4.08	3.98	3.89	3.79	3.69	3.59	3.50
23	5.02	4.92	4.83	4.74	4.65	4.55	4.46	4.37	4.27	4.18	4.09	4.00	3.90	3.81	3.72	3.62	3.53	3.44	3.34
24	4.81	4.72	4.63	4.54	4.45	4.36	4.27	4.18	4.10	4.01	3.92	3.83	3.74	3.65	3.56	3.47	3.38	3.29	3.21
25	4.62	4.53	4.44	4.36	4.27	4.19	4.10	4.02	3.93	3.85	3.76	3.68	3.59	3.50	3.42	3.33	3.25	3.16	3.08
26	4.44	4.36	4.27	4.19	4.11	4.03	3.95	3.86	3.78	3.70	3.62	3.53	3.45	3.37	3.29	3.21	3.12	3.04	2.96
27	4.27	4.19	4.12	4.04	3.96	3.88	3.80	3.72	3.64	3.56	3.48	3.40	3.32	3.25	3.17	3.09	3.01	2.93	2.85
28	4.12	4.05	3.97	3.89	3.82	3.74	3.66	3.59	3.51	3.43	3.36	3.28	3.21	3.13	3.05	2.98	2.90	2.82	2.75
29	3.98	3.91	3.83	3.76	3.68	3.61	3.54	3.46	3.39	3.32	3.24	3.17	3.09	3.02	2.95	2.87	2.80	2.73	2.65
30	3.85	3.78	3.70	3.63	3.56	3.49	3.42	3.35	3.28	3.21	3.13	3.06	2.99	2.92	2.85	2.78	2.71	2.64	2.56
31	3.72	3.65	3.58	3.52	3.45	3.38	3.31	3.24	3.17	3.10	3.03	2.96	2.90	2.83	2.76	2.69	2.62	2.55	2.48
32	3.61	3.54	3.47	3.41	3.34	3.27	3.21	3.14	3.07	3.01	2.94	2.87	2.80	2.74	2.67	2.60	2.54	2.47	2.40

rear →

Table 8.2: Development table in meters (for a tire circumference of 213.7 cm)

When choosing your cogs, a gear table is especially useful to avoid overlapping developments generated in the small and large chain rings. For flat races, many racers prefer straight blocks (12-13-14-15-16-17-18-19), which permit very fine adjustments to the development. The gear table is also useful to avoid exceeding the highest permissible development in the junior classes under 18 years old (not applicable in the U.S. anymore). To be absolutely certain, you can do a roll test to help you determine the exact wheel circumference, which you can then use in your own development calculations.

Here are the current (1996) German gear restrictions for the individual classes:

Males				Females			
Class	Age	Track	Road	Class	Age	Track	Road
Juniors	9/10	5.66 m (42x16)	5.66 m (42x16)	Juniors	9/10	5.66 m (42x16)	5.66 m (42x16)
Juniors	11/12	6.10 m (48x17)	5.66 m (42x16)	Juniors	11/12	6.10 m (48x17)	5.66 m (42x16)
Juniors	13/14	6.45 m (48x16)	6.10 m (42x15)	Juniors	13/14	6.45 m (48x16)	6.10 m (42x15)
Juniors	15/16	7.01 m (52x16)	7.01 m (52x16)	Juniors	15/16	7.01 m (52x16)	7.01 m (52x16)
Juniors	17/18	free	7.93 m (52x14)	Juniors	17/18	free	7.40 m (52x15)
Under 23	19-22	free	free				
Elite	23 +	free	free	Women	19 +	free	free
Seniors 1	30 +	free	free	Seniors 1	30 +	free	free
Seniors 2	41 +	free	free	Seniors 2	41 +	free	free
Seniors 3	51 +	free	free	Seniors 3	51 +	free	free

Table 8.3: Restrictions of transmissions and age-groups (Bund Deutscher Radfahrer, Union Cycliste International, 01.01.1998). The choice of transmission depends on the length of chain and not on the number of cogs. The transmissions mentioned above are proposals and have to be checked individually.

Top: Relaxed climbing position (brake hood grip): with a fluid style, Miguel Indurain leads a group up a mountain pass.
Bottom: In the drops: in an aerodynamic position with a high cadence, this rider focuses on the finish line.

Time trialing: you can win only with peak fitness and the perfect mental attitude, since time trialing - also called the „truth test" - is among the hardest disciplines in cycling.

The ability to time trial well is also useful during solo breakaways. Pacing yourself is crucial for time trialing. (Among the cycling pros, there are obvious time trial specialists.)
Here: D. Thurau

Attacking in the drops with complete concentration

Paris-Roubaix

8.8 Overcoming Obstacles

While riding on roads or paths, your safe progress may be impeded by many different obstacles, such as holes, cracks, bumps, branches, train tracks, or curbs. A little bit of practice will enable you to jump over most of these obstacles. First, place your crank arms in a horizontal position and grip the handlebars either on the brake hoods or in the drops. Next, rise out of the saddle and shift your weight lower (bend your elbows, flatten out your back); then, pull up on the handlebars and pedals, raising the bike up off the ground as evenly as possible by lifting up your upper body and pulling up your feet (bending your knees) without turning the handlebars. When landing, let your body give a little to cushion the impact.

To learn this technique, attempt first to lift only your front or only your back wheel. When you become comfortable with this skill, combine the two motions into a jump. If you want to jump over a high obstacle, ride fairly fast (30 km/hr) towards it to allow you to jump high enough and, above all, far enough. On the other hand, approach high curbs slowly, pulling up your front wheel first and following it with your back wheel. Cross train tracks perpendicularly if possible, but never at a sharp angle. If you must ride over rough ground, such as bumps in the road, shift your weight, as mentioned in the section on braking, to the back wheel by stretching out your arms and sliding off the back of the saddle.

8.9 Teaching Juniors Proper Technique

As already outlined in the previous sections, riding technique training should be an important part of the total training program for beginning cyclists and young junior riders. The younger (in training age as well as calendar age) the rider, the more riding technique he should be taught to prepare him for all potentially dangerous situations that may arise during training or racing. Technically difficult movements, such as jumping, physical contact while riding, or track standing, can easily be mastered by young athletes, who have great motor learning skills. Ten to fourteen year-olds are in their so-called "golden age of learning". The tour rider or the occasional cyclist should not be bashful about trying some of these exercises; he can improve his bike handling and traffic safety enormously by learning such skills.

Negotiating an obstacle course can be a lot of fun for Juniors 15-16 in particular, although they may get some bruises. Practice on a firm grass field first before switching to asphalt to make these exercises less painful. There are few restrictions to your imagination when designing these exercises; practice the exercises or tasks individually before combining them or timing yourself. You can design grass games such as "bicycle soccer" or "tag".

Even riding on the track is part of well-rounded training in cycling.

While riding in a group on a car-free road or a large parking lot (preferably when the store is closed), you can practice tapping your front wheel against the back wheel of the rider in front of you, side-to-side physical contact (bumping, leaning on each other), and pace lining. Individual exercises that you can practice as well are riding with no hands, jumping, and track standing. All of these exercises improve your bicycle handling skills: some hone specific techniques, while others contribute to an improvement in general handling abilities.

8.10 Safety in Traffic

How safe a rider is in traffic depends a lot on his technical riding skills. As long as you obey the traffic laws, ride defensively and with foresight, and have good bicycle handling skills, you will usually be safe. In many critical situations, avoiding the obstacle is much better than slamming on the brakes and risking a collision.

New studies have shown that a large percentage of bicycle accidents are caused by rider inattention or poor road conditions (holes, etc.). Cyclists should always ride with watchful eyes and a clear head and react defensively by perceiving all dangerous traffic situations as personal threats. Wearing a hard-shell helmet is an obvious requirement for which there are no convincing arguments to the contrary. Older cyclists who have ridden many years without a helmet may understandably have difficulty getting used to wearing one regularly now. However, most juniors habitually wear helmets not only in races, but also during training rides. The new models are technologically more advanced and look and fit much better, so that arguments against wearing helmets are no longer valid.

Riding Alone

When riding alone, always leave a safe distance of one-half to one meter between you and the edge of the road, so that you have room to swerve over. Pay attention not only to oncoming traffic, but also to traffic behind you by occasionally glancing over your shoulder. If you are riding on a street that is so narrow that a passing car would endanger you and oncoming traffic, ride closer to the center of the lane to discourage drivers from trying to pass when cars are approaching from the opposing direction. This behavior is often life-saving in city traffic.

Although bicycle paths must be used by law, you should decide whether using the bike path in city traffic is worth the additional risk.

Using a bicycle path at speeds around 20 km/hr is no problem; however, riding faster on such a path may pose serious risks. These paths are dangerous not in and of themselves, but because of the poor foresight and planning of traffic engineers. As seen in several cities, the bicycle path problem can be resolved in the cyclists' favor, but this solution would without a doubt affect automobile traffic. Using bicycle paths in the countryside normally poses no problems.

Training in a Group

Most fundamentals of training alone are also applicable to group training. It is important for a group to form a compact structure, rather than expanding to cover an area five meters wide and one hundred meters long. On heavily traveled streets, ride in single file. On quieter streets, two abreast is the norm for training rides. When riding two abreast, cyclists pair up and ride together until they finish their turn at the front. After several harder pedal strokes (to make sure they are clear of the wheel behind them), the rider on the left drifts back on the left side, while the one on the right falls back on the right side. Once they reach the end, they get back into the double pace line and follow the rider ahead of them until they reach the front again. Avoid surging at the front and try to maintain the previous speed to keep the pace as even as possible. "Surging", which prevents a steady, safe pace, is one of the most common mistakes that beginners make when riding in a group.

Do not ride directly behind the back wheel of the rider in front of you, but rather off to the side a bit to avoid hitting his wheel when the pace changes and to enable you to even out speed variations without braking. Do not stare at the back wheel in front of you, but rather look forward at the shoulder-level of those in front of you. If you want to get out of the saddle while riding in a group, for example during a climb, do so smoothly and carefully to avoid endangering those behind you by suddenly throwing back your bike. Warn others about obstacles in time (by calling out or pointing) and try to steer the group around them.

During a Race
During a race, you should ride in the top third of the pack to avoid the crashes that usually occur in the middle or at the end of the field. If you are not confident about your riding skills, ride on the outside of the pack, where you have more room to move than in the crowded middle. Only ride close enough to the edge of the street or the curb so that you still have a little room for emergency situations. As already mentioned, fast turns are usually safer on the inside of the field. Even when cornering, you should not ride directly behind, but rather slightly off to the side of, the wheel of the rider in front of you. In potentially dangerous situations, you should always have one finger on the brake. Sudden pile-ups usually happen when the pace is very slow and riders lose concentration.

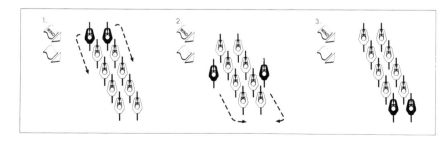

Figure 8.2: The double pace line

9 Tactics

9.1 Drafting and Pace Lining

Drafting

Drafting is one of the most fundamental skills in cycling and must, therefore, be mastered, since only the energy saved while drafting permits high average speeds during long tours and races. A rider's work load reduction in the draft is between 20 and 40%, depending on many factors, such as speed, wind conditions, and the size of the riders.

Wind resistance increases with the square of the speed; this formula means that as speed increases, wind resistance rises significantly faster than the speed itself. An American study at the University of Florida showed that the oxygen consumption, and therefore the stress on the circulatory system, of a rider drafting at a speed of about 30 km/hr is approximately 18% lower than that of the rider exposed to the wind. At a speed of 40 km/hr, oxygen consumption is already 27% less than it is in the wind; in a pack, for example in a race, the intensity may even be 39% less than it is at the front of the peleton. Drafting behind a truck or tractor increases this value to up to a maximum of 60%. Skilled use of the draft can save a lot of energy. Despite this fact, you still should not shun all work, since this type of riding goes against the unwritten rule that every cyclist has a "duty" to do his share of the work at the front.

When riding in a group or peleton, paying attention to several rules will save you much strength without causing you to be labeled a "wheel sucker". Wheel suckers are those riders who do little or no work during the race, but beat the stronger riders in the final sprint or when sprinting for primes. This phenomenon explains the occasionally very impressive results of weaker riders who have good sprints.

The goal of drafting is to "stick" as closely as possible, but as safely as necessary, to the back wheel of the rider in front of you. During even-paced rides and flaw-lessly-executed group rides, such as team time trials, gaps of only a few centimeters are the norm. In training groups or during races, you should draft, as already mentioned, off to the side with a 20 to 50 cm gap; the more insecure you are, the more space you should leave between you and the riders in front of

Drafting

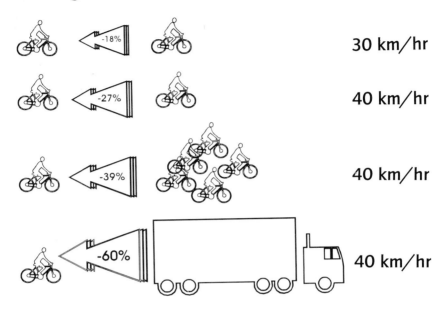

30 km/hr

40 km/hr

40 km/hr

40 km/hr

Figure 9.1: Reduction in oxygen consumption in the draft at different speeds

and beside you. By drafting off to the side, you avoid running into the wheel in front of you, get a better view of the road, and do not have to brake with every small change in pace, but rather only have to reduce the pressure on your pedals a bit.

When finishing a pull at the front of an echelon, let yourself drop back on the side into the wind; this side may be difficult to ascertain if the wind is weak or undetectable. If there is little wind, the riders must first find the best draft, so until the group has become organized, leave larger gaps. Clear hand signals and commands are very useful. Be especially careful when riding with beginners, since they are not used to pace lining and may suddenly swerve over when they are finished pulling; under these circumstances, it is not uncommon for a whole group to crash.

The Gutter

Guttering is a phenomenon feared by tour riders as well as racers that occurs whenever a strong wind hits a pack or group of riders at an angle or from the side. The gutter is on the side of the street opposite the wind direction. Several riders will take turns drafting by forming an echelon in one lane or across the whole street (in races), while the left-over riders line up in the gutter like beads on a string. These riders get only a minimal draft from the rider in front of them, so that they must work very hard and often pay the price by getting dropped.

To avoid becoming a victim of the gutter, you must ride in the front half of the field, since the riders in the middle or at the end of the peleton have no chance of catching the first echelon, unless they form their own echelon. If you are caught in the gutter, you *Alex Zuelle, surrounded by teammates* should form another echelon or several echelons as soon as possible to try to keep up with the front group. It is often difficult, however, to organize this group of riders into a rotation, because many riders are already riding at their physical limits and may not be able to take their turn at the front. The near-exhaustion of these riders in the gutter greatly increases the risk of accidents; this crashing risk is another good reason never to ride at the back of a pack.

Echelons and gutter-riding are especially common in the windy spring classics. The wind disperses the sometimes very large starting fields so much that it is not uncommon for only a few riders to finish the race.

Echelon/Pace-Line

Small groups of riders generally adopt a drafting formation in which riders take turns at the front. Riders who have just finished their turn at the front drop back diagonally to the last position, drafting off the riders in front of them in the process. The higher the speed and the more riders there are in the group, the shorter the individual pulls. The transitions to the rotating echelon or rotating pace line are smooth.

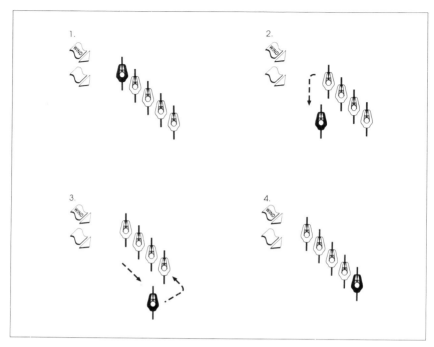

Figure 9.2: The echelon

Now the rotation of a 3 to 6 rider group will be described: if there is a cross-wind, the riders line up in a diagonal with their shoulders even with the hips of the rider in front of them. The more head-on the wind is, the less the wheels of the riders overlap and the longer the pace line becomes. The front rider maintains the same speed until he is relieved by the rider behind him.

When the rider in front has finished his turn, he pulls off into the wind, lets himself drop back slowly behind the other riders, taking care not to lose too much speed, and then gets behind the last rider by pedaling a little harder on the wind-protected side. The pulls at the front are between 30 seconds and several minutes long. To prevent shattering the group apart, stronger athletes should not pull faster, but rather longer, than weaker riders. A steady pace is essential for the effective functioning of a group, since even a single rider who does not want to or cannot do his share will disturb the group, intentionally or because of his weakness, thereby precluding the smooth collaboration and ultimate success of the group.

During a race, the riders must put aside their own self interests and devote all their energy to serving the group. Even tour riders can derive more pleasure from a training ride or a tour in a well-functioning group.

Riders who do not wish to or cannot do any work allow a gap to open up for the rider who has just finished his pull at the front. All team time trials use either the echelon or the rotating pace line.

The technique of the **double pace** line was already discussed in chapter 8.10. The double pace line is the recommended organization for larger training groups.

The Rotating Echelon

The rotating echelon is common in the Belgian Spring Classics, often during adverse weather conditions. A larger group of riders forms a rotating echelon when they are either in a breakaway or in the gutter and wish to catch back up to the field or lead group. Tour riders rarely use this formation.

A rotation needs at least five riders to function somewhat smoothly. The rotation is characterized by short pulls and high speeds, since each pull is only as long as it takes for the second position rider to pass the one in front of him. This formation is composed of two rows that are riding at different speeds: as the row of riders that is exposed to the wind drops back one by one, it provides a draft for the riders in the faster row. Once you approach the lead, ride past the rider pulling off in front of you, move into the wind out of the faster row, let yourself drop back into the slower row, and finally return to the faster row for another rotation. When you drop back, immediately seek the draft of the rider beginning to drop back in front of you; the key to an efficient rotation is equally small distances between the riders, since gaps and pace changes destroy the rhythm of a rotation.

The riders trace the path of an ellipse as they move through the rotating echelon, and depending on the wind direction and strength, the rotation may be drawn out in length or spread out over the entire width of the road. Practice the formation of a rotating echelon or pace line during training until you achieve perfection.

In order for a rotation to function properly, it must be composed of experienced riders, who have mastered the technique of a rotation. During a race, inexperienced riders are often unable to bridge a gap to a relatively slow-moving pack due to their inability to form a functioning pace line or rotation. Even in breakaways containing highly conditioned athletes, various reasons may occasionally prevent

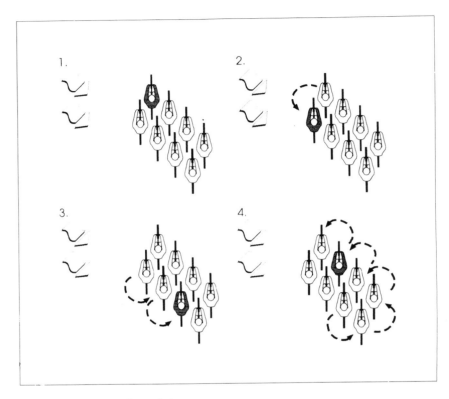

Figure 9.3: The rotating echelon

the establishment of a functioning formation (lack of skill, personal and team interests, low levels of fitness). There are several special situations that can occur during a race in connection with a rotating formation:

The Gatekeeper

The gatekeeper is a rider drafting at the end of an echelon or a rotation who opens up a gap for riders dropping back from the lead, giving them reentry to the draft formation. The task of the gatekeeper is to protect the echelon in front of him. If no one would assume this role, the riders in the gutter behind the echelon could easily enter the formation and displace riders from the group into the gutter or destroy the smooth functioning of the formation. The gatekeeper is a teammate or a rider accepted by the group.

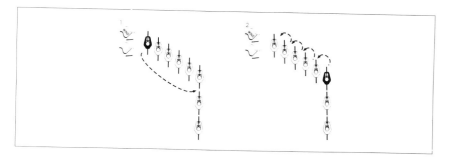

Figure 9.4: The gatekeeper allows riders dropping back after their turn at the front to reenter the draft formation.

Pulling off on the Side Opposite the Wind

If there is no gatekeeper, you can employ another, albeit rarely-used, technique: instead of pulling off into the wind, do so opposite the wind and drift towards the back in front of the echelon. Once you arrive in the gutter, your spot in the echelon is secure, since riders trying to draft here cannot defend their position against a rider drifting back towards them and must make room for you. Sometimes, rather than being in the echelon, you are struggling in the gutter and would like to have a place in the echelon. There are only two ways to fulfill your wish: either initiate a new echelon or try to force your way into the echelon by taking advantage of a rider's inattention.

Dropping Wheel Suckers

In most groups, there are several riders who, after a while, for various reasons, do not wish to or cannot work any longer. Often, the group attempts to drop these riders, who draft at the very back, by forcing them into the gutter and increasing the pace a bit, so that they either get dropped or agree to work.

Group Disruptions

If you have a teammate up the road, you can disrupt the group's organization. You may slow down the pace when you take a pull, pull off to the wrong side, ride in the gutter when you are in front, or open up gaps in the pace line. After a while, the other riders will notice such tactics and will no longer let you into the echelon.

9.2 Before the Race

During the week before a race, you should attempt to pre-ride the race course and memorize the most important sections. You should pay attention to cross-wind stretches (guttering), in which echelons will probably form, or sections that are ideal for launching attacks and consider this information when planning race strategy. If you are unable to see the course in person, use a map and a course profile to memorize the terrain.

Shortly before the race, look at the rider roster to get an overview of the participants and memorize the race numbers of the strong riders, on whom you might base part of your strategy. After a thorough warm-up (30-40 min), which should be longer the shorter the race is, and the other pre-race preparations (mental preparation, stretching, putting oil on your legs, eating and drinking) calmly claim your spot on the starting line as close to the front as possible; in the C class, lining up near the front often means being at the starting line 15 minutes before the beginning of the race. Pass the time you spend waiting with a few stretching exercises.

9.3 The Unfolding of the Race

Particularly races on short circuits, begin at high speeds, which causes problems for quite a few riders. Those not thoroughly warmed-up do not stand a chance. Long road races are usually relatively calm in the beginning; you can use this time to warm up by pedaling at a high cadence. The individual tactical race situations will be discussed in detail later; the advice given is designed to help less experienced riders learn basic strategies. Knowing tactical skills and tricks is not a guarantee that you will be able to apply them in practice. This knowledge is best combined with tactical talent or an instinct for the right opportunity, both of which are difficult to convey to others.

Figure 9.5: Typical rider formation at medium speeds: at high speeds the riders are single file like beads on a string.

9.4 Pack Riding

The race is decided at the front of the field and in the breakaway groups. Therefore, you should stay in the top third of the pack, where you can actively participate in the outcome of the race. In the last third of the pack, the pace changes are more pronounced (braking, sprinting out of turns), the danger of crashing is elevated due to the carelessness of tired riders, and the chance of getting dropped or guttered is much greater.

In hilly terrain, the leaders set the pace and string out the field; the first riders up the mountain can calmly concentrate on the descent, while the last ones often have to risk everything to try to keep up. Poor climbers should try to get as close to the front as possible before the ascent begins; this provides them with an opportunity to set the pace up the climb, but also leaves room to drift back if necessary while still maintaining a good chance of arriving at the top with the main pack. If you are able to climb a hill at the front of the pack or a group of riders, your confidence grows and you feel strong, since you set the pace. Hills are tactically very important sections of races, since breakaway groups or individual riders can often get away on ascents. As a rule, attacks are initiated on hills, no matter how short, since drafting plays a smaller roll here than on the flats.

9.5 The Breakaway or Solo Attack

While winning breakaways are rare in races for riders under 16 years old and the outcome is often decided by field sprints, breakaways (group and individual) are much more common in races for juniors 17-18, amateurs, and women. Young riders should be taught that it takes more skill to place in a race by breaking away than by winning the final sprint.

The Attack
The purpose of an attack or breakaway attempt is to separate yourself from your opponents (peleton or small group) to win a prime, bridge up to another breakaway, or place in or win the race. There are many reasons why riders attack. Many breakaway attempts are, however, initiated in unfavorable locations or at the wrong time, so that they basically just amount to a waste of energy. This statement does in no way mean that only the last decisive attack is wise, since many of the other attacks during the course of the race could have been successful. In the end,

the principle still holds that he who risks nothing also stands to gain nothing. Attempting to break away in unfavorable locations only to please your coach, assistant, or parents, is not wise and wastes precious energy.

When Should You Attack?
There is no definitive answer to this question, since there are many times at which a breakaway attempt could succeed. The most promising times are the following:

- after an unsuccessful attack, as soon as the riders have been caught,
- when the pace is slow and riders are not concentrating,
- when you feel good,
- when opponents look tired or distracted.

An old rule also states, however, that you should attack when you yourself are suffering and in pain, since your opponents are also struggling and may not want to or be able to react to your attack. There are usually many attacks during a race, only one of which, however, leads to victory.

Where Is the Best Place for an Attack?
The choice of location depends on the type of rider: a climber will always attack on a steep hill, while a good descender will attack on a descent or in the last few meters before the top of a climb, and a good time trialist will try to ride away on a flat section. It is important to have high performance expectations for the special attack situation and to await the proper time. Tactically favorable places are shortly before a turn, after a turn, in a cross-wind section (guttering), in technically difficult sections (turns, poor road conditions), and, as already mentioned, on a hill or during a descent. Attacks that occur following crashes or mechanicals or in the feed zone are unsportsmanlike and implicitly forbidden.

How Should You Attack?
The attack should be a surprise to your opponents. Therefore, it would not be wise to attack from the front of a field or group of riders, since the surprise effect is practically zero. Only a very strong rider can succeed by attacking from the front, and only if he does so on a hill. Sometimes, however, you can slowly roll off the front, and when there are several meters between yourself and the pack, you can start riding hard.

In a group of riders off the front, the last position is the best from which to attack; in a pack of riders, the attack should be initiated on the outside from a position somewhere in the top third. When trying to pull away from a group of riders, let yourself drift back a bit, choose the appropriate gear, and attack, moving toward the side opposite the wind direction (when cross-winds are a factor) to provide your pursuers with as little a draft as possible. By surprising the other riders and attacking at high speed, you should be able to quickly create a 20 to 50 m gap that you now have to widen. The attack itself must be explosive and you must give it "everything that you have"; only after the first 500-1,000 m, which you should ride at top speed in a high gear, should you look back and decide whether to continue or to let the pack catch you again.

The first phase of a breakaway attempt is characterized by a very high heart rate and high oxygen uptake; part of the energy is provided by the anaerobic pathway, which generates lactic acid and leads to acidification of the musculature. It is important not to ride too fast and to become too anaerobic, since this could prevent you from successfully continuing. Only if you have experimented with this type of riding during training and know how hard you can push your legs or, better yet, what heart rate you can maintain for a certain amount of time, can you be sure that a lactic acid build-up won't impede further progress.

The Solo Breakaway

Probably the most rewarding experience a cyclist can have is to cross the finish line first after a short or long solo breakaway; however, this is also one of the hardest victories a cyclist can accomplish. Optimally, one should ride at a constant effort, not unlike that required during a time trial. While maintaining a high cadence in a large gear and staying as aerodynamic as possible, ride at 85-95% of your maximum heart rate, focusing on the finish line or prime.

There are few tactical considerations in this situation; important is only the careful rationing of energy to avoid getting caught shortly before the finish. Poor sprinters, in particular, attempt solo breakaways shortly before the end of a race.

The Breakaway

A breakaway consists of at least two riders working more or less together to reach the finish line. More or less means that often not all the riders in the group participate, drafting, instead, due to team tactics or personal reasons. The previously discussed draft formations are useful in this situation. When more experienced riders organize the breakaway and give brief commands to get the echelon or pace line rolling, the chance for a successful breakaway is increased. Often riders in a breakaway may have conflicting intentions or goals, usually condemning the group to failure. If a breakaway is being formed and you are not sure whether to make the effort to join the group, you should pay attention to its composition. Are all of the important teams, and from them the strongest riders, represented? Is the successful rider X who can sense the right breakaway present? If the answers to these questions are yes, you should attempt to reach the group.

9.6 The Finish of the Race

The outcome of a race is almost always determined by a sprint at the end; the only exception is when a single rider approaches the finish. Even if only two riders sprint for the win or for a place, a lot of tactical minutia are important, since without tactics only a physically completely superior rider can win. The pack sprint, which will be elaborated on next, is even more difficult from a tactical standpoint.

During a sprint, you have to make tactical decisions so quickly that there is little time to think. Only the experienced athlete can use a number of different tactics to his advantage, enabling him to perform well even when fitness levels are less than optimal. Tactical training is therefore very important for beginners, since it reduces the advantage that experienced racers would otherwise have over them in this regard.

There are two types of sprinters: the sprinter that needs a relatively long distance (500 m) to achieve top speed and the rider who can reach his top speed in a short distance (100-200 m). Riders who can reach top speed quickly can, for example, win a sprint after being in fifth position coming around the final turn before the finish. Between these two extremes are many intermediate sprinter types.

Riders who claim they cannot sprint mostly belong to the category of cyclists who need a long time to reach their top speed. Their individual top speed is usually also lower than that of good sprinters. For these riders, developing a better sprint involves improving their tactical skills, in addition to more speed, speed-strength, and strength-endurance training.

The Two-man Sprint

If two riders have enough of a lead, they often play tactical games, in which they ride very slowly and watch each other. The sprinter who needs a long time to achieve top speed will try to keep the pace high and begin his sprint early, while the quick sprinter waits as long as possible and then passes the other rider in the last few meters. In general, the rear position is the most favorable, since it enables you to react to your opponent's actions. You should try to stick to your opponent's back wheel, so that you can carry out your own tactics and not depend on your opponent's tactical mistakes.

The sprint situation is tactically more interesting when there is wind. Normally, both riders will then ride in the gutter; the rear one must ride into the wind to come around the rider in front of him. If you initiate the sprint from the rear position, you should move over into the gutter again as quickly as possible to give your opponent as little of a draft as possible. However, even if you initiate the sprint from the front, you still must ride in the gutter at the edge of the road.

In a full-fledged sprint, the rider in front can allow a teammate behind him to pass in the draft. By moving over a bit towards the middle of the street, he can

Figure 9.6: Two-man sprint: 1. The rider in the back remains in the draft as long as possible and then sprints past the other rider. 2. The rider in back lets a gap "open up", attacks suddenly, and passes the leader with such high speed that he cannot catch up. 3. The gate opening technique during a sprint.

open up a temporary gate so that the rider behind him can pass. If another rider tries to squeeze by as well, the rider closes the gate again by moving back to the edge of the street or the curb, forcing his opponents to soft-pedal but not endangering them. This brief action is generally enough to save first place, since other riders must now attempt to pass into the wind shortly before a rapidly-approaching finish line.

The Group Sprint (three or more riders)

Most of the tactics just discussed also apply to a group sprint. Usually, intermediate race sprints will identify the strongest sprinter in the group. If you are not the strongest sprinter, you should try to follow the best sprinter's back wheel in the last kilometers and to jump when he jumps; even if you do not stand a chance of passing him, you can still try to stay in his draft to place well. Poor sprinters usually try to breakaway in the last few kilometers; it is not too rare for such attempts to succeed when others are not paying attention. The attack should be initiated suddenly from the back of the pack to surprise the other riders.

If the sprint has not yet begun (600-200 m before the finish line), even a weak sprinter can use the surprise effect to get such a large gap that he may be able to hang onto first place. If a poor sprinter cannot be successful with this tactic, he should at least begin the sprint near the front, from where he can achieve better results than if he were to start the sprint in last place.

When sprinting from the middle of the pack, watch out that you do not get boxed in so that you cannot use your full sprint. The ideal positions for a sprint are second through fourth, since you will rarely get boxed in there. Once you decide on your strategy (for example, attacking from the back of the group), invest all your energy into it, rather than making a half-hearted attempt. Such commitment requires the courage to bet everything on one attempt and risk coming in dead last. The absolute willpower to carry out such an all-out effort usually allows you to mobilize your last energy reserves and helps you succeed (chapter 7, "Psychology: Winning Occurs in Your Head)". If you hesitate, you have generally already lost.

The Field Sprint

A field sprint is an impressive, difficult to predict spectacle, in which crashes frequently occur. Since the danger of getting boxed in is very great in a pack sprint, you must be in the front of the field (second row) for the last kilometers.

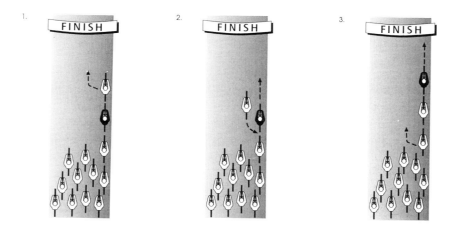

Figure 9.7: In the final sprint, a rider opens the "gate" and then quickly shuts it again immediately behind his teammate by riding over to the right side of the road; the other riders in the field must take the long way around (into the wind) to pass both riders.

Only from such a position can you react to sudden attacks and surges and choose the right back wheel for the final sprint. The same rules as for the two-man sprint apply here (opening and closing the gate; guttering). Sprinters with strong teams to back them up are clearly at an advantage, since it is almost impossible to penetrate the formation of a team leading out their sprinter for the victory. An unattached rider should ride close to the back wheel of a well-positioned sprinter. When the outcome of a race will be decided by a field sprint, all sprinters congregate at the front of the field. An outsider with a poor sprint has a chance to ruin the sprinters' plans with a well-timed attack. If no team is leading out their sprinter, the pace is usually not high enough to make a breakaway attempt impossible. The sprinters at the front of the field may hesitate to counter-attack, because they do not wish to spoil their chance in the final sprint.

It is very useful to have a teammate lead you out in the gutter and then open up a gap to let you through. You must ride a straight line during all sprints to avoid endangering other riders. Riding zigzags is both unsportsmanlike as well as dangerous. Riders often make the mistake of stopping their sprint several meters before the finish line, which not infrequently results in the loss of a place or the victory.

Bike Throw

In a field sprint, often several riders are side-by-side immediately before the finish line, necessitating a bike throw. To explosively push your bicycle forwards, stretch out your arms and legs and simultaneously slide back in your saddle. The winner in a cycling race is he whose front wheel crosses the finish line first in an upright position. Proper timing is important for the bike throw, since initiating it too late or too early will cause you to lose valuable centimeters and possibly the victory. You should practice throwing your bike during training rides.

9.7 Team Tactics

As already mentioned, cycling is not only a classical individual sport, but also involves team tactics. In professional cycling, this team collaboration is so pronounced that riders can hardly win without the support of their team. The individual top riders need the support of their team colleagues for a sprint, a break-away attempt on a hill, or just to stay in the lead group. Even in amateur men's and women's racing, stronger teams usually do well, not only in the German Bundesliga, but also in the C-class and even in junior 17-18 and 15-16 races. The drawback of having extremely strong teams is that they can completely dominate the smaller races, winning a majority of the primes and prize money, and racing may become boring for others. Smaller teams or unattached individuals have only minimal chances of placing well. The team should discuss their strategy before the race, with the understanding that this plan may have to be modified under certain circumstances. It is often unwise to designate a rider before the race for whom all others must work, since he may have a bad day. Instead, you should decide whom to work for during the course of the race.

If several riders from a team are in a breakaway, their teammates in the pack must either try to slow down the field by curbing the pace at the front (before turns, for example), or, what is usually more effective, thwart the breakaway attempts of others. To thwart breakaway attempts, immediately follow riders' attacks, but do not work with them once you get in their draft until they either reach the leading breakaway or get "swallowed up" again into the pack. Use this team strategy until the breakaway group with one or more teammates has built up an insurmountable lead. If, however, you were able to catch up to your teammates in the breakaway by drafting off of an opponent, you may then launch your own attack. The important thing is that riders on the same team do not attack during a teammate's breakaway attempt.

To give their designated sprinter the best prospects, the team should keep the pace in the last few kilometer so high that breakaway attempts become impossible. During the last few meters, they can use the already mentioned "gate method" to make it difficult for other riders to pass their sprinter. If two or even three riders from the same team are in a breakaway group, they should take turns attacking in the last few kilometers until finally one of them can get away alone.

9.8 The Tactics of Different Types of Races

Criteriums
Criteriums usually have smaller field sizes than road races. In Germany, there are several point laps scattered throughout the race with 5, 3, 2, and 1 points, and these points are added to the double-value ones for the finishing sprint. (In the U.S., similar points races exist (usually on the track), but in typical criteriums, placing is determined only by the final sprint.) The frequent point laps and intermediately-placed primes keep the pace of the criterium very high. Riding near the front of the field may help you maintain an overview of the race, which can sometimes be fairly confusing. In small packs, you can rest for a few laps in the middle or at the back of the field, since you can work your way back to the front again within a lap. Tactically inexperienced riders should learn from the sprinters or criterium specialists. Poor sprinters who cannot be competitive in the fast sprints should attack after a prime or a point lap and try to stay in front for several laps, since this strategy is the only way that they can get points. Team strategy is most difficult in criteriums. Only teams that have a good perspective on the whole race (ideally with the help of an assistant who writes down the points) can place several riders near the front. The assistant calls out strategic advice, since only he knows the exact point totals of all riders.

Circuit Races

The tactical situation for circuit races, especially on short courses, is similar to that for criteriums. Race-determining breakaways rarely occur at the beginning of the race; usually decisive moves do not occur until the middle or even the last few laps of the race. The success of a breakaway group depends heavily on the number of riders, since experience has shown again and again that a group that is too large (usually over eight) rarely has a chance to make it to the finish line due to the many and varied interests of its members. In large groups, the number of riders who do not work increases; riders can hide in the back of the group and in this way prevent smooth collaboration. Groups of three to six riders are ideal. In this type of racing as well, attacks after competitive prime laps have a high success rate.

Road Races

In general, road races have large to extremely large field sizes. Therefore, you should ride near the front in strategically promising locations (cross-wind sections, hills) to avoid getting dropped if the field gets torn apart. The main pack usually gets divided into many smaller segments; larger groups still have a chance to catch the leaders. The tactics of the strongest teams greatly influence high caliber road races. The information mentioned above about guttering and draft formation is especially pertinent to road racing.

Individual Time Trials

There are very few tactical rules for individual time trialing. The most important one is to pace yourself so that you do not experience a sudden performance decline. You should ride with a high pedal cadence (+/- 100 revolutions per minute) in large or very large gears; shift infrequently to avoid disrupting your rhythm. Make use of every draft (walls, bushes, trees, etc.), and take the ideal line in the turns. Time trial training is critical for good time trial performance, since only by knowing your individual endurance performance limits, can you ride at the highest possible pace that you can maintain for a given distance without exceeding your limits and causing a collapse in performance. Mental pre-race preparation is important for time trialing (see chapter 7). The goal is to create a performance enhancing, positive, even slightly aggressive, but nevertheless relaxed attitude. Even during the race, the cyclist must stay mentally and physically (upper body) relaxed.

Team Time Trials

Most of the general information pertaining to time trials was already discussed in the section on individual time trials. However, several additional strategic aspects apply uniquely to team time trials. If possible, the team should be composed of equally strong riders that are also approximately the same physical size. If there are large size differences, a smaller rider should always ride behind a slightly larger athlete. The rotation (see section on draft formations) must be practiced to perfection during training, and the rider order should always be the same in both practice and actual competition.

Riders should take pulls of 20 to 30 seconds, after which they pull off and draft off of their teammates while letting themselves drop to the back. When you reach the front, do not briskly increase the pace, since otherwise the rider who just finished working will have problems getting into the draft again. Maintaining a steady pace is critical for success, since pace fluctuations hurt the weakest rider on the team and may even cause him to get dropped. Although you may still do well with only three riders, you should nevertheless attempt to finish the race with a complete team. During training, a team must test and determine exactly the maximum pace that it can maintain, so that it can ride precisely at this pace when racing.

Index of Abbreviations

ADP	adenosine diphosphate
ATP	adenosine triphosphate
BDR	Bund Deutscher Radfahrer (German cycling federation)
BE	basic endurance
BTR	bicycle tour rider
Ca	calcium
CNS	central nervous system
CO	compensatory training
CP	competition period
CSE	competition-specific endurance
EGG	electrocardiogram
Fe	iron
HMV	heart minute-volume
K	potassium
kcal	kilocalorie
Mg	magnesium
MHR	maximum heart rate
mmol/L	chemical unit of concentration
MTB	mountain bike
Na	sodium
PC	personal computer
PNS	peripheral nervous system
PP	preparation period
Rev	revolutions (pedal cadence)
Se	selenium
SE	strength-endurance training
SS	speed-strength training
ST	speed training
tB	back chain ring teeth number
tF	front chain ring teeth number
TP	transition period
UV	ultraviolet
VO_2 max	maximum oxygen uptake
Zn	zinc

Glossary

adaptation: the body's adjustment to training stress

aerobic metabolism: energy-liberating process that can only occur in the presence of oxygen

anaerobic metabolism: energy-liberating process that does not require oxygen

citric acid cycle: the metabolic enzyme system found in mitochondria

cog: a single gear on the back wheel

complex sugar: a carbohydrate formed by many simple sugars (such as glucose); must first be cleaved before being absorbed in the intestines

concentric: work in which muscles shorten against the load placed on them; contraction (dynamic)

dehydration: loss of body water, for example during cycling, which leads to a drop in performance

dynamic: dynamic muscle work moves joints to produce physical work (opposite: static)

eccentric: pliant (yielding) muscle work; lengthening (always dynamic)

enzyme: protein that increases the rate of metabolic reactions; there are many different types

glycogen: carbohydrate storage form in the body (complex sugar; animal starch)

gutter: forms primarily during races on the side of the road opposite the wind direction; the riders who are stacked behind each other get less of a draft

heart rate: highest possible heart rate during maximal exertion

intensity: measure of training stress; controlled by heart rate or body feeling

lactic acid: the acid of milk sugar; metabolic product of anaerobic, lactic acid-producing energy liberation; accumulates during high levels of exertion and forces exercise cessation

lactic acid tolerance: the ability to tolerate high concentrations of lactic acid (pain) in the bloodstream

macrocycle: cycle within the periodization of 4 to 8 weeks duration maximum

maximum oxygen uptake: the body's highest possible oxygen uptake during maximal exertion

metabolism: all the chemical reactions that the substances and nutrients in the body go through

mileage: the training mileage is measured by the number of kilometers ridden or the time spent training

microcycle: a week-long training plan

micro-trauma: miniscule injury

mitochondria: powerhouse of the cell

mobilization: heightening the excitement level (psychologically)

muscle contraction: the shortening of a muscle

muscular imbalance: strength discrepancy between two muscles or muscle groups, i.e. between stomach and back musculature

peleton: a field of riders

periodization: division of the training year into several sections that foster the development and/or maintenance of certain conditioned abilities

preventative: prophylactic, usually health-related prophylactic measures

regeneration: recovery; repairing the body; important for the training process

rehabilitative: repairing the body, usually following a sickness or injury

relaxation: resting

repeat: a number used during interval and strength training that represents the number of times an exercise is performed per set

resting pulse: lowest pulse (heart rate) when completely relaxed; usually measured in the mornings

rotating echelon: a draft formation, adopted mainly during races, in which all riders except the leader are protected from the wind

set: a number used during interval and strength training for specifying the amount of training; a set is composed of a number of repeats

simple sugars: building blocks of the complex carbohydrates; can be absorbed from the small intestine without further digestive processes

spinning: the smooth, fluid pedaling technique

sport-induced damage: damage to a structure caused by repetitively occuring, excessively high stress

sports injury: an injury caused by a sudden force

static: without externally visible movement; the joint angles do not change

steady state: state of balance

visualization: part of a mental training program in which a movement procedure is imagined

Index

Literary References

Anderson, K.: *Cycling for Women*, Emmaus 1989.

Appel, H.-J.; Stang-Voss, C.: *Funktionelle Anatomie*. Berlin 1991.

Baecker, K.: *Nutrition for Cyclist*. Emmaus 1991.

Baumann, S.: *Psychologie im Sport*. Aachen 1993.

Bohlmann, J.T.: „Injuries in Competitive Cycling". in: *The Physician and Sportsmedicine* 1981.

Breuer-Schüder, R.: *Mehr Wissen Mehr Leisten*. Bruchhausen-Vilsen 1986.

Burke, E.R.: *Medical and Scientific Aspects Of Cycling*. Champaign 1988.

Edwards, S.: *Leitfaden zur Trainingskontrolle*. Aachen 1993.

Ericson, M. et all.: „Power Output and Work in Different Muscle Group during Ergometer Cycling". in: *Eur. J. appl. Physiol*. 55 (1986), S. 229-235.

Geis, K.R.; Hamm, M.: *Handbuch Sportler Ernährung*. Hamburg 1990.

Harre, D.: *Trainingslehre*. Berlin 1985.

Haushalter, G.: *Cyclisme*. Paris 1990.

Hull, M.L.: „Measurement of Pedal Loading in Bicycling". in: *Journal of Biomechanics*, 14 ∕12), 834-856.

Jacobsen, G.: *Progressive Relaxation*. Chicago 1938.

Judet, H.: *Médicine du cyclisme*. Mason 1983.

Jung, K.: *Sport und Ernährung*. Aachen 1984.

Konopka, P.: *Radsport*. München 1988.

Kuipers, H.: *Wielrennen*. Haarlem 1989.

La Fortuna, M.: *Biomechanical Investigation of Pedalling Techniques of Elite and Recreational Cyclists*. Canberra 1989.

Link, K.: *Radrennsport*. Böblingen 1986.

Mac Callum, P.: *Spinning*. Cincinnati 1993.

Marées, de H.: *Sportphysiologie*. Köln 1989.

Markworth, P.: *Sportmedizin*. Hamburg 1986.

Matheny, F.: *Beginning Bicycle Racing*. Brattleboro 1988.

Naltnikowa, M.J.: *Die spezielle Ausdauer des Sportlers*. Berlin 1976.

Neumann, G.: *Alles unter Kontrolle; Ausdauertraining*. Aachen 1993.

Nöcker,J.: *Die Ernährung des Sportlers*. Schorndorf 1987.

Piednoir, F: *La bicyclette, cyclisme et cyclotourisme*. Paris 1990.

Radcliffe, J.C.: *Sprungkrafttraining*. Aachen 1991.

Rost, R.: *Sport- und Bewegungstherapie bei inneren Krankheiten*. Köln 1991.

Schmidt, A.: „Stretching für Radfahrer" in *Radfahren extra* (2) Bielefeld. 1993.

Schulte, K.-L. (Hrsg.): *Kardiales Risiko beim Sport*. Darmstadt 1991.

Sleamaker, R.: *Systematisches Leistungstraining*. Aachen 1991.

Sloane, E.: *Complete Book of Cycling*. New York 1988.

Smolik, H.C.: *Rund ums Rennrad*. München 1990.

Tobias, M.; Sullivan, J.: *The Complete Stretching Book*. London 1992.

Vetter, W.L.: „Aerobic Dance Injuries". in: *The Physician and Sportsmedicine* 1985.
Whitt, F.R.: *Bicycling Science*. Cambridge 1974.
Zintl, F.: *Ausdauertraining*. München 1990.
Zorn, H.: *Radsport*. Hamburg 1984.

Addresses

BDR
Bund Deutscher Radfahrer
Otto-Fleck-Schneise 4
D-60528 Frankfurt/Main
Tel.: 069/678922

South Africa
South African Cycling Organisation
P.O. Box 271
Table View 7439
Rep. South Africa

Australia
Australian Cycling Fed. Inc
14 Telopea Avenue
2140 Homebush West, NSW
Australia

Canada
Ass. Cycliste Canadienne
1600 Promenade James
Naismith Drive
Gloucester Ontario K1B5N4
Canada

Ireland
Federation of Irish Cyclists
Kelly Roche House
619, North Circular Road
Dublin 1
Ireland

New Zealand
Cycling New-Zealand Federation Inc.
P.O. Box 1057
Wellington
New Zealand

USA
USA Cycling, Inc.
One Olympic Plaza
Colorado Springs CO, 80909-577
USA

Great Britain
British Cycling Federation
National Cycling Centre
Stuart Street
M11 4DQ Manchester
Great Britain

Japan
Japan Cycling Federation
C/o Nihon Jitansha-Kaikan
1-9-15 Akasaka, Minato-Ku
Tokyo 107